POL MARTIN's SUPREME *Cuisine*

BRIMAR

Editor Angela Rahaniotis

Copy Editor Sylvie Beaudoin

Coordinator Josée Halna du Fretay

Graphic Design Zapp

Typesetting Conversion Plus Inc.

Photography Melissa du Fretay,
　　　　　　　Studio Pol Martin (Ontario) Ltd.

Electrical appliance courtesy of KitchenAid ®

BRIMAR PUBLISHING INC.
338 St. Antoine St. East
Montreal, Canada
H2Y 1A3
Telephone: (514) 954-1441
Fax: (514) 954-1443

ISBN 2-89433-026-X

Printed and bound in Canada
by Metropole Litho Inc.

CONTENTS

AVOCADO AND APPLE SALAD
(SERVES 4)

2	ripe avocados, halved, pitted, peeled and sliced	2
2	apples, cored and sliced with skin	2
1 tsp	Dijon mustard	5 mL
2 tbsp	lemon juice	30 mL
4 tbsp	olive oil	60 mL
1 tbsp	chopped fresh parsley	15 mL
¼ cup	slivered toasted almonds	50 mL
	salt and pepper	

■ Place sliced avocados and apples in bowl; set aside.

■ Place mustard, lemon juice and oil in small bowl; season well. Using whisk, mix until thick.

■ Pour dressing over avocados and apples; sprinkle with parsley. Add almonds, season and toss gently. Serve.

1 SERVING:	383 CALORIES	21 g CARBOHYDRATE	4 g PROTEIN
	32 g FAT	4.8 g FIBER	

COLD HALIBUT WITH ASSORTED VEGETABLES
(SERVES 2)

1	cooked halibut steak, flaked	1
½	large tomato, quartered	½
1 cup	cooked cauliflower florets	250 mL
2 tbsp	chopped fresh parsley	30 mL
6	stuffed green olives, sliced	6
8	cooked baby carrots	8
2 tbsp	wine vinegar	30 mL
1	garlic clove, smashed and chopped	1
3 tbsp	olive oil	45 mL
	salt and pepper	
	slices hard-boiled egg	

■ Place fish in bowl with tomato, cauliflower, half the parsley, olives and carrots; season well.

■ Place vinegar, garlic, remaining parsley, salt and pepper in separate bowl. Whisk together. Incorporate oil gradually while whisking constantly.

■ Pour vinaigrette over salad ingredients and toss gently. Serve with slices of hard-boiled egg and lettuce leaves, if desired.

1 SERVING:	450 CALORIES	26 g CARBOHYDRATE	22 g PROTEIN
	29 g FAT	8.0 g FIBER	

CARROT SALAD
WITH TOASTED ALMONDS

(SERVES 4)

3 tbsp	mayonnaise	45 mL
2 tbsp	heavy cream	30 mL
1 tbsp	chopped fresh parsley	15 mL
4	carrots, pared, sliced in julienne and cooked	4
1	Boston lettuce, washed and dried	1
¼ cup	toasted almonds	50 mL
	few drops Tabasco sauce	
	few drops lemon juice	
	salt and pepper	

■ Mix mayonnaise, cream, Tabasco, lemon juice and parsley together in large bowl. Season to taste.

■ Add carrots to bowl and mix gently.

■ Arrange lettuce leaves on serving platter. Spoon carrots in center of lettuce and top with toasted almonds. Serve.

1 SERVING:	183 CALORIES	8 g CARBOHYDRATE	3 g PROTEIN
	16 g FAT	3.4 g FIBER	

POTATO AND TUNA FISH SALAD

(SERVES 4)

6.5-oz	can tuna, drained	184-g
3	large cooked potatoes, still hot, cubed	3
4 tbsp	cooked chopped red onion	60 mL
2	green onions, chopped	2
1	bell pepper, cubed	1
1	celery stalk, diced	1
2 tbsp	wine vinegar	30 mL
2 tbsp	lemon juice	30 mL
1½ tbsp	Dijon mustard	25 mL
¼ cup	heavy cream	50 mL
	salt and pepper	

■ Place tuna in large bowl. Add vegetables and mix.

■ Pour vinegar and lemon juice in another bowl. Add mustard, salt and pepper; mix together with whisk.

■ Whisk in cream. Pour sauce over salad and toss well. Marinate 15 minutes before serving.

1 SERVING:	238 CALORIES	30 g CARBOHYDRATE	16 g PROTEIN
	6 g FAT	3.2 g FIBER	

PURPLE LETTUCE SALAD

(SERVES 4)

1	small radicchio lettuce, washed and well dried	1
1	Boston lettuce, washed and well dried	1
1	endive, washed and well dried	1
½ cup	stuffed green olives (optional)	125 mL
2	hard-boiled eggs, sliced	2
1 tbsp	Dijon mustard	15 mL
1	blanched garlic clove, smashed and chopped	1
3 tbsp	wine vinegar	45 mL
½ cup	olive oil	125 mL
2 tbsp	heavy cream, whipped	30 mL
1½ cups	croutons	375 mL
	salt and pepper	

■ Arrange lettuces and endive in large salad bowl, tearing leaves into smaller pieces if necessary. Add olives and eggs; set aside.

■ Place mustard, garlic and vinegar in small bowl; season and mix together using whisk.

■ Incorporate oil in thin stream while whisking constantly. Add whipped cream and mix well. Correct seasoning.

■ Pour dressing over salad and toss until evenly coated. Add croutons, mix once more and serve.

1 SERVING:	387 CALORIES	11 g CARBOHYDRATE	6 g PROTEIN
	36 g FAT	1.7 g FIBER	

BUTTERMILK AND PARMESAN CHEESE SALAD DRESSING

(SERVES 8 – 10)

1½ cups	buttermilk	375 mL
1 tbsp	smashed green peppercorns	15 mL
3 tbsp	grated Parmesan cheese	45 mL
¼ cup	mayonnaise	50 mL
2 tbsp	sour cream	30 mL
1 tbsp	chopped fresh parsley	15 mL
	few drops Tabasco sauce	
	few drops lemon juice	
	dash paprika	
	salt	

■ Place all ingredients in bowl and mix together. Correct seasoning and serve over fresh salad greens.

1 SERVING:	65 CALORIES	3 g CARBOHYDRATE	2 g PROTEIN
	5 g FAT	0 g FIBER	

MAYONNAISE
(SERVES 4 TO 6)

2	egg yolks	2
1 tsp	Dijon mustard	5 mL
1¼ cups	olive oil	300 mL
	juice of 1 lemon	
	salt and pepper	

■ Place egg yolks in bowl. Add mustard and mix well. Season with salt and pepper.

■ Add oil, drop by drop, mixing constantly with whisk. When mayonnaise begins to thicken, add oil in steady stream, whisking constantly.

■ Add lemon juice only after mayonnaise is very thick.

Note: To keep mayonnaise for 2 days in refrigerator, add 1 tbsp (15 mL) hot water. Whisk well.

1 SERVING:	519 CALORIES	1 g CARBOHYDRATE	1 g PROTEIN
	57 g FAT	0 g FIBER	

Place egg yolks in bowl.

Add mustard.

Mix well. Season with salt and pepper.

Add oil while mixing constantly with whisk.

Add lemon juice only after mayonnaise is very thick.

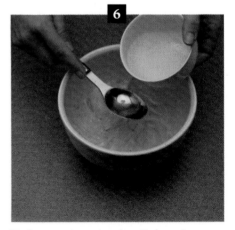

To keep mayonnaise 2 days in refrigerator, incorporate 1 tbsp (15 mL) hot water.

CREAMY MUSTARD VINAIGRETTE

(SERVES 4)

1	shallot, finely chopped	1
2 tbsp	Dijon mustard	30 mL
2 tbsp	lemon juice	30 mL
½ cup	heavy cream	125 mL
	pinch of paprika	
	salt and pepper	

■ Place shallot, mustard and lemon juice in bowl. Season with salt and pepper; mix well with whisk.

■ Incorporate cream in a thin stream while whisking constantly. Add paprika, mix and correct seasoning.

■ Serve over salad.

1 SERVING:	120 CALORIES	4 g CARBOHYDRATE	1 g PROTEIN
	11 g FAT	0 g FIBER	

HERBED POTATO SALAD

(SERVES 4)

4	large potatoes, cooked in skins, peeled and diced	4
1	onion, finely chopped	1
2	hard-boiled eggs, chopped	2
2 tbsp	chopped fresh parsley	30 mL
1 tsp	chopped fresh tarragon	5 mL
3 tbsp	mayonnaise	45 mL
	juice ¼ lemon	
	salt and pepper	

■ Place potatoes, onion and eggs in large bowl. Add parsley and tarragon; mix well.

■ Add mayonnaise and lemon juice; mix well. Season, mix once more and serve.

1 SERVING:	275 CALORIES	38 g CARBOHYDRATE	6 g PROTEIN
	11 g FAT	0 g FIBER	

SHRIMP AND TOMATO REMOULADE

(SERVES 6 TO 8)

8	small tomatoes, hollowed	8
¾ lb	cooked shrimp, peeled, deveined and chopped	375 g
½	stalk celery, diced small	½
2	green onions, finely chopped	2
2 tbsp	chopped pimento	30 mL
1 tsp	horseradish	5 mL
1 tbsp	Dijon mustard	15 mL
2 tbsp	chopped fresh parsley	30 mL
3 tbsp	wine vinegar	45 mL
¼ cup	olive oil	50 mL
	juice of ½ lemon	
	salt, pepper, paprika	

■ Season cavities of tomatoes with salt and pepper; set aside.

■ Place shrimp, celery, green onions and pimento in bowl. Season with salt and pepper. Set aside.

■ Mix horseradish, mustard and parsley together in another bowl. Season with salt, pepper and paprika. Whisk in vinegar. Add oil in thin stream, mixing constantly with whisk.

■ Pour dressing over shrimp mixture and mix well. Stir in lemon juice, and stuff tomatoes with mixture. Serve.

1 SERVING:	156 CALORIES	7 g CARBOHYDRATE	14 g PROTEIN
	8 g FAT	1.0 g FIBER	

SPANISH SALAD
(SERVES 4)

1	bunch fresh watercress, washed and well dried	1	
1	Boston lettuce, washed and well dried	1	
2	endives, washed and well dried	2	
1	apple, cored and sliced	1	
1 cup	cantaloupe balls	250 mL	
2 tbsp	tarragon vinegar	30 mL	
2 tbsp	mayonnaise	30 mL	
2 tbsp	sour cream	30 mL	
	juice ½ lemon		
	pinch sugar		
	salt and pepper		

■ Place watercress in large bowl. Tear lettuce leaves into pieces and add to bowl with endives. Add apple slices and cantaloupe balls; season well.

■ Mix together vinegar, mayonnaise, sour cream, lemon juice and sugar in small bowl. Season well and pour over salad ingredients.

■ Toss until evenly coated, then serve.

1 SERVING:	110 CALORIES	13 g CARBOHYDRATE	3 g PROTEIN
	5 g FAT	2.5 g FIBER	

HOT WHITE BEAN SALAD

(SERVES 4)

1 tbsp	butter	15 mL
2	shallots, chopped	2
1	garlic clove, smashed and chopped	1
2 cups	cooked white beans	500 mL
1 tbsp	chopped fresh parsley	15 mL
2 tbsp	white wine vinegar	30 mL
1 tsp	Dijon mustard	5 mL
5 tbsp	olive oil	75 mL
	salt and pepper	

■ Heat butter in saucepan over medium heat. Add shallots and garlic; cook 2 minutes.

■ Add beans and parsley. Season and cook 4 minutes over low heat, stirring occasionally.

■ Transfer contents of saucepan to bowl.

■ Place vinegar and mustard in another bowl; mix well. Pour in oil and incorporate with whisk.

■ Pour vinaigrette over beans, mix and serve.

1 SERVING:	317 CALORIES	26 g CARBOHYDRATE	8 g PROTEIN
	21 g FAT	7.7 g FIBER	

JULIENNE OF GRUYÈRE CHEESE SALAD

(SERVES 4)

½ lb	Gruyère cheese, sliced in julienne	250 g
1	celery stalk, sliced in julienne	1
½ cup	pecan halves	125 mL
½ cup	walnut halves	125 mL
1 tbsp	chopped fresh parsley	15 mL
1 tbsp	chopped lemon rind	15 mL
2	green onions, finely chopped	2
1	recipe Creamy Mustard Vinaigrette (see page 14)	1
	salt and pepper	

■ Mix all salad ingredients together in bowl.

■ Pour in vinaigrette and mix well. Correct seasoning.

■ Serve on lettuce leaves.

1 SERVING:	605 CALORIES	10 g CARBOHYDRATE	24 g PROTEIN
	53 g FAT	2.4 g FIBER	

CLEARWATER CITY CAESAR SALAD

(SERVES 6)

1 tbsp	Dijon mustard	15 mL
4	anchovy filets, puréed	4
3	blanched garlic cloves, puréed	3
2	egg yolks	2
3 tbsp	wine vinegar	45 mL
⅓ cup	olive oil	75 mL
4 tbsp	grated Parmesan cheese	60 mL
2	large heads Romaine lettuce, washed and dried	2
1¼ cups	garlic croutons	300 mL
5	slices well-cooked bacon, chopped	5
	juice of 1 lemon	
	few drops Worcestershire sauce	
	salt and pepper	

■ Rub inside of large salad bowl with garlic clove. Place mustard, anchovies, garlic purée and lemon juice in bowl. Mix well to make a paste.

■ Add Worcestershire sauce and egg yolks; mix well with whisk.

■ Add vinegar and mix well. Incorporate oil in thin stream while whisking constantly. Add half of Parmesan and mix again.

■ Tear lettuce leaves into smaller pieces and add to salad bowl containing dressing. Season well and toss until evenly coated. Sprinkle with more lemon juice, if desired.

■ Add croutons and bacon; toss salad again. Sprinkle with remaining cheese and serve.

1 SERVING:	218 CALORIES	9 g CARBOHYDRATE	8 g PROTEIN
	17 g FAT	2.5 g FIBER	

Rub inside of large salad bowl with garlic clove.

Place mustard, anchovies, garlic purée and lemon juice in bowl.

Mix well to make a paste.

Add Worcestershire sauce and egg yolks; mix well with whisk.

Add vinegar and mix well.

Incorporate oil in thin stream while whisking constantly.

PORT ST. AUGUSTINE SALAD

(SERVES 4 TO 6)

½ lb	green beans, pared and cooked	250 g
2	tomatoes, cored and quartered	2
2	hard-boiled eggs, quartered	2
½ cup	green peas, cooked	125 mL
½ cup	mayonnaise	125 mL
1	large head Romaine lettuce, washed and dried	1
	few drops Worcestershire sauce	
	few drops lemon juice	
	salt and pepper	

■ Place beans, tomatoes, eggs and peas in large bowl. Season with salt and pepper.

■ Add mayonnaise, Worcestershire sauce and lemon juice. Mix well and correct seasoning.

■ Serve on lettuce leaves.

1 SERVING:	260 CALORIES	12 g CARBOHYDRATE	6 g PROTEIN
	21 g FAT	4.7 g FIBER	

IMPERIAL SALAD

(SERVES 4)

1 lb	green beans, pared and cooked	500 g
2	carrots, pared, sliced in julienne and blanched	2
1	apple, peeled and sliced in julienne	1
¼ cup	Egg Yolk Vinaigrette (see page 28)	50 mL
	lemon juice	
	salt and pepper	

■ Combine vegetables with apple in large bowl. Season with salt and pepper; sprinkle with lemon juice.

■ Add vinaigrette and mix well. Serve.

1 SERVING:	188 CALORIES	18 g CARBOHYDRATE	3 g PROTEIN
	12 g FAT	5.4 g FIBER	

SALAD BEATRICE

(SERVES 4)

1	whole chicken breast, cooked	1
2	potatoes, cooked in skins	2
1	bunch fresh asparagus, cooked	1
⅓ cup	mayonnaise	75 mL
	few drops Worcestershire sauce	
	salt and pepper	

■ Remove and discard skin from chicken breast. Bone and slice meat in julienne.

■ Peel potatoes and slice. Cut asparagus into 1-in (2.5-cm) pieces.

■ Place chicken, potatoes and asparagus in large bowl; season with salt and pepper.

■ Add mayonnaise and mix well. Add Worcestershire sauce and mix again. Serve on lettuce leaves.

1 SERVING:	276 CALORIES	18 g CARBOHYDRATE	17 g PROTEIN
	15 g FAT	2.7 g FIBER	

MARINE CABBAGE SALAD

(SERVES 6 TO 8)

1	small white cabbage	1
1	large carrot, pared and grated	1
6 tbsp	white vinegar	90 mL
1 cup	cold water	250 mL
⅓ cup	mayonnaise	75 mL
½ tsp	dry mustard	2 mL
¼ cup	milk	50 mL
	juice of ½ lemon	
	few drops Tabasco sauce	
	pinch of sugar	
	salt and white pepper	

■ Core cabbage. Cut head in quarters and slice each quarter thinly. Place sliced cabbage in bowl; add carrot, lemon juice and 3 tbsp (45 mL) vinegar. Pour in water and mix well. Let marinate 1 hour.

■ Place mayonnaise in small bowl. Add mustard and remaining vinegar; season with salt and pepper. Mix well.

■ Incorporate milk, Tabasco and sugar. Season to taste and mix well.

■ Squeeze out excess liquid from marinated cabbage. Place cabbage in clean bowl and add mayonnaise sauce. Mix and correct seasoning. Serve.

1 SERVING:	87 CALORIES	3 g CARBOHYDRATE	1 g PROTEIN
	8 g FAT	1.0 g FIBER	

RICE AND SHRIMP SALAD
(SERVES 4)

2 cups	cooked rice	500 mL
1 cup	diced fresh pineapple	250 mL
1 cup	cooked crab meat	250 mL
½ lb	cooked shrimp, peeled, deveined and halved	250 g
2	tomatoes, peeled, seeded and diced (optional)	2
½ cup	cooked corn, well drained	125 mL
½ cup	salad dressing of your choice	125 mL
	salt and pepper	
	dash paprika	

■ Mix all ingredients (except salad dressing) together in large bowl. Season well, pour in dressing and marinate 10 minutes.

■ Serve on lettuce leaves or in hollowed-out pineapple halves.

1 SERVING:	435 CALORIES	37 g CARBOHYDRATE	29 g PROTEIN
	19 g FAT	3.1 g FIBER	

SALAD BAGATELLE

(SERVES 4)

1	large bunch fresh asparagus, cooked	1
3	carrots, pared, sliced in julienne and blanched	3
½ lb	fresh mushrooms, cleaned and sliced	250 g
¼ cup	Mousseline Mayonnaise (see page 44)	50 mL
	lemon juice	
	salt and pepper	

■ Cut asparagus into 1-in (2.5-cm) pieces. Place in bowl with carrots and mushrooms. Season with salt and pepper.

■ Add Mousseline Mayonnaise and mix.

■ Add lemon juice, mix and correct seasoning.

1 SERVING:	168 CALORIES	12 g CARBOHYDRATE	4 g PROTEIN
	12 g FAT	4.4 g FIBER	

EGG YOLK VINAIGRETTE

(SERVES 4 TO 6)

1	egg yolk	1
1 tbsp	Dijon mustard	15 mL
1 tbsp	chopped fresh parsley	15 mL
2 tbsp	chopped shallot	30 mL
¼ cup	red wine vinegar	50 mL
¾ cup	olive oil	175 mL
	few drops lemon juice	
	salt and pepper	

■ Place egg yolk in bowl. Add mustard and mix.

■ Add parsley, shallot and vinegar. Season with salt and pepper; mix well with whisk.

■ Add oil in thin stream, mixing constantly with whisk. Add few drops of lemon juice, mix and correct seasoning. The vinaigrette should be thick.

Note: This vinaigrette will keep for 3 days in the refrigerator.

1 SERVING:	330 CALORIES	2 g CARBOHYDRATE	1 g PROTEIN
	36 g FAT	0 g FIBER	

Place egg yolk in bowl.

Add mustard.

Mix with whisk.

Add parsley and shallot.

Add vinegar. Season with salt and pepper; mix well with whisk.

Add oil in thin stream, while whisking constantly.

MIXED CAULIFLOWER SALAD
(SERVES 4)

1	head cauliflower, cooked and in florets	1
8	cherry tomatoes, halved	8
1	red apple, thinly sliced with skin	1
2	carrots, pared, julienned and cooked	2
12	cooked green beans, halved	12
4	artichoke bottoms, sliced	4
2	small cooked onions, diced	2
1 tbsp	chopped fresh parsley	15 mL
½ cup	French dressing	125 mL
	salt and pepper	
	lemon juice to taste	
	lettuce leaves	
	quartered hard-boiled eggs	

■ Place all vegetables and apple in large bowl; sprinkle with parsley. Pour in French dressing and toss until evenly coated.

■ Season and add lemon juice to taste; toss again.

■ Serve in salad bowl lined with lettuce leaves and decorate with eggs.

1 SERVING:	278 CALORIES	27 g CARBOHYDRATE	7 g PROTEIN
	16 g FAT	5.3 g FIBER	

VEGETABLE PARTY SALAD

(SERVES 6)

2	cooked potatoes, diced	2
2	cooked carrots, diced	2
½ lb	cooked green beans, diced	250 g
¼	cooked turnip, diced	¼
½	green pepper, diced	½
½	red pepper, diced	½
1 tbsp	chopped fresh chives	15 mL
⅓ cup	mayonnaise	75 mL
3 tbsp	chili sauce	45 mL
1 tbsp	celery seeds	15 mL
	salt and pepper	
	lemon juice to taste	

■ Mix all diced vegetables together in large salad bowl. Season, add chives, mix well and set aside.

■ Mix mayonnaise with chili sauce, celery seeds, lemon juice, salt and pepper.

■ Pour mayonnaise mixture over vegetables, mix well, correct seasoning and serve.

1 SERVING:	164 CALORIES	18 g CARBOHYDRATE	2 g PROTEIN
	9 g FAT	2.3 g FIBER	

THREE-BEAN SALAD

(SERVES 4 TO 6)

½ cup	cooked chickpeas	125 mL
½ cup	cooked red kidney beans	125 mL
⅓ cup	cooked black beans	75 mL
¼ tsp	finely chopped chili pepper	1 mL
2	green onions, chopped	2
12	cherry tomatoes, halved	12
1	shallot, finely chopped	1
1	green pepper, diced	1
1	garlic clove, smashed and chopped	1
1 tbsp	tomato paste (optional)	15 mL
3 tbsp	wine vinegar	45 mL
1 tbsp	Dijon mustard	15 mL
7 tbsp	olive oil	105 mL
	juice of ½ lemon	
	salt and pepper	

■ Place chickpeas and beans in bowl. Add chili pepper, green onions, tomatoes, shallot and green pepper. Season with salt and pepper; mix well and set aside.

■ Place garlic in another bowl. Add salt, pepper, tomato paste, vinegar and mustard; mix well.

■ Pour in oil and incorporate with whisk. Correct seasoning.

■ Pour vinaigrette over salad ingredients and mix well. Add lemon juice and mix again. Marinate 30 minutes before serving.

1 SERVING:	289 CALORIES	23 g CARBOHYDRATE	6 g PROTEIN
	20 g FAT	1.4 g FIBER	

CHICKEN PASTA SALAD WITH GRUYÈRE
(SERVES 4)

3 cups	cooked pasta (penne, spiral, etc.)	750 mL
1 cup	cooked green peas	250 mL
1	whole chicken breast, cooked, skinned and diced	1
1 cup	diced Gruyère cheese	250 mL
1 tbsp	curry powder	15 mL
⅓ cup	light mayonnaise ("low-cal")	75 mL
	salt and pepper	
	juice ½ lemon	
	dash paprika	

■ Place pasta, peas, chicken and Gruyère in bowl and mix together. Add curry powder, remaining seasonings and mayonnaise; mix well.

■ Serve chilled.

1 SERVING:	520 CALORIES	35 g CARBOHYDRATE	34 g PROTEIN
	27 g FAT	2.2 g FIBER	

WARM CHICKEN BREAST AND RICE SALAD

(SERVES 4 TO 6)

3 tbsp	olive oil	45 mL
1	whole chicken breast, skinned, boned and cubed	1
½	green pepper, sliced	½
1	zucchini, sliced	1
1	garlic clove, smashed and chopped	1
1 tbsp	soy sauce	15 mL
2 cups	cooked rice	500 mL
4	large olives, pitted and chopped	4
2 tbsp	chopped pimento	30 mL
1 tbsp	chopped parsley	15 mL
1 tbsp	wine vinegar	15 mL
	lemon juice	
	salt and pepper	

■ Heat 1 tbsp (15 mL) olive oil in frying pan over high heat. Add cubed chicken and cook 3 minutes. Add green pepper, zucchini and garlic; mix well. Continue cooking 4 minutes.

■ Mix in soy sauce and cook 1 minute.

■ Transfer chicken and vegetables to large bowl. Add remaining ingredients and season well. Mix and marinate 15 minutes before serving.

1 SERVING:	222 CALORIES	20 g CARBOHYDRATE	13 g PROTEIN
	10 g FAT	1.6 g FIBER	

LA CANAILLE

(SERVES 4)

3	tomatoes, cored and quartered	3
1	bunch fresh asparagus, cooked and cut in 1-in (2.5-cm) pieces	1
1	red onion, sliced in rings	1
1	celery stalk, sliced in julienne of 1 in (2.5 cm)	1
1	banana, sliced	1
1 cup	cooked rice	250 mL
¼ cup	mayonnaise seasoned with mustard	50 mL
2 tbsp	sour cream	30 mL
	few drops Worcestershire sauce	
	salt and pepper	

■ Mix vegetables, banana and rice together in large bowl. Season with salt and pepper.

■ Place mayonnaise in another bowl. Add sour cream and Worcestershire sauce; mix well. Season to taste.

■ Pour mayonnaise mixture over salad and mix well. Serve.

1 SERVING:	225 CALORIES	28 g CARBOHYDRATE	5 g PROTEIN
	11 g FAT	4.5 g FIBER	

SALAD ANDALUSIA
(SERVES 4 TO 6)

2	shallots, chopped	2	
1 tbsp	chopped fresh parsley	15 mL	
1 tbsp	Dijon mustard	15 mL	
1	garlic clove, smashed and chopped	1	
3 tbsp	red wine vinegar	45 mL	
½ cup	olive oil	125 mL	
1	hard-boiled egg, chopped	1	
1 tbsp	whipped cream	15 mL	
3	tomatoes, cored and quartered	3	
2	green peppers, sliced in julienne	2	
½	red onion, sliced in rings	½	
1 cup	cooked white rice	250 mL	
	salt and pepper		

■ Place shallots and parsley in bowl. Add mustard, garlic and vinegar; mix well. Season with salt and pepper.

■ Add oil in thin stream, mixing constantly with whisk.

■ Add chopped hard-boiled egg and mix. Incorporate whipped cream.

■ Place vegetables and rice in large bowl. Mix to combine and season to taste.

■ Add vinaigrette, mix well and serve.

1 SERVING:	308 CALORIES	18 g CARBOHYDRATE	4 g PROTEIN
	25 g FAT	2.0 g FIBER	

Place shallots and parsley in bowl.

Add mustard and garlic.

Add wine vinegar and mix well. Season with salt and pepper.

Add oil in thin stream while whisking constantly.

Add chopped hard-boiled egg.

Incorporate whipped cream.

BOSTON FRUIT SALAD

(SERVES 4)

1	large Boston lettuce, washed and dried	1
2 cups	strawberries, washed, hulled, and halved	500 mL
1 cup	mandarin segments	250 mL
1	pear, peeled and sliced	1
4 tbsp	mayonnaise	60 mL
3 tbsp	sour cream	45 mL
¼ cup	grated coconut	50 mL
	few drops of lemon juice	
	freshly ground pepper	

■ Tear lettuce leaves into smaller pieces and place in bowl. Add strawberries, mandarin segments, pear slices, mayonnaise and sour cream. Mix well.

■ Add lemon juice and season with pepper. Mix again.

■ Sprinkle with grated coconut and serve.

1 SERVING:	219 CALORIES	20 g CARBOHYDRATE	2 g PROTEIN
	15 g FAT	4.7 g FIBER	

BROILED PEPPER SALAD

(SERVES 4)

1	yellow pepper, halved	1
1	red pepper, halved	1
1	green pepper, halved	1
4 tbsp	olive oil	60 mL
2	garlic cloves, smashed and chopped	2
1	dry shallot, chopped	1
2 tbsp	chopped fresh parsley	30 mL
1 tsp	chopped fresh tarragon	5 mL
3 tbsp	tarragon vinegar	45 mL
	juice ½ lemon	
	salt and pepper	

■ Preheat oven at broil.

■ Place peppers cut-side-down in baking dish. Sprinkle each with few drops of olive oil and season well. Place on middle rack in preheated oven and cook 10 to 15 minutes. Remove and set aside.

■ Place garlic, shallot, parsley, tarragon, remaining oil, vinegar and lemon juice in small bowl. Season and mix well, using whisk.

■ Pour dressing over peppers, season and marinate until cooled.

1 SERVING:	145 CALORIES	6 g CARBOHYDRATE	1 g PROTEIN
	13 g FAT	1.0 g FIBER	

MIXED BEAN SALAD WITH GREEN VINAIGRETTE
(SERVES 4)

1 cup	canned kidney beans, well drained	250 mL
1 cup	canned chickpeas, well drained	250 mL
1 lb	fresh green beans, pared and cooked	500 g
3	hard-boiled eggs	3
2	dry shallots, finely chopped	2
2 tbsp	chopped fresh parsley	30 mL
1 tsp	tarragon	5 mL
1	garlic clove, smashed and chopped	1
3 tbsp	wine vinegar	45 mL
6 tbsp	olive oil	90 mL
	salt and pepper	
	juice ½ lemon	
	few drops Tabasco sauce	

■ Mix kidney beans, chickpeas and green beans together in large bowl.

■ Slice hard-boiled eggs in half and remove yolks; set aside. Chop whites and add to beans in bowl. Season well.

■ Place remaining ingredients, except egg yolks, in small bowl and quickly whisk together just until blended.

■ Pour dressing over salad ingredients, mix well and marinate 15 minutes at room temperature.

■ To serve, spoon salad onto plates; force egg yolks through fine sieve onto beans.

1 SERVING: 488 CALORIES 45 g CARBOHYDRATE 17 g PROTEIN 27 g FAT 4.9 g FIBER

BROCCOLI AND POTATO SALAD

(SERVES 4)

1	small head broccoli, cooked	1	
2	large potatoes, cooked in skins, peeled and diced	2	
1	celery stalk, sliced	1	
2 tbsp	wine vinegar	30 mL	
6 tbsp	olive oil	90 mL	
1 tbsp	chopped fresh parsley	15 mL	
	salt and pepper		
	paprika		

■ Cut cooked broccoli into florets and place in large bowl. Add the potatoes and celery; season well.

■ Mix vinegar, oil, salt and pepper together in small bowl. Pour over broccoli and toss to evenly coat.

■ Season with salt, pepper and paprika. Sprinkle with parsley and serve.

1 SERVING:	280 CALORIES	22 g CARBOHYDRATE	3 g PROTEIN
	20 g FAT	2.1 g FIBER	

WHITE CABBAGE SALAD
(SERVES 6)

1	medium white cabbage	1
2	carrots, pared and grated	2
1	green pepper, sliced	1
1 tbsp	chopped fresh parsley	15 mL
½ cup	cider vinegar	125 mL
¼ cup	sugar	50 mL
¼ cup	olive oil	50 mL
½ tsp	celery salt	2 mL
½ tsp	celery seeds	2 mL
2	garlic cloves, peeled and pressed to remove garlic juice	2
	lemon juice	
	salt and pepper	

■ Core cabbage. Cut cabbage head into quarters. Slice cabbage and place in saucepan with boiling, salted water. Cover and blanch 3 minutes.

■ Drain cabbage and chill 1 hour in cold water.

■ Drain cabbage again and squeeze out excess water. Place cabbage in bowl; add carrots and green pepper. Season well.

■ Place remaining ingredients, including garlic juice, in small saucepan. Boil 3 minutes. Pour marinade over cabbage and mix well. Marinate 1 hour before serving.

1 SERVING:	98 CALORIES	12 g CARBOHYDRATE	1 g PROTEIN
	6 g FAT	1.5 g FIBER	

ARTICHOKE HEARTS SALAD
(SERVES 4 TO 6)

3 tbsp	mayonnaise	45 mL	
1 tbsp	curry powder	15 mL	
6	cooked artichoke hearts, quartered	6	
3	green onions, chopped	3	
1 cup	cubed pineapple	250 mL	
1½ cups	cooked rice	375 mL	
½	stalk celery, diced	½	
1 cup	pitted black olives	250 mL	
	lemon juice		
	few drops Worcestershire sauce		
	salt, pepper, paprika		

- Mix mayonnaise with curry powder. Set aside.

- Place artichoke hearts, green onions, pineapple, rice, celery and olives in bowl. Pour mayonnaise over salad ingredients and mix well.

- Add lemon juice, Worcestershire sauce, salt, pepper and paprika. Mix well.

- Serve on lettuce leaves.

1 SERVING:	190 CALORIES	25 g CARBOHYDRATE	3 g PROTEIN
	9 g FAT	2.1 g FIBER	

MOUSSELINE MAYONNAISE
(SERVES 4)

2	egg yolks	2	
1 tbsp	Dijon mustard	15 mL	
1 tsp	wine vinegar	5 mL	
1 tbsp	curry powder	15 mL	
1 tsp	chopped shallot	5 mL	
1 tsp	chopped fresh parsley	5 mL	
1¼ cups	olive oil	300 mL	
¼ cup	whipped cream	50 mL	
	salt and pepper		

■ Place egg yolks in bowl. Add mustard, vinegar, curry powder, shallot and parsley. Incorporate with whisk.

■ Add oil in thin stream, mixing constantly with whisk. Season with salt and pepper.

■ Fold in whipped cream. Serve mayonnaise with vegetables, fish or salads.

1 SERVING:	658 CALORIES	0 g CARBOHYDRATE	1 g PROTEIN
	73 g FAT	0 g FIBER	

Place egg yolks in bowl and add mustard.

Add vinegar.

Add curry powder.

Add shallot and parsley; mix well.

Add oil in thin stream, mixing constantly with whisk.

Fold in whipped cream.

COUNTRYSIDE POTATO SALAD

(SERVES 4)

2	garlic cloves, smashed and chopped	2
3 tbsp	wine vinegar	45 mL
½ cup	olive oil	125 mL
3	potatoes, cooked in skins and still hot	3
10	slices mild salami, cut into julienne	10
4 tbsp	chopped red onion	60 mL
2	green onions, chopped	2
1 tbsp	chopped fresh parsley	15 mL
4 tbsp	chopped pimento	60 mL
	salt and pepper	

■ Place garlic, vinegar and oil in bowl. Season with salt and pepper. Whisk together for 1 minute.

■ Peel, then slice potatoes thick. Place in mixing bowl.

■ Add remaining salad ingredients and toss. Pour in vinaigrette and toss again. Season well and marinate 15 minutes before serving.

1 SERVING:	509 CALORIES	31 g CARBOHYDRATE	10 g PROTEIN
	39 g FAT	1.0 g FIBER	

VEGETABLE SHELL SOUP

(SERVES 6 TO 8)

3 tbsp	butter	45 mL
3	medium onions, diced small	3
3	celery stalks, diced small	3
1 tsp	herbes de Provence*	5 mL
4	carrots, pared and diced small	4
½	turnip, peeled and diced small	½
½ tsp	thyme	2 mL
½ tsp	basil	2 mL
3	large potatoes, peeled and diced small	3
8 cups	chicken stock, heated	2 L
2	bay leaves	2
4 tbsp	tomato paste	60 mL
1 cup	small shell noodles	250 mL
	salt and pepper	

■ Heat butter in large saucepan over medium heat. Add onions, celery and herbes de Provence; season well. Cover and cook 15 minutes over low heat.

■ Stir in carrots, turnip, thyme and basil; season to taste. Mix well, cover and continue cooking 5 minutes.

■ Add potatoes, chicken stock, bay leaves and tomato paste. Mix and bring to boil.

■ Add noodles and cook, partly covered, 15 minutes over medium-high heat. Serve hot.

*A mixture of thyme, rosemary, bay leaf, basil and savory.

1 SERVING:	207 CALORIES	35 g CARBOHYDRATE	3 g PROTEIN
	6 g FAT	2.2 g FIBER	

KIDNEY BEAN VEGETABLE SOUP

(SERVES 4 TO 6)

1 tbsp	olive oil	15 mL
1	onion, chopped	1
½	stalk celery, sliced	½
5 cups	light beef stock, heated	1.2 L
1 cup	cooked kidney beans	250 mL
1	green pepper, diced medium	1
1	red pepper, diced medium	1
1 cup	frozen peas	250 mL
1 cup	corned beef, cubed	250 mL
1 cup	cooked corn kernels	250 mL
1 tsp	basil	5 mL
¼ tsp	thyme	1 mL
1	bay leaf	1
	salt and pepper	

■ Heat oil in saucepan over medium heat. Add onion and celery; cook 5 minutes over low heat.

■ Add beef stock and mix well. Add remaining ingredients. Season with salt and pepper; bring to boil. Cook 12 minutes over medium heat. Serve.

1 SERVING:	174 CALORIES	24 g CARBOHYDRATE	9 g PROTEIN
	5 g FAT	9.0 g FIBER	

CREAM OF CARROT SOUP
(SERVES 4 TO 6)

3 tbsp	butter	45 mL
1	medium onion, chopped	1
6	carrots, pared and thinly sliced	6
1	celery stalk, thinly sliced	1
½ tsp	basil	2 mL
1 tbsp	chopped fresh parsley	15 mL
3 tbsp	flour	45 mL
5 cups	chicken stock, heated	1.2 L
	salt and pepper	

■ Heat butter in large saucepan over medium heat. Add onion, cover and cook 5 minutes over low heat.

■ Add carrots, celery, basil and parsley; season well. Mix and cook 6 minutes, partly covered, over medium heat.

■ Mix in flour until well incorporated. Pour in chicken stock, correct seasoning and bring to boil, partly covered. Reduce heat to low and cook soup 20 minutes.

■ Pass soup through food mill or purée in blender. Serve hot.

1 SERVING:	119 CALORIES	12 g CARBOHYDRATE	2 g PROTEIN
	7 g FAT	2.3 g FIBER	

HOT CORNED BEEF AND CHEESE SANDWICHES
(SERVES 4)

8	slices rye bread	8
16	thin slices corned beef	16
1½ cups	sauerkraut	375 mL
½ cup	grated Swiss cheese	125 mL
½ cup	grated Cheddar cheese	125 mL
2 tbsp	butter	30 mL
	Dijon mustard to taste	
	freshly ground pepper	

■ Spread Dijon mustard to taste over slices of bread. Build sandwiches with two slices of corned beef topped with sauerkraut.

■ Mix Swiss and Cheddar cheeses together; divide between sandwiches. Season with pepper and close sandwiches. Press top slice down with spatula.

■ Spread top slice of each sandwich with butter. Place remaining butter in large frying pan and melt over medium heat.

■ When hot, set sandwiches in pan, buttered-side-up, and cook 2 minutes. Turn sandwiches over and continue cooking 2 minutes or long enough to melt cheese.

■ Slice and serve hot.

---

1 SERVING: 539 CALORIES   31 g CARBOHYDRATE   44 g PROTEIN
               27 g FAT   1.2 g FIBER

ROAST TURKEY BREAST WITH SPROUTS ON PUMPERNICKEL
(SERVES 2)

4	slices pumpernickel bread	4
2 tbsp	mayonnaise	30 mL
6	thin slices roast turkey breast	6
4	slices Havarti cheese	5
4	slices avocado	4
	alfalfa sprouts	
	salt and pepper	

■ Spread slices of bread with mayonnaise. Build sandwiches with turkey, cheese and alfalfa sprouts. Be sure to season meat well.

■ Top each sandwich with slice of avocado. Serve.

1 SERVING:	677 CALORIES	38 g CARBOHYDRATE	33 g PROTEIN
	44g FAT	2.0 g FIBER	

BRONX BOMBER

(SERVES 1)

3	slices rye bread
	thin slices of corned beef
	thin slices of roast beef
	thin slices of roast turkey breast
	mayonnaise and mustard to taste
	coleslaw
	lettuce leaves, washed and dried
	salt and pepper

3

■ Spread slices of bread with mayonnaise and mustard. Cover bottom slice of bread with lettuce leaves. Top with several slices of meat and season well. Add second slice of bread and finish building sandwich with remaining meat and third slice of bread.

■ Serve with coleslaw.

1 SERVING:	489 CALORIES	41 g CARBOHYDRATE	34 g PROTEIN
	21 g FAT	2.6 g FIBER	

WINTER SOUP
(SERVES 4 TO 6)

1 tbsp	butter	15 mL	
2	onions, chopped	2	
1	celery stalk, diced	1	
3	medium carrots, pared and sliced	3	
3	potatoes, peeled, halved and sliced	3	
5 cups	light chicken stock, heated	1.2 L	
14-oz	can black-eyed peas, drained	398-mL	
1 cup	elbow macaroni	250 mL	
	salt and pepper		

■ Prepare a bouquet garni consisting of: thyme, basil, parsley and 2 bay leaves. Set aside.

■ Heat butter in large saucepan over medium heat. Add onions and celery; cover and cook 4 minutes.

■ Mix in carrots and season with salt and pepper. Cook 5 minutes uncovered.

■ Add potatoes and chicken stock. Season and drop in bouquet garni. Bring to boil and cook 12 minutes over medium heat.

■ Add remaining ingredients. Bring to boil and cook 12 minutes at medium-low.

Note: This soup will keep for 3 days in refrigerator.

1 SERVING:	243 CALORIES	48 g CARBOHYDRATE	6 g PROTEIN
	3 g FAT	4.8 g FIBER	

Cook onions and celery in hot butter. Cover saucepan and cook 4 minutes.

Mix in carrots and season with salt and pepper. Cook 5 minutes uncovered.

Add potatoes.

Add chicken stock and season.

Drop in bouquet garni and bring to boil.

Add remaining ingredients.

BLACK BEAN SOUP

(SERVES 6 TO 8)

1 cup	dried black beans	250 mL
¼ lb	bacon, diced	125 g
1	onion, diced	1
1	meaty ham bone	1
7 cups	light beef stock, heated	1.8 L
1	bouquet garni*	1
2	garlic cloves, smashed and chopped	2
	salt and pepper	

■ Soak beans in cold water for 12 hours. Drain and set aside.

■ Place bacon in large saucepan and cook 3 minutes over medium heat.

■ Add onion, cover, and continue cooking 8 minutes. Stir once or twice during cooking process.

■ Add beans and remaining ingredients. Mix well and bring to boil. Cook 3 hours, partly covered, over medium heat, stirring occasionally.

*Tie together thyme, basil, parsley and a bay leaf.

1 SERVING:	160 CALORIES	8 g CARBOHYDRATE	10 g PROTEIN
	10 g FAT	2.6 g FIBER	

BEAUFORT CHOWDER

(SERVES 4 TO 6)

2 oz	salt pork, diced	60 g
2	onions, finely chopped	2
1	peeled whole garlic clove	1
2	large tomatoes, peeled, seeded and diced	2
3	potatoes, peeled and diced	3
5 cups	fish stock	1.2 L
½ tsp	thyme	2 mL
1 tsp	chopped fresh parsley	5 mL
2	red snapper filets, cut in ½-in (1.2-cm) wide strips	2
½ lb	shrimp, shelled and deveined	250 g
	pinch of crushed chilies	
	lime juice	
	salt and pepper	

■ Place salt pork in saucepan. Cook 4 minutes over medium heat. Remove salt pork and discard.

■ Add onions and garlic to hot pan and cook 4 minutes over medium heat.

■ Add tomatoes, mix well, and cook 2 minutes.

■ Add potatoes, fish stock and seasonings. Bring to boil and cook 10 minutes over medium heat. Do not cover.

■ Add fish and shrimp, mix and cook 4 minutes over low heat. Add few drops of lime juice. Serve with toasted garlic bread.

1 SERVING:	280 CALORIES	29 g CARBOHYDRATE	18 g PROTEIN
	10 g FAT	1.2 g FIBER	

PROSCIUTTO AND CANTALOUPE CANAPÉS

(SERVES 8 TO 10)

Mild Garlic Butter

5	garlic cloves, unpeeled	5
½ lb	soft butter	250 g
	few drops Tabasco sauce	
	few drops lemon juice	

Canapés

½	cantaloupe	½
6 oz	thinly sliced prosciutto	200 g
	slices of baguette, toasted	
	lemon juice	
	freshly ground pepper	

■ Blanch unpeeled garlic cloves in boiling water for 6 minutes. Drain and peel. Purée cloves.

■ Place puréed garlic in bowl with butter, Tabasco and lemon juice. Mix well.

■ Cut half cantaloupe into quarters. Re-cut each quarter into 1-in (2.5-cm) wide pieces. Set aside.

■ Spread garlic butter over toasted baguette slices. Top with prosciutto and piece of cantaloupe. Sprinkle canapés with few drops of lemon juice. Season with freshly ground pepper.

1 SERVING: 329 CALORIES   13 g CARBOHYDRATE   5 g PROTEIN
29 g FAT   1.0 g FIBER

SHRIMP CANAPÉS

(SERVES 10)

1½ lbs	cooked shrimp, shelled, deveined and chopped	750 g	
3 tbsp	chopped pimento	45 mL	
2	garlic cloves, blanched and puréed	2	
1 tbsp	celery seeds	15 mL	
¼ lb	soft butter	125 g	
3 tbsp	mayonnaise	45 mL	
	few drops Worcestershire sauce		
	few drops lemon juice		
	pinch cayenne pepper		
	salt and pepper		

■ Place all ingredients in food processor and blend 1 minute.

■ Transfer mixture to clean bowl, cover and refrigerate at least 1 hour.

■ Serve with toasted bread.

1 SERVING:	254 CALORIES	2 g CARBOHYDRATE	16 g PROTEIN
	20 g FAT	0 g FIBER	

GRUYÈRE MUSHROOM BROIL
(SERVES 4)

2	Italian-type buns	2	
2 tbsp	butter	30 mL	
¾ lb	fresh mushrooms, cleaned and sliced	375 g	
½ lb	fresh oyster mushrooms, cleaned and sliced	250 g	
1	shallot, chopped	1	
¼ cup	sherry	50 mL	
½ tsp	basil	2 mL	
1 cup	light white sauce, heated	250 mL	
1 cup	light cream	250 mL	
1 cup	grated Gruyère cheese	250 mL	
	pinch nutmeg		
	paprika		
	salt and pepper		

■ Cut buns in half lengthwise. Hollow insides of buns by scooping out half of the bread. Toast bread shells in oven, then set aside.

■ Melt butter in large frying pan over medium-high heat. Add both types of mushrooms; season with salt and pepper. Cook 6 minutes over high heat.

■ Add shallot, mix and continue cooking 3 minutes over high heat.

■ Stir in sherry, seasonings, white sauce and cream. Cook 5 minutes over low heat.

■ Preheat oven at 400 °F (200 °C).

■ Arrange toasted bun shells on cookie sheet. Spoon in mushroom mixture and top with cheese. Brown 3 minutes in oven. Serve.

1 SERVING:	354 CALORIES	25 g CARBOHYDRATE	14 g PROTEIN
	22 g FAT	4.5 g FIBER	

CUCUMBER CANAPÉS

(SERVES 4 TO 6)

1	small cucumber	1
4 oz	cream cheese	125 g
¼ tsp	paprika	1 mL
1 tsp	horseradish	5 mL
1 tbsp	mayonnaise	15 mL
½	baguette, thinly sliced and toasted	½
	salt and pepper	

■ Cut cucumber in half, lengthwise. Set one half aside. Peel other half, seed and grate flesh into bowl. Add cheese, paprika, horseradish and mayonnaise to grated cucumber. Season and mix well.

■ Seed remaining cucumber and slice thinly without peeling.

■ Spread cucumber/cheese mixture over toasted rounds of bread and top with slices of cucumber. Serve.

1 SERVING:	204 CALORIES	19 g CARBOHYDRATE	5 g PROTEIN
	12 g FAT	1.0 g FIBER	

CREAMY POTATO SOUP
(SERVES 4 TO 6)

4	large potatoes, peeled and cubed	4
½	onion, finely chopped	½
⅓	stalk celery, diced	⅓
3 cups	water	750 mL
4 cups	milk, heated	1 L
1 tsp	chervil	5 mL
	pinch nutmeg	
	salt and pepper	

■ Place potatoes, onion and celery in saucepan. Add water and season with salt and pepper. Partly cover and bring to boil. Cook 18 minutes over medium heat or according to size of potatoes. Potatoes should be fully cooked.

■ Drain vegetables, reserving liquid in pan, and set aside.

■ Return saucepan with liquid to stove. Cook over high heat to reduce liquid by ¾.

■ Turn off heat. Pour milk into saucepan and stir. Add cooked vegetables, nutmeg, salt and pepper. Cook 4 minutes over very low heat. Note: Do not allow milk to boil at this point.

■ Sprinkle with chervil and serve.

1 SERVING:	231 CALORIES	39 g CARBOHYDRATE	10 g PROTEIN
	4 g FAT	0 g FIBER	

Place potatoes, onion and celery in saucepan.

Add water.

Drain cooked vegetables.

Reduce cooking liquid over high heat.

Add hot milk.

Add cooked vegetables.

SPLIT YELLOW PEA SOUP
(SERVES 4 TO 6)

2 tbsp	bacon fat	30 mL
1	medium onion, chopped	1
2	celery stalks, diced	2
1	large carrot, pared and diced	1
1¼ cups	dry split yellow peas, soaked 8 hours in cold water	300 mL
6 cups	chicken stock, heated	1.5 L
1	bay leaf	1
½ tsp	basil	2 mL
1 tsp	chopped fresh parsley	5 mL
1 cup	cooked ham, in julienne	250 mL
2 tbsp	soft butter	30 mL
	salt and pepper	
	few drops Worcestershire sauce	

■ Heat bacon fat in large saucepan over medium heat. Add onion and cook 3 minutes.

■ Stir in celery and carrot; cover and cook 4 minutes, stirring once or twice.

■ Stir in drained soaked peas. Add chicken stock and all seasonings including bay leaf. Add ham; partly cover and cook soup 45 minutes over medium heat. Stir several times.

■ Add Worcestershire sauce and butter; mix well and serve hot.

1 SERVING:	207 CALORIES	14 g CARBOHYDRATE	11 g PROTEIN
	12 g FAT	1.0 g FIBER	

NAVY BEAN SOUP

(SERVES 4 TO 6)

1 cup	dried navy beans	250 mL
2 oz	salt pork, diced medium	60 g
2	onions, diced	2
½	stalk celery, diced	½
½ tsp	oregano	2 mL
1	bay leaf	1
1	large carrot, pared and diced large	1
	salt and pepper	

■ Place beans in large bowl and cover with hot water. Soak 2 hours.

■ Place salt pork in large saucepan over medium heat. Cook 3 minutes. Add onions and celery; cook 4 minutes over low heat.

■ Drain beans and add to onions in saucepan. Add seasonings. Pour in enough cold water to cover beans by 3 in (8 cm). Bring to boil. Cook 1½ hours, partly covered, over medium heat. Stir occasionally.

■ Add diced carrot and correct seasoning. Continue cooking 1 hour, stirring occasionally.

1 SERVING: 168 CALORIES 16 g CARBOHYDRATE 5 g PROTEIN
9 g FAT 4.8 g FIBER

CREAM OF ARTICHOKE BOTTOMS
(SERVES 4)

4 tbsp	butter	60 mL
2	shallots, finely chopped	2
8	fresh artichoke bottoms, washed	8
4 tbsp	flour	60 mL
5 cups	chicken stock, heated	1.2 L
½ cup	heavy cream (optional)	125 mL
1 tbsp	chopped fresh parsley	15 mL
	few drops lemon juice	
	croutons	
	salt and pepper	

■ Heat butter in saucepan over medium heat. Add shallots and artichoke bottoms. Season with salt and pepper, cover and cook 18 minutes over low heat.

■ Mix in flour and continue cooking 3 minutes.

■ Pour in chicken stock and stir to mix. Bring to boil, then cook 20 minutes over low heat.

■ Purée soup. Stir in cream, parsley and lemon juice.

■ Serve with croutons.

1 SERVING:	325 CALORIES	25 g CARBOHYDRATE	5 g PROTEIN
	23 g FAT	1.0 g FIBER	

SPLIT PEA SOUP

(SERVES 4 TO 6)

2 tbsp	butter	30 mL
1	onion, finely chopped	1
1	celery stalk, diced	1
2	carrots, pared and diced	2
1	meaty ham bone	1
1⅓ cups	split peas, rinsed in cold water	325 mL
6 cups	vegetable stock	1.5 L
1	bay leaf	1
¼ tsp	thyme	1 mL
5	sprigs fresh parsley	5
1 tsp	mustard seeds	5 mL
¼ tsp	ground cloves	1 mL
	salt and pepper	

■ Melt butter in large saucepan over medium heat. Add onion, celery and carrots. Cover and cook 7 minutes over low heat.

■ Add remaining ingredients; season with salt and pepper. Bring to boil. Cook 3 hours, partly covered, over low heat. Stir occasionally.

■ Remove ham bone.

■ Serve with croutons.

1 SERVING:	128 CALORIES	16 g CARBOHYDRATE	5 g PROTEIN
	5 g FAT	1.0 g FIBER	

SHE-CRAB SOUP

(SERVES 4 TO 6)

2 cups	milk	500 mL
¼ tsp	mace	1 mL
2 cups	crab meat, fresh or frozen, flaked	500 mL
3 tbsp	butter	45 mL
2 cups	light cream	500 mL
½ cup	crushed soda crackers	125 mL
2 tbsp	sherry	30 mL
	pinch cayenne pepper	
	salt and pepper	
	chopped fresh parsley	

■ Pour milk into top half of double boiler. Add mace and cook 8 minutes over low heat.

■ Add crab meat, butter and cream. Season with salt, pepper and cayenne pepper. Stir and cook 15 minutes over low heat. Stir occasionally during cooking.

■ Remove from heat. Add crushed crackers and let stand several minutes to thicken soup.

■ Stir in sherry just before serving.

■ Sprinkle with parsley and serve.

1 SERVING: 351 CALORIES   13 g CARBOHYDRATE   16 g PROTEIN
26 g FAT   0 g FIBER

WATERCRESS SOUP WITH POTATO

(SERVES 4 TO 6)

2 tbsp	butter	30 mL
1	onion, sliced	1
1	garlic clove, smashed and chopped	1
2	bunches fresh watercress, washed and chopped	2
½ tsp	thyme	2 mL
1 tsp	oregano	5 mL
1 tbsp	chopped fresh parsley	15 mL
4	large potatoes, peeled and sliced	4
5 cups	light chicken stock, heated	1.2 L
½ cup	sour cream	125 mL
	salt and pepper	

■ Heat butter in saucepan over medium heat. Add onion and garlic; cook 4 minutes over low heat.

■ Add watercress and seasonings. Mix, cover and cook 8 minutes over low heat. Stir occasionally.

■ Add potatoes and chicken stock. Season and bring to boil. Cook 30 minutes, partly covered, over medium heat.

■ Force soup through sieve into bowl. Incorporate sour cream.

■ If desired, sprinkle with paprika before serving.

1 SERVING:	221 CALORIES	33 g CARBOHYDRATE	4 g PROTEIN
	8 g FAT	1.0 g FIBER	

EGG-DROP CHICKEN SOUP

(SERVES 4)

5 cups	chicken stock, heated	1.2 L	
2	eggs, well beaten	2	
1 tsp	chopped fresh parsley	5 mL	
	freshly ground pepper		
	few drops Worcestershire sauce		

■ Pour chicken stock into saucepan and bring to boil.

■ Meanwhile, place eggs in small bowl. Add parsley, pepper and Worcestershire sauce; beat together well.

■ Reduce heat under soup to medium. Pour egg mixture into liquid and stir quickly; cook 30 seconds.

■ Remove from heat and serve at once.

1 SERVING:	47 CALORIES	1 g CARBOHYDRATE	5 g PROTEIN
	3 g FAT	0 g FIBER	

SAVANNAH'S FRESH OKRA SOUP

(SERVES 4 TO 6)

1 tbsp	olive oil	15 mL
1	celery stalk, diced	1
1	medium onion, chopped	1
3	tomatoes, peeled and diced	3
½ tsp	thyme	2 mL
1 tsp	basil	5 mL
½ tsp	celery seeds	2 mL
1	meaty ham bone	1
6 cups	vegetable or light chicken stock, heated	1.5 L
2 cups	fresh okra, cleaned and cut in two	500 mL
	pinch sugar	
	few drops Worcestershire sauce	
	salt and pepper	

- Heat oil in saucepan. Add celery and onion; cook 5 minutes over medium heat.

- Add tomatoes and all seasonings. Mix and cook 2 minutes.

- Add ham bone and stock. Bring to boil.

- Stir in okra and continue cooking 45 minutes over medium heat. Stir occasionally.

- Serve over steamed rice.

1 SERVING:	80 CALORIES	11 g CARBOHYDRATE	2 g PROTEIN
	3 g FAT	3.3 g FIBER	

CREAM OF EGGPLANT SOUP
(SERVES 4 TO 6)

2 tbsp	butter	30 mL
1	onion, finely chopped	1
1	zucchini, diced	1
3 tbsp	flour	45 mL
1	medium eggplant, peeled and diced	1
½ tsp	sugar	2 mL
4 cups	light chicken stock, heated	1 L
½ cup	sour cream	125 mL
	paprika	
	salt and pepper	

■ Melt butter in saucepan over medium heat. Add onion and zucchini; cover and cook 5 minutes over low heat.

■ Mix in flour; continue cooking 3 minutes over low heat.

■ Add eggplant, sugar and chicken stock. Sprinkle in paprika, mix and bring to boil. Cook 45 minutes over low heat.

■ Force soup through sieve into bowl. Season and stir in sour cream.

Note: Do not reheat soup after sour cream has been added.

1 SERVING:	122 CALORIES	10 g CARBOHYDRATE	2 g PROTEIN
	8 g FAT	1.4 g FIBER	

Add onion and zucchini to hot butter in saucepan. Cover and cook 5 minutes over low heat.

Mix in flour; continue cooking 3 minutes over low heat.

Add eggplant and sugar.

Add chicken stock and paprika.

Force cooked soup through sieve into bowl.

Add sour cream.

SHE-CRAB SOUP
À LA MODE
(SERVES 4 TO 6)

2 tbsp	butter	30 mL
1	onion, grated	1
1	celery stalk, grated	1
¼ tsp	mace	1 mL
2 tbsp	flour	30 mL
2 cups	milk	500 mL
1½ cups	crab meat, fresh or frozen, flaked	375 mL
½ cup	light cream	125 mL
2 tbsp	sherry	30 mL
	salt and pepper	

■ Heat butter in saucepan over medium heat. Add onion, celery and mace. Mix and cook 6 minutes over low heat.

■ Sprinkle in flour and mix well. Cook 2 minutes. Season with salt and pepper.

■ Incorporate milk using whisk. Season again, then bring to boil. Cook 8 minutes over low heat, stirring occasionally.

■ Add crab meat and simmer 5 minutes.

■ Incorporate cream and simmer 2 minutes.

■ Add sherry, mix and simmer 1 minute. Serve.

1 SERVING:	201 CALORIES	11 g CARBOHYDRATE	12 g PROTEIN
	12 g FAT	0 g FIBER	

CHUNKY SUMMER SQUASH AND POTATO SOUP

(SERVES 4)

1 tbsp	butter	15 mL
1	onion, sliced	1
2	shallots, sliced	2
¼ tsp	thyme	1 mL
1	bay leaf	1
1 tsp	basil	5 mL
1 tsp	celery seeds	5 mL
3	potatoes, peeled and sliced	3
5 cups	vegetable stock, heated	1.2 L
1	yellow summer squash, halved lengthwise and sliced	1
	salt and pepper	

■ Heat butter in saucepan over medium heat. Add onion and shallots. Cook 7 minutes, stirring once. Season with salt and pepper.

■ Add seasonings and mix well. Add potatoes and vegetable stock. Season to taste. Bring to boil and cook 8 minutes over medium heat.

■ Stir in summer squash and continue cooking 8 minutes. Serve.

---

1 SERVING: 183 CALORIES   35 g CARBOHYDRATE   4 g PROTEIN
3 g FAT   1.1 g FIBER

Chicken Gumbo

CHICKEN GUMBO
(SERVES 6 TO 8)

4½ lbs	chicken, cleaned	2 kg
12 cups	cold water	3 L
1	large onion, quartered	1
2	carrots, pared and cut in two	2
2	celery stalks, diced large	2
1	bay leaf	1
4	parsley sprigs	4
	salt and pepper	

■ Place chicken in large pot. Add water and bring to boil. Boil 8 to 10 minutes over medium heat. Skim foam off liquid during cooking process.

■ Add remaining ingredients and season well. Partly cover and cook 1 to 1¼ hours.

■ When chicken is cooked, remove from pot and set aside.

■ Leave pot on stove over medium heat. Continue cooking liquid 20 minutes. Strain and set aside.

1 tbsp	butter	15 mL
1	large onion, diced	1
2	carrots, pared and diced	2
1 cup	corn kernels	250 mL
1 cup	frozen peas	250 mL
¼ lb	green beans, pared and cut in three	125 g
12	fresh okra, pared and halved	12
½ lb	fresh mushrooms, cleaned and halved	250 g
3	tomatoes, peeled and diced	3
½ tsp	basil	2 mL
	salt and pepper	

■ Melt butter in large saucepan over medium heat. Add onion and carrots. Cover and cook 5 minutes without letting onion brown.

■ Add remaining ingredients and stir. Add 6-7 cups (1.6-1.7 L) of reserved cooking liquid from chicken. Season and cook 15 minutes over medium-low heat. Stir occasionally.

■ Meanwhile, remove skin from chicken and cut meat into cubes. Add meat to soup. Simmer 8 minutes over low heat. Serve.

1 SERVING:	196 CALORIES	27 g CARBOHYDRATE	16 g PROTEIN
	3 g FAT	9 g FIBER	

CAULIFLOWER SOUP
(SERVES 4 TO 6)

3 tbsp	butter	45 mL
1	large onion, thinly sliced	1
1	small cauliflower, in small florets	1
½ tsp	basil	2 mL
3	parsley sprigs	3
3 tbsp	flour	45 mL
6 cups	chicken stock, heated	1.5 L
1	bay leaf	1
	salt and pepper	

■ Heat butter in large saucepan over medium heat. Add onion, partly cover, and cook 6 minutes over low heat.

■ Stir in cauliflower, basil and parsley sprigs; season well. Cook 8 minutes, partly covered, over low heat.

■ Mix in flour until well incorporated; continue cooking 2 minutes uncovered.

■ Pour in chicken stock, add bay leaf and season; bring to boil. Cook soup, partly covered, 25 minutes over low heat.

■ Pass soup through food mill or purée in blender before serving.

1 SERVING:	105 CALORIES	8 g CARBOHYDRATE	2 g PROTEIN
	7 g FAT	1.3 g FIBER	

POTAGE ST-GERMAIN

(SERVES 6-8)

1 tbsp	butter	15 mL
1	large onion, chopped	1
2	celery stalks, sliced	2
1	green pepper, chopped	1
2 cups	split green peas, well washed	500 mL
10 cups	light chicken stock, heated	2.5 L
1 tsp	chopped fresh rosemary	5 mL
1 tsp	chopped fresh thyme	5 mL
1 tsp	chopped fresh lovage	5 mL
1 tbsp	chopped fresh parsley	15 mL
3 tbsp	heavy cream	45 mL
	salt and pepper	

■ Heat butter in large saucepan over medium heat. Cook onion, celery and green pepper, covered, 4 minutes.

■ Reduce heat to low and continue cooking 6 to 7 minutes.

■ Mix in split peas and season. Pour in chicken stock and add seasonings; pepper well. Partly cover and bring to boil over medium heat.

■ Reduce heat to medium-low and cook 1¼ to 1½ hours.

■ Force soup through sieve or food mill, incorporate cream and serve.

1 SERVING:	123 CALORIES	16 g CARBOHYDRATE	6 g PROTEIN
	4 g FAT	0 g FIBER	

ONION SOUP AU GRATIN
(SERVES 4)

2 tbsp	butter	30 mL
3	Spanish onions, thinly sliced	3
1 cup	dry white wine	250 mL
5 cups	beef stock, heated	1.2 L
1	bouquet garni (thyme, bay leaf, basil and parsley)	1
1 cup	grated Gruyère or Emmentaler cheese	250 mL
	cayenne pepper	
	salt and pepper	
	large slices of toasted French bread	

■ Heat butter in saucepan over medium heat. Add onions and brown 35 minutes over medium-low heat. Stir several times during cooking, and do not allow onions to burn.

■ Pour in wine and cook 6 minutes over high heat.

■ Add beef stock, bouquet garni and cayenne pepper. Season with salt and pepper. Stir and cook soup 30 minutes over medium heat. Do not cover.

■ Place 2 tbsp (30 mL) of grated cheese in bottom of each ovenproof soup bowl. Ladle in soup and add toasted bread. Top with remaining cheese.

■ Set bowls on ovenproof platter and place in middle of preheated oven set at broil. Brown 8 minutes. Serve.

1 SERVING:	258 CALORIES	15 g CARBOHYDRATE	9 g PROTEIN
	13 g FAT	1.3 g FIBER	

Add onions to hot butter in saucepan.

Brown onions for 35 minutes. Do not allow onions to burn.

Pour in wine and cook 6 minutes over high heat.

Add beef stock, bouquet garni and cayenne pepper. Season with salt and pepper. Continue cooking.

Place cheese in bottom of each soup bowl.

Ladle soup into bowls.

CREAM OF GREEN ONION SOUP

(SERVES 4 TO 6)

3 tbsp	butter	45 mL
16	green onions, chopped	16
3 tbsp	flour	45 mL
4½ cups	chicken stock, heated	1.1 L
2	large potatoes, peeled and sliced	2
½ tsp	thyme	2 mL
1 tsp	basil	5 mL
1 tsp	tarragon	5 mL
1 tbsp	chopped fresh parsley	15 mL
	salt and pepper	

■ Melt butter in saucepan over medium heat. Add green onions and cook 6 minutes over low heat.

■ Mix in flour and cook 1 minute.

■ Whisk in chicken stock. Add potatoes and seasonings. Cook 30 minutes over medium-low heat, stirring occasionally.

■ Remove from heat and force soup through coarse sieve into bowl. Sprinkle with parsley and serve.

1 SERVING:	96 CALORIES	7 g CARBOHYDRATE	2 g PROTEIN
	7 g FAT	1.5 g FIBER	

CAROLINA BEEF AND BEANS

(SERVES 4 TO 6)

¾ cup	dried black beans	175 mL
4 cups	cold water	1 L
1 tsp	olive oil	5 mL
¾ lb	beef short ribs, cut up	375 g
1	large onion, diced	1
½	stalk celery, diced	½
1	garlic clove, peeled	1
1	bay leaf	1
½ tsp	basil	2 mL
1 tbsp	chopped fresh parsley	15 mL
1	large carrot, pared and diced	1
	salt and pepper	

■ Place beans in saucepan and pour in water. Bring to boil over medium heat. Boil 7 minutes. Remove saucepan from heat and let stand 1 hour.

■ Heat oil in large saucepan over medium heat. Add short ribs and sear 4 minutes.

■ Add onion and celery; mix well and continue cooking 4 minutes.

■ Add garlic, seasonings and carrot. Drain beans and add to saucepan. Correct seasoning. Add 5 cups (1.2 L) cold water, stir and bring to boil. Partly cover and cook 1½ hours over medium heat. Stir occasionally.

1 SERVING:	219 CALORIES	9 g CARBOHYDRATE	25 g PROTEIN
	9 g FAT	3.2 g FIBER	

Beaufort Bisque

BEAUFORT BISQUE
(SERVES 4 TO 6)

⅓ lb	fresh scallops, washed	150 g
⅓ lb	fresh shrimp, shelled and deveined	150 g
3 tbsp	butter	45 mL
1	small onion, finely chopped	1
½	stalk celery, diced	½
3 tbsp	flour	45 mL
3 cups	fish or light chicken stock, heated	750 mL
¼ tsp	ground fennel seed	1 mL
1 cup	milk or light cream, heated	250 mL
¼ cup	sherry	50 mL
1 tsp	chopped fresh parsley	5 mL
	lemon juice	
	paprika	
	salt and pepper	

- Place scallops and shrimp in large sauté pan. Add lemon juice and pour in enough water to cover. Place sheet of waxed paper over seafood and bring to boil.

- As soon as water starts to boil, remove sauté pan from heat. Let seafood stand in hot liquid for 1 minute.

- Using slotted spoon, remove seafood from liquid and set aside. Reserve cooking liquid.

- Heat butter in saucepan over medium heat. Add onion and celery; cook 4 minutes over low heat.

- Sprinkle in flour, mix and cook 1 minute.

- Using whisk, incorporate fish or chicken stock and reserved cooking liquid. Season with salt, pepper and fennel. Cook 8 minutes over low heat.

- Incorporate hot milk and simmer 3 minutes.

- Add seafood and simmer 2 minutes over low heat.

- Add sherry and simmer another 2 minutes.

- Sprinkle with parsley and paprika. Serve.

1 SERVING: 185 CALORIES   9 g CARBOHYDRATE   17 g PROTEIN
9 g FAT   0 g FIBER

ALI CAT SANDWICHES

(SERVES 4)

8	slices pumpernickel bread	8
8	thin slices cooked pork	8
8	slices Havarti cheese	8
8	lettuce leaves	8
¼ cup	Apple and Raisin Chutney (see page 92)	50 mL
	mayonnaise to taste	
	mustard to taste	

■ Spread each slice of bread with mayonnaise and mustard to taste.

■ On half the bread slices, build sandwiches with slice of pork, slice of cheese, lettuce leaf and layer of chutney. Repeat layers, top with second bread slice and cut sandwiches in half.

■ Serve with potato chips and pickles.

1 SERVING:	629 CALORIES	64 g CARBOHYDRATE	28 g PROTEIN
	29 g FAT	2.5 g FIBER	

BREEZEWOOD VEGETABLE SOUP
(SERVES 6)

1 tbsp	butter	15 mL
1	small onion, chopped	1
1	large carrot, pared and diced	1
¼	cabbage, washed and sliced	¼
¼ lb	fresh green beans, pared and cut in three	125 g
½ cup	frozen corn kernels	125 mL
½ cup	cooked black beans	125 mL
¼ cup	frozen peas	50 mL
4	slices corned beef, diced	4
4 cups	beef stock, heated	1 L
1 cup	tomato juice	250 mL
	few drops Worcestershire sauce	
	salt and pepper	

■ Melt butter in medium saucepan over medium heat. Add onion and carrot; cover and cook 6 minutes over low heat.

■ Add cabbage, mix and continue cooking 3 minutes.

■ Add remaining ingredients and mix well. Bring to boil, then cook 10 minutes over medium heat.

■ Serve with garlic bread.

1 SERVING:	136 CALORIES	14 g CARBOHYDRATE	6 g PROTEIN
	6 g FAT	4.2 g FIBER	

WINDOW'S RED PEPPER SOUP
(SERVES 4)

4 tbsp	butter	60 mL
1	onion, sliced	1
1	shallot, sliced	1
1 tbsp	paprika	15 mL
4	red peppers, seeded and sliced	4
½ tsp	cayenne pepper	2 mL
½ tsp	thyme	2 mL
1 tsp	basil	5 mL
1 tsp	oregano	5 mL
4½ tbsp	flour	65 mL
4½ cups	light chicken stock, heated	1.1 L
1 tbsp	tomato paste	15 mL
2 tbsp	heavy cream	30 mL
	salt and pepper	

■ Heat butter in large saucepan. When hot, add onion, shallot and paprika; mix and cook 6 minutes over low heat.

■ Add peppers and season with salt and pepper. Add all remaining seasonings and cover. Cook 20 minutes over low heat, stirring occasionally.

■ Mix in flour and continue cooking 2 minutes. Do not cover.

■ Pour in chicken stock and mix to incorporate. Increase heat to medium. Mix in tomato paste, then cook 15 minutes over medium-low heat.

■ Purée soup in food processor, then pour into bowl. Stir in cream and serve.

1 SERVING:	209 CALORIES	16 g CARBOHYDRATE	3 g PROTEIN
	15 g FAT	1.4 g FIBER	

CREAMY SUMMER SQUASH SOUP

(SERVES 4 TO 6)

4 tbsp	butter	60 mL
1	onion, sliced	1
2	yellow summer squash, sliced	2
4 tbsp	flour	60 mL
4½ cups	light chicken stock, heated	1.1 L
½ tsp	thyme	2 mL
1 tsp	basil	5 mL
½ tsp	celery seeds	2 mL
¼ tsp	paprika	1 mL
	salt and pepper	

■ Melt butter in saucepan over medium heat. Add onion and cook 3 minutes over low heat.

■ Add summer squash and season well. Cover and cook 6 minutes over low heat.

■ Sprinkle in flour and mix well. Cook 1 minute.

■ Stir in chicken stock and seasonings. Correct seasoning and bring to boil. Cook 20 minutes over low heat.

■ Force soup through sieve into bowl. Serve.

1 SERVING: 133 CALORIES 9 g CARBOHYDRATE 2 g PROTEIN
10 g FAT 1.4 g FIBER

VICHYSSOISE
(SERVES 4 TO 6)

1 tbsp	butter	15 mL
1	Spanish onion, sliced	1
3	leeks, white part only, washed and sliced	3
3	parsley sprigs	3
½ tsp	thyme	2 mL
1 tsp	basil	5 mL
4	potatoes, peeled and sliced	4
4 cups	light chicken stock, heated	1 L
½ cup	heavy cream	125 mL
	salt and pepper	

■ Heat butter in sauté pan over medium heat. Add onion and cook 7 minutes over low heat, stirring once during cooking.

■ Add leeks, parsley and seasonings. Cover and cook 7 minutes over low heat.

■ Add remaining ingredients, except cream. Season, mix and cook 30 minutes. Stir occasionally.

■ Pass soup through food mill. Incorporate cream and refrigerate.

■ Serve soup cold and if desired, garnish with chopped fresh chives.

1 SERVING:	276 CALORIES	40 g CARBOHYDRATE	5 g PROTEIN
	11 g FAT	5.0 g FIBER	

Cook onion in hot butter.

Add leeks, parsley and seasonings. Cover and continue cooking over low heat.

Add potatoes.

Add chicken stock and season well. Mix and cook soup 30 minutes.

Pass soup through food mill.

Incorporate cream and refrigerate.

APPLE AND RAISIN CHUTNEY

(SERVES 10)

¾ cup	white vinegar	175 mL
5	apples, cored, peeled and sliced	5
⅔ cup	brown sugar	150 mL
¼ cup	chopped lemon rind	50 mL
¼ cup	chopped orange rind	50 mL
½ cup	chopped candied ginger	125 mL
¼ cup	sliced seedless green grapes	50 mL
1	garlic clove, smashed and chopped	1
1	mango, peeled and sliced	1
¼ tsp	mustard seeds	1 mL
¼ tsp	powdered ginger salt and pepper	1 mL

■ Place vinegar in saucepan and bring to boil over medium heat. Add apples and partly cover; cook 5 minutes.

■ Mix in remaining ingredients and continue cooking, partly covered, for 13 minutes. Stir several times during cooking.

■ Cool and serve with meat, or use as a sandwich spread.

1 SERVING:	123 CALORIES	31 g CARBOHYDRATE	0 g PROTEIN
	0 g FAT	1.7 g FIBER	

HALF CHICKEN ON THE GRILL

(SERVES 4)

2	chickens, 2½ lbs (1.2 kg) each, cut in half	2
2	portions Thick Barbecue Sauce (see page 137)	2
1	lemon, halved	1
	oil	
	salt and freshly ground pepper	

- Preheat oven to 375 °F (190 °C).

- Leave skin on chicken.

- Place chicken halves in roasting pan and season well. Rub lemon over chicken skin and brush with oil. Cook 20 minutes in oven.

- Preheat barbecue at medium.

- Oil grill. Remove chickens from roasting pan and place on grill, skin-side up. Brush with barbecue sauce and cover. Cook 10 to 12 minutes.

- Turn chickens over and baste again. Cover and continue cooking 10 to 12 minutes.

- Serve with a salad and grilled vegetables.

---

1 SERVING:	484 CALORIES	3 g CARBOHYDRATE	70 g PROTEIN
	20 g FAT	0 g FIBER	

COUNTRY TURKEY STUFFING

1 cup	long-grain rice	250 mL
2 cups	cold water	500 mL
6 tbsp	butter	90 mL
1	onion, finely chopped	1
1	large stalk celery, finely chopped	1
2 tbsp	chopped fresh parsley	30 mL
½ tsp	sage	2 mL
½ tsp	thyme	2 mL
2	eggs, well beaten	2
4	slices white bread, crusts removed, cubed and soaked in milk	4
2 cups	canned chestnuts, well drained and chopped	500 mL
1 tsp	ground fresh pepper	5 mL
	salt	

■ Spread rice in bottom of frying pan. Brown the rice over low heat.

■ Pour water into saucepan and add pinch of salt. Bring to boil. Add browned rice to water, cover and cook 15 minutes over low heat.

■ Melt butter in another saucepan over low heat. Add onion, celery, parsley, sage and thyme. Mix and cook 4 minutes over low heat.

■ Remove saucepan from heat. Add eggs, drained bread, chestnuts, pepper, salt and rice. Mix well. Stuff turkey with mixture.

---

1 SERVING: 2097 CALORIES   288 g CARBOHYDRATE   36 g PROTEIN
89 g FAT   8.8 g FIBER

ROAST CHICKEN WITH MUSHROOM GRAVY

(SERVES 4)

3½-lb	chicken, cleaned and trussed	1.6-kg
2 tbsp	melted butter	30 mL
1	onion, finely chopped	1
½ lb	fresh mushrooms, cleaned and diced	250 g
1 tsp	chopped fresh parsley	5 mL
½ tsp	tarragon	2 mL
1½ cups	beef stock, heated	375 mL
1 tbsp	tomato paste	15 mL
1 tbsp	cornstarch	15 mL
3 tbsp	cold water	45 mL
	juice of 1 lemon	
	salt and pepper	

■ Preheat oven to 425 °F (220 °C).

■ Place chicken in roasting pan and season with salt and pepper. Brush skin with melted butter and lemon juice. Roast 30 minutes in oven.

■ Reduce heat to 350 °F (180 °C). Continue cooking chicken 1 hour and 15 minutes.

■ Check if chicken is cooked by inserting a skewer in thickest part of leg. Juices should be clear, not pink.

■ Remove cooked chicken from roasting pan and set aside. Discard ⅔ of fat from roasting pan. Place pan on stove burner over high heat. Add onion and cook 3 minutes, stirring frequently.

■ Add mushrooms and seasonings; mix well. Cook 4 minutes over high heat.

■ Mix in beef stock and tomato paste. Continue cooking 3 minutes.

■ Dissolve cornstarch in cold water; stir into mushroom sauce and cook 1 minute.

■ Serve roast chicken with gravy. Accompany with roasted potatoes.

1 SERVING:	451 CALORIES	8 g CARBOHYDRATE	62 g PROTEIN
	19 g FAT	1.9 g FIBER	

Brush skin of chicken with melted butter.

After cooked chicken is removed from pan, discard ⅔ of fat left in pan.

Place pan on burner over high heat. Add onion and cook 3 minutes, stirring frequently.

Add mushrooms and seasonings; mix well. Cook 4 minutes over high heat.

Mix in beef stock and tomato paste. Continue cooking 3 minutes.

Stir in dissolved cornstarch.

SAUCE FOR MEAT AND CHICKEN

(SERVES 4 TO 5)

2½ tbsp	butter	40 mL
1 lb	fresh mushrooms, cleaned and sliced thick	500 g
2	shallots, finely chopped	2
1 tbsp	chopped fresh parsley	15 mL
½ tsp	oregano	2 mL
1 cup	dry white wine	250 mL
1½ cups	beef stock, heated	375 mL
1½ tbsp	tomato paste	25 mL
1½ tbsp	cornstarch	25 mL
3 tbsp	cold water	45 mL
3 tbsp	heavy cream (optional)	45 mL
	few drops of Worcestershire sauce	
	few drops of Tabasco sauce	
	salt and pepper	

■ Heat butter in sauté pan over medium heat. Add mushrooms, shallots, parsley and oregano. Cook 10 minutes. Season with salt and pepper.

■ Add wine and cook 4 minutes over high heat.

■ Incorporate beef stock, tomato paste, Worcestershire and Tabasco sauces. Cook 8 to 10 minutes over low heat.

■ Dissolve cornstarch in cold water; stir into sauce and cook 2 minutes.

■ If desired, add cream and cook 2 minutes.

■ Serve with red meat, chicken, veal or lamb.

1 SERVING:	138 CALORIES	11 g CARBOHYDRATE	3 g PROTEIN
	9 g FAT	2.7 g FIBER	

DELICIOUS BROILED CHICKEN

(SERVES 4)

3 tbsp	melted butter	45 mL
3 tbsp	olive oil	45 mL
2	dry shallots, finely chopped	2
2 tbsp	chopped fresh parsley	30 mL
2	garlic cloves, smashed and chopped	2
¼ tsp	crushed chilies	1 mL
3½-lb	chicken, cleaned and cut into 8 pieces	1.6-kg
	juice 1 lemon	
	salt and pepper	

■ Preheat oven to 350 °F (180 °C).

■ Combine melted butter and oil in small bowl; set aside.

■ Place shallots, parsley, garlic and crushed chilies in mortar. Mix well and add lemon juice; mix again. Stir half of butter/oil mixture into chilies mixture; set aside.

■ Season chicken pieces well. Brush leftover butter/oil mixture over chicken and place skin-side down in roasting pan. Change oven setting to broil and cook chicken 6 in (15 cm) from broiler element for 8 minutes.

■ Baste chicken, turn pieces over and continue broiling 8 minutes. Turn pieces over again and change oven setting to 350 °F (180 °C); cook 15 minutes, basting frequently.

■ About 4 minutes before chicken is cooked, spread shallot/chilies mixture over chicken pieces. Spoon cooking juices over meat and serve.

1 SERVING:	516 CALORIES	5 g CARBOHYDRATE	61 g PROTEIN
	28 g FAT	0 g FIBER	

SHERRIED PORK TENDERLOIN
(SERVES 4)

2	small pork tenderloins, trimmed of fat and sliced ½ in (1.2 cm) thick	2
3 tbsp	dry sherry	45 mL
2 tbsp	cornstarch	30 mL
1 tbsp	soy sauce	15 mL
1 tbsp	freshly chopped ginger root	15 mL
1 tbsp	olive oil	15 mL
2 tbsp	vegetable oil	30 mL
12	large fresh mushrooms, cleaned and cut in 3	12
1	large green pepper, sliced thick	1
1	celery stalk, thinly sliced	1
1	apple, cut in wedges	1
6 oz	drained bamboo shoots, sliced	200 g
	juice ½ lemon	
	salt and pepper	

■ Place pork in large bowl. Stir together sherry, cornstarch, soy sauce, ginger, olive oil and lemon juice; pour over pork. Season well. Marinate 30 minutes.

■ Heat 1 tbsp (15 mL) vegetable oil in large frying pan over high heat. Add half of meat and stir-fry 3 minutes. Remove and repeat for remaining meat. Set seared pork aside.

■ Add mushrooms to frying pan along with green pepper and celery. Cook 3 minutes over medium-high heat.

■ Add remaining 1 tbsp (15 mL) vegetable oil to pan. Add apple and bamboo shoots; correct seasoning. Cook 3 to 4 minutes over high heat.

■ Return pork to pan, reheat 30 seconds and serve.

---

1 SERVING:	327 CALORIES	14 g CARBOHYDRATE	38 g PROTEIN
	13 g FAT	2.5 g FIBER	

Sherried Pork Tenderloin

ROASTED BONELESS LOIN OF VEAL

(SERVES 4)

1 tbsp	olive oil	15 mL
1½ lbs	boneless loin of veal	750 g
1 tsp	butter	5 mL
1	onion, finely chopped	1
½	stalk celery, diced small	½
½ tsp	basil	2 mL
½ tsp	tarragon	2 mL
1 tbsp	chopped fresh parsley	15 mL
1 cup	dry white wine	250 mL
1¼ cups	chicken stock, heated	300 mL
1 tbsp	cornstarch	15 mL
3 tbsp	cold water	45 mL
	salt and pepper	

■ Preheat oven to 375 °F (190 °C).

■ Heat oil in cast iron frying pan over high heat. Add veal and sear on both sides. Transfer veal to roasting pan.

■ Season meat with salt and pepper. Spread butter over top of meat and cook in oven 20 minutes per lb (500 g).

■ When meat is cooked, remove from roasting pan and keep hot.

■ Place roasting pan on burner over high heat. Add onion, celery and all seasonings. Cook 3 minutes.

■ Pour in wine and cook 5 minutes over high heat.

■ Incorporate chicken stock and bring to boil.

■ Dissolve cornstarch in cold water; stir into sauce. Cook 2 minutes.

■ Pass sauce through sieve into bowl. Discard vegetables and serve sauce with roast.

1 SERVING:	455 CALORIES	5 g CARBOHYDRATE	42 g PROTEIN
	25 g FAT	0 g FIBER	

Have butcher prepare boneless loin of veal.

Sear both sides of meat in hot oil in cast iron frying pan.

Transfer veal to roasting pan and spread butter over top of meat. Cook in oven.

Remove cooked veal from pan. Add onion, celery and all seasonings to juices in pan. Cook 3 minutes.

Pour in wine and cook 5 minutes over high heat. Incorporate chicken stock and bring to boil.

Pass sauce through sieve into bowl. Discard vegetables and serve sauce with veal.

BEEF SIRLOIN AND VEGETABLES ON SKEWERS
(SERVES 4)

1½ lbs	beef sirloin steak, cubed	750 g
2 tbsp	teriyaki sauce	30 mL
2 tbsp	wine vinegar	30 mL
2	garlic cloves, blanched and chopped	2
1 tbsp	chopped fresh ginger	15 mL
¼ tsp	pepper	1 mL
8	large shallots, peeled and blanched	8
2	stalks Chinese cabbage, in 1-in (2.5-cm) pieces	2
1	yellow summer squash, halved lengthwise and sliced	1
4	jalapeño peppers	4
	juice of 1 lemon	
	salt	

■ Place beef in bowl. Add teriyaki sauce, vinegar, garlic, ginger, lemon juice and pepper. Mix well and marinate 1 hour.

■ Preheat barbecue at high.

■ Alternate beef, whole shallots, Chinese cabbage and summer squash on skewers. End each skewer with whole jalapeño pepper. Brush skewers with marinade.

■ Oil grill. Add skewers and cook 2 minutes each side, uncovered. Season to taste and baste with marinade during cooking Serve with vegetables.

1 SERVING:	323 CALORIES	13 g CARBOHYDRATE	47 g PROTEIN
	9 g FAT	2.3 g FIBER	

SKEWERS OF SHRIMP AND RED ONION

(SERVES 4)

1 oz	roasted red pepper, puréed	30 g
2 tbsp	olive oil	30 mL
2 tbsp	lemon juice	30 mL
½ tsp	cayenne pepper	2 mL
2	garlic cloves, blanched and puréed	2
1 tsp	fennel seed	5 mL
½ tsp	pepper	2 mL
24	large shrimp, shelled, deveined and washed	24
1	large red onion, in wedges	1
	salt and pepper	

■ Mix all ingredients, except shrimp and onion, together in bowl.

■ Place shrimp in bowl and add marinade. Mix and marinate 1 hour.

■ Preheat barbecue at medium.

■ Alternate shrimp and onion on skewers.

■ Oil grill and add skewers. Cover and cook 3 to 4 minutes on each side. Season to taste and baste during cooking.

■ Serve with salad or rice.

1 SERVING:	80 CALORIES	3 g CARBOHYDRATE	11 g PROTEIN
	3 g FAT	0 g FIBER	

BONELESS ROUND ROAST

(SERVES 4 TO 6)

½ tsp	pepper	2 mL
¼ tsp	cayenne pepper	1 mL
½ tsp	ground cloves	2 mL
1 tsp	thyme	5 mL
1 tsp	basil	5 mL
2	garlic cloves, smashed and chopped	2
5-lb	boneless round roast	2.3-kg
2 tbsp	olive oil	30 mL
2	onions, diced	2
1	celery stalk, diced	1
3 tbsp	flour	45 mL
1½ cups	beef stock, heated	375 mL
3 tbsp	tomato paste	45 mL
½ cup	sherry wine	125 mL
	salt	

- Preheat oven to 350 °F (180 °C).

- Place all seasonings and garlic in small bowl; mix well.

- Cut some small incisions in roast. Fill slits with seasonings.

- Heat oil in large ovenproof casserole over medium heat. Add meat and sear on all sides. Season with salt and pepper. Remove meat from casserole and set aside.

- Add vegetables to casserole and cook 5 minutes.

- Stir in flour and cook 5 minutes over low heat to brown flour.

- Incorporate beef stock and tomato paste. Mix well, then return roast to casserole. Season with salt, cover and cook 2½ to 3 hours in oven.

- Fifteen minutes before end of cooking time, pour in the sherry wine.

- Serve with assorted vegetables.

1 SERVING: 521 CALORIES   9 g CARBOHYDRATE   73 g PROTEIN
19 g FAT   0 g FIBER

Place all seasonings and garlic in small bowl; mix well.

Cut some small incisions in roast. Fill slits with seasonings.

Sear meat on all sides in hot oil. Season with salt and pepper.

Remove seared meat and set aside.

Cook vegetables in casserole for 5 minutes.

Mix in flour and cook 5 minutes over low heat to brown flour.

HICKORY SPARERIBS WITH WHISKY SAUCE
(SERVES 6 TO 8)

8 lbs	pork spareribs	3.6 kg		*Sauce*		
1 tsp	pepper	5 mL		3 tbsp	butter	45 mL
1 tsp	paprika	5 mL		1	celery stalk, chopped	1
1 tsp	cayenne pepper	5 mL		1	large onion, chopped	1
1 tsp	thyme	5 mL		2	garlic cloves, smashed and chopped	2
1 tsp	basil	5 mL		4 tbsp	flour	60 mL
4	garlic cloves, blanched, peeled and puréed	4		3 cups	beef stock, heated	750 mL
½ cup	hickory liquid smoke seasoning	125 mL		¼ cup	vinegar	50 mL
				5½-oz	can tomato paste	156-mL
2 tbsp	olive oil	30 mL		¼ cup	brown sugar	50 mL
				3 tbsp	whisky	45 mL
					salt and pepper	

■ Place spareribs in saucepan containing boiling water. Cook 18 minutes. Remove and pat dry.

■ Mix remaining ingredients together. Brush mixture over spareribs and marinate 15 minutes.

■ Preheat oven to 350 °F (180 °C).

■ Heat butter in saucepan over medium heat. Add vegetables and garlic; cook 6 minutes.

■ Add flour and mix well. Cook 5 minutes over low heat.

Cook spareribs 18 minutes in boiling water.

Brush marinade over spareribs.

To make sauce, cook vegetables and garlic in hot butter for 6 minutes.

(continued)

■ Incorporate beef stock, vinegar, tomato paste and brown sugar. Mix well and season to taste. Cook sauce 16 minutes over low heat.

■ Mix in whisky.

■ Arrange spareribs in large baking dish. Pour sauce over and cook 45 minutes in oven. Turn spareribs over twice during cooking process.

■ Serve.

1 SERVING:	954 CALORIES	18 g CARBOHYDRATE	108 g PROTEIN
	50 g FAT	0 g FIBER	

Add flour and mix well. Cook 5 minutes over low heat.

Incorporate beef stock and vinegar.

Add tomato paste and brown sugar.

SPICY GRILLED LAMB CHOPS
(SERVES 4)

⅓ tsp	ground ginger	1.5 mL
¼ tsp	allspice	1 mL
1 tsp	curry powder	5 mL
1 tsp	oregano	5 mL
1 cup	tomato sauce	250 mL
3 tbsp	cider vinegar	45 mL
3	garlic cloves, smashed and chopped	3
8	lamb chops, 2.5 cm (1 in) thick, trimmed of fat	8
	salt and pepper	

■ Place all ingredients, except lamb chops, in saucepan. Boil 10 minutes.

■ Place lamb chops in deep glass dish and pour sauce over. Marinate 1 hour.

■ Preheat barbecue at medium-high.

■ Oil grill and add lamb chops. Cover and cook 6 to 7 minutes on each side. After meat is seared, season well and baste with marinade during cooking.

1 SERVING:	430 CALORIES	5 g CARBOHYDRATE	56 g PROTEIN
	21 g FAT	0 g FIBER	

MARINADE FOR STEAK

4	garlic cloves, smashed and chopped	4
3 tbsp	olive oil	45 mL
3 tbsp	teriyaki sauce	45 mL
	few drops sesame oil	
	juice of 1 lemon	
	freshly ground pepper	

■ Place all ingredients in bowl and mix together.

■ Spread mixture over both sides of steaks and arrange side by side in glass dish. Cover with plastic wrap and refrigerate 3 hours.

■ Grill or pan fry steaks as desired.

Note: This recipe yields enough marinade for 4 steaks.

1 SERVING:	401 CALORIES	6 g CARBOHYDRATE	1 g PROTEIN
	42 g FAT	0 g FIBER	

BARBECUED FRESH CORN

(SERVES 4 TO 12)

4 to 12	ears of corn
	soft butter
	salt

4 to 12

■ Do not husk corn. Place ears in cold water and soak 7 to 8 minutes.

■ Preheat barbecue at medium.

■ Place corn on grill and cover. Cook 10 minutes, turning ears over 3 times during cooking.

■ Serve with butter and salt.

---

1 SERVING: 123 CALORIES   19 g CARBOHYDRATE   2 g PROTEIN
                    4 g FAT   3.6 g FIBER

BARBECUED SPARERIBS WITH TOMATO-HONEY SAUCE
(SERVES 4)

2 tbsp	olive oil	30 mL
1	large onion, chopped	1
3	garlic cloves, smashed and chopped	3
⅓ cup	cider vinegar	75 mL
5½-oz	can tomato paste	156-mL
4 tbsp	honey	60 mL
½ tsp	thyme	2 mL
½ tsp	basil	2 mL
¼ cup	Worcestershire sauce	50 mL
½ cup	beef stock, heated	125 mL
4 lbs	pork spareribs	1.8 kg
	salt and pepper	

■ Heat oil in sauté pan over medium heat. Add onion and garlic; cook 5 minutes over low heat.

■ Add cider vinegar, increase heat to high and cook 3 minutes.

■ Mix in tomato paste, honey, seasonings, Worcestershire sauce and beef stock. Cook 12 minutes over medium heat.

■ Pour sauce over spareribs and marinate 15 minutes.

■ Preheat oven to 375 °F (190 °C).

■ Arrange spareribs, with fat side up, in large ovenproof frying pan. Baste generously with marinade and season. Cook 1 hour in oven.

■ Baste pork every 10 minutes with marinade. If the sauce begins sticking to the pan during cooking, add a little water.

1 SERVING: 843 CALORIES   28 g CARBOHYDRATE   95 g PROTEIN
39 g FAT   0 g FIBER

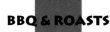

GRILLED STUFFED PORK TENDERLOINS
(SERVES 4)

Stuffing

3 tbsp	butter	45 mL
½	stalk celery, diced	½
½	onion, chopped	½
½ tsp	rosemary	2 mL
1 tbsp	chopped fresh basil	15 mL
6	fresh mushrooms, chopped	6
2 tbsp	Madeira wine	30 mL
½ cup	breadcrumbs	125 mL
	salt and pepper	

■ Heat butter in sauté pan over medium heat. Add celery and onion; cook 5 minutes over low heat.

■ Add seasonings and cook 2 minutes over medium heat.

■ Add mushrooms; continue cooking 4 minutes.

■ Add wine and cook another 2 minutes.

■ Mix in breadcrumbs and cook 1 minute. Remove from heat and transfer mixture to food processor; blend 30 seconds.

2	medium pork tenderloins, fat removed	2
1 tbsp	olive oil	15 mL
1 tsp	teriyaki sauce	5 mL
	juice of 1 lemon	
	freshly ground pepper	

■ Cut each tenderloin open lengthwise to prepare for stuffing. Do not cut through the entire thickness of the meat. Place opened tenderloins between sheets of waxed paper. Pound with mallet to flatten.

■ Spread stuffing over tenderloins, roll and secure with string.

■ Mix oil, teriyaki sauce, lemon juice and pepper together. Brush mixture over pork.

■ Preheat barbecue at medium. Oil grill and add stuffed pork tenderloins. Cover and cook 30 minutes. Season to taste and turn tenderloins over 2 to 3 times during cooking. Baste 5 to 6 times with oil mixture.

1 SERVING:	371 CALORIES	11 g CARBOHYDRATE	38 g PROTEIN
	19 g FAT	1.4 g FIBER	

Cook celery and onion in hot butter for 5 minutes over low heat.

Add seasonings and cook 2 minutes over medium heat.

Add mushrooms and cook 4 minutes. Add wine and cook another 2 minutes. Mix in breadcrumbs and cook 1 minute.

Cut each tenderloin open lengthwise to prepare for stuffing. Do not cut through the entire thickness of the meat.

Place opened tenderloins between sheets of waxed paper. Pound with mallet to flatten.

Spread stuffing over surface of meat.

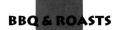

BARBECUE SAUCE #1

(MAKES SAUCE FOR 5-6 LBS [2.3-2.7 KG] OF MEAT)

3 tbsp	butter	45 mL
1	large onion, finely chopped	1
3	green onions, chopped	3
3	garlic cloves, smashed and chopped	3
1 cup	white wine vinegar	250 mL
1 cup	water	250 mL
½ cup	ketchup	125 mL
¼ cup	lime juice	50 mL
¼ cup	brown sugar	50 mL
2 tbsp	chili sauce	30 mL
1 tbsp	dry mustard	15 mL
2 tbsp	Worcestershire sauce	30 mL
½ tsp	cayenne pepper	2 mL
1 tsp	pepper	5 mL
1 tsp	thyme	5 mL
1 tsp	basil	5 mL
1 tsp	oregano	5 mL
	salt	

■ Heat butter in saucepan over medium heat. Add both types of onions and garlic. Cook 5 minutes over low heat, without letting onions brown.

■ Add remaining ingredients and mix well. Bring to boil. Reduce heat to low and cook sauce for 18 minutes.

1 RECIPE:	707 CALORIES	89 g CARBOHYDRATE	7 g PROTEIN
	36 g FAT	3.0 g FIBER	

BARBECUE SAUCE #2

(MAKES SAUCE FOR 5-6 LBS [2.3-2.7 KG] OF MEAT)

4 tbsp	butter	60 mL
1	large onion, finely chopped	1
5	garlic cloves, smashed and chopped	5
1 cup	dry white wine	250 mL
1 tbsp	brown sugar	15 mL
1 cup	tomato sauce	250 mL
½ cup	ketchup	125 mL
1 tbsp	horseradish	15 mL
2 tsp	dry mustard	10 mL
2 tbsp	chili powder	30 mL
½ tsp	cayenne pepper	2 mL
½ tsp	pepper	2 mL
1 tsp	celery salt	5 mL
	salt	

■ Heat butter in saucepan over medium heat. Add onion and garlic; cook 6 minutes over low heat.

■ Pour in wine and cook 2 minutes over high heat.

■ Add remaining ingredients and bring to boil. Cook 18 minutes over low heat.

1 RECIPE:	1055 CALORIES	80 g CARBOHYDRATE	9 g PROTEIN
	61 g FAT	1.8 g FIBER	

BARBECUE SAUCE #3

(MAKES SAUCE FOR 5-6 LBS [2.3-2.7 KG] OF MEAT)

1	red bell pepper	1
1	green chili pepper	1
4 tbsp	butter	60 mL
1	large red onion, finely chopped	1
3	shallots, chopped	3
4	garlic cloves, smashed and chopped	4
1 cup	white vinegar	250 mL
1 cup	water	250 mL
¼ cup	honey	50 mL
½ cup	chili sauce	125 mL
1 tbsp	chili powder	15 mL
1 tsp	oregano	5 mL
1 tsp	basil	5 mL
2	bay leaves, crushed	2
½ tsp	cayenne pepper	2 mL
1 tsp	pepper	5 mL
2 tbsp	lime juice	30 mL
½ cup	chopped pecans	125 mL
	salt	

■ Purée red and chili peppers in food processor. Set aside.

■ Heat butter in saucepan over medium heat. Add onion, shallots and garlic. Cook 6 minutes over low heat, without browning.

■ Pour in vinegar and bring to boil over medium heat. Continue cooking 3 minutes.

■ Add remaining ingredients, except pepper purée and pecans. Correct seasoning and bring to boil. Cook sauce 13 minutes over low heat.

■ Stir in pecans and pepper purée. Continue cooking 5 minutes.

1 RECIPE:	1333 CALORIES	85 g CARBOHYDRATE	12 g PROTEIN
	105 g FAT	3.1 g FIBER	

SPICY RIB ROAST
(SERVES 6)

½	stalk celery, diced	½
1	jalapeño pepper, chopped	1
4	shallots, chopped	4
3 tbsp	butter	45 mL
2	garlic cloves, blanched and puréed	2
½ tsp	cayenne pepper	2 mL
1 tsp	pepper	5 mL
1 tsp	thyme	5 mL
4 lbs	boneless rib roast	1.8 kg
	salt	

Sauce

1	celery stalk, diced large	1
1	large onion, diced large	1
½ tsp	thyme	2 mL
1	bay leaf	1
1½ cups	beef stock, heated	375 mL

■ Preheat oven to 400 °F (200 °C).

■ Place celery, jalapeño pepper and shallots in small bowl. Add butter, garlic and seasonings; mix well.

■ Trim excess fat from roast. Make at least 6 incisions, 1 in (2.5 cm) deep, in meat. Fill slits with spicy butter mixture and place meat in roasting pan.

■ Sear roast in oven 35 minutes at 400 °F (200 °C). Reduce heat to 375 °F (190 °C) and continue cooking 1 hour and 40 minutes. After 15 minutes of cooking at lower temperature, season meat well.

■ Eighteen minutes before the rib roast is cooked, add vegetables and seasonings for sauce to roasting pan.

■ When cooked, remove meat from pan and set aside.

■ Place roasting pan on stove over high heat. Cook 3 minutes. If necessary, remove excess fat.

■ Incorporate beef stock and continue cooking 6 minutes.

■ Strain sauce and serve with roast.

1 SERVING:	563 CALORIES	6 g CARBOHYDRATE	67 g PROTEIN
	30 g FAT	0 g FIBER	

Place celery, jalapeño pepper and shallots in small bowl. Add butter, garlic and seasonings; mix well.

Trim excess fat from meat.

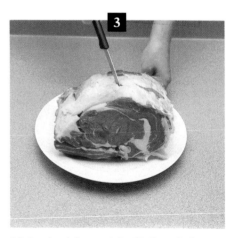

Make incisions, 1 in (2.5 cm) deep, in meat.

Fill slits with spicy butter mixture.

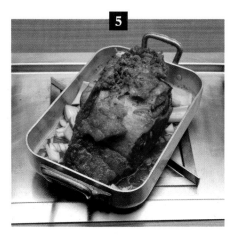

Eighteen minutes before the rib roast is cooked, add vegetables and seasonings to roasting pan.

When cooked, remove meat from pan. Incorporate beef stock.

Pork Tenderloin with Apples

PORK TENDERLOIN WITH APPLES

(SERVES 4)

1 tbsp	butter	15 mL
2	garlic cloves, blanched and puréed	2
3	green onions, chopped	3
1	apple, peeled and finely chopped	1
¼ tsp	cayenne pepper	1 mL
1 tsp	chopped fresh basil	5 mL
2	slices French bread, crusts removed, bread cubed and soaked in milk	2
2 tbsp	grated Gruyère cheese	30 mL
2	pork tenderloins, trimmed of fat	2
	salt and pepper	
	oil	

■ Heat butter in saucepan over medium heat. Add garlic and green onions; cook 2 minutes.

■ Add apple and seasonings. Cook 4 minutes.

■ Squeeze excess milk from bread. Add bread to apple mixture in saucepan. Stir in cheese and remove pan from heat.

■ Transfer stuffing to food processor; process to mix.

■ Cut each tenderloin open lengthwise to prepare for stuffing. Do not cut through entire thickness of meat.

■ Place opened tenderloins between sheets of waxed paper. Pound with mallet to flatten.

■ Spread stuffing over tenderloins, roll and secure with string. Brush meat with oil.

■ Preheat barbecue at medium.

■ Oil grill and add pork tenderloins. Cover and cook 30 minutes. Season to taste. Turn tenderloins 2 to 3 times during cooking.

■ Serve with yellow summer squash, if desired.

1 SERVING:	292 CALORIES	11 g CARBOHYDRATE	37 g PROTEIN
	11 g FAT	1.5 g FIBER	

GRILLED BACK BACON WITH GARLIC

(SERVES 4)

1 tbsp	olive oil	15 mL
½ tsp	honey	2 mL
1	garlic clove, blanched and puréed	1
½ tsp	Worcestershire sauce	2 mL
8	slices back bacon, ¼ in (0.65 cm) thick	8
	juice of ½ lemon	
	freshly ground pepper	

- Mix all ingredients, except bacon, together in bowl.

- Brush mixture over both sides of bacon slices.

- Preheat barbecue at medium.

- Oil grill and add bacon slices. Cover and cook 3 to 4 minutes on each side.

- Serve with sautéed potatoes.

1 SERVING:	111 CALORIES	1 g CARBOHYDRATE	11 g PROTEIN
	7 g FAT	0 g FIBER	

GRILLED CHICKEN LEGS WITH BARBECUE SAUCE
(SERVES 4)

4	chicken legs, skinned	4
½	recipe Barbecue Sauce #1 (see page 116)	½
	salt and freshly ground pepper	

■ Slash meat on legs in several places. Place legs on plate and cover with barbecue sauce. Marinate 2 hours in refrigerator.

■ Preheat barbecue at medium-low.

■ Oil grill and add chicken legs. Cover and cook 20 minutes. If chicken is cooking too fast, open cover slightly. Turn legs once and baste frequently.

■ Transfer legs to upper grill of barbecue. Cover and continue cooking 25 minutes. Turn legs once and baste frequently. Season to taste.

■ Serve with grilled yellow summer squash.

1 SERVING:	351 CALORIES	22 g CARBOHYDRATE	27 g PROTEIN
	17 g FAT	1.0 g FIBER	

ROASTED CORNISH HENS WITH WHITE WINE
(SERVES 4)

2	large Cornish hens, cleaned and trussed	2
⅓ cup	unsalted butter	75 mL
2	shallots, chopped	2
½ cup	dry white wine	125 mL
1 cup	chicken stock, heated	250 mL
1 tbsp	cornstarch	15 mL
3 tbsp	cold water	45 mL
1 tbsp	chopped fresh parsley	15 mL
1 tbsp	chopped fresh tarragon	15 mL
	salt and pepper	

Caramelized Apricots

12	apricots, halved and pitted	12
1 tbsp	butter	15 mL
1 tsp	brown sugar	5 mL
2 tbsp	water	30 mL

■ Preheat oven to 450 °F (230 °C).

■ Season cavities of hens with salt and pepper. Spread butter over hens and season skin generously. Place in roasting pan and cook 30 to 40 minutes. Baste during cooking.

■ Prick hens in thickest part of leg. Juice should run clear when cooked. Remove hens from roasting pan and set aside.

■ Place roasting pan on stove over medium heat. Add shallots and cook 2 minutes.

■ Pour in wine and cook 4 minutes.

■ Add chicken stock and simmer 3 minutes.

■ Dissolve cornstarch in cold water; stir into sauce using whisk. Add seasonings.

■ Serve sauce with Cornish hens. Accompany with baked potatoes and Caramelized Apricots.

■ Place all apricot ingredients in saucepan and cook 7 to 8 minutes over medium heat.

1 SERVING: 745 CALORIES   18 g CARBOHYDRATE   72 g PROTEIN
40 g FAT   2.3 g FIBER

Spread butter over hens.

Remove cooked hens from roasting pan. Place pan on stove over medium heat. Add shallots and cook 2 minutes.

Pour in wine and cook 4 minutes.

Add chicken stock and simmer 3 minutes.

Stir dissolved cornstarch into sauce using whisk.

Add seasonings.

LAMB KEBABS DIJONNAISE

(SERVES 4)

Marinade

4 tbsp	olive oil	60 mL
4 tbsp	dry white wine	60 mL
1 tbsp	lemon juice	15 mL
2	garlic cloves, smashed and chopped	2
1 tbsp	Dijon mustard	15 mL
½ tsp	pepper	2 mL
¼ tsp	cayenne pepper	1 mL
1 tbsp	tarragon	15 mL
	salt	

Kebabs

1 lb	loin of lamb, fat removed and meat cut in 1-in (2.5-cm) cubes	500 g
8	slices lemon	8
1	large red onion, in wedges	1
8	bay leaves	8
12	1-in (2.5-cm) pieces zucchini	12

■ Mix all marinade ingredients together in large bowl. Add lamb and marinate 1 hour.

■ Preheat barbecue at high.

■ Alternate pieces of lamb and remaining ingredients on skewers. Fold lemon slices in half before threading. Brush kebabs with marinade.

■ Oil grill and add kebabs. Cook 6 minutes on each side, uncovered. Season to taste and baste with marinade during cooking.

1 SERVING:	344 CALORIES	14 g CARBOHYDRATE	37 g PROTEIN
	16 g FAT	3.6 g FIBER	

BARBECUED PORK CHOPS

(SERVES 4)

⅓ cup	cider vinegar	75 mL
¼ cup	ketchup	50 mL
1½ tbsp	brown sugar	25 mL
½	onion, finely chopped	½
1 tsp	rosemary	5 mL
1 tsp	Worcestershire sauce	5 mL
½ tsp	pepper	2 mL
4	pork chops, ¾-in (2-cm) thick, trimmed of fat	4

■ Mix all ingredients, except pork, together in bowl. Pour mixture into small saucepan and cook 5 minutes over medium heat. Remove from stove and let cool.

■ Brush pork with mixture and marinate 15 minutes.

■ Preheat barbecue at medium.

■ Oil grill and add pork chops. Cook, uncovered, 8 to 9 minutes on each side. Baste chops with marinade 4 to 5 times during cooking.

■ Serve with new potatoes cooked in foil.

1 SERVING:	221 CALORIES	9 g CARBOHYDRATE	21 g PROTEIN
	11 g FAT	0 g FIBER	

STUFFED ROAST TURKEY
(SERVES 6)

Turkey

10-lb	turkey, cleaned	4.5-kg
1	recipe Country Turkey Stuffing (see page 95)	1
½ lb	Hot Chili Pepper Butter (see page 136)	125 g
	juice of 1 lemon	
	salt and pepper	

Sauce

1	onion, cubed	1
1	celery stalk, cut in large pieces	1
1 tsp	basil	5 mL
½ tsp	celery seeds	2 mL
½ tsp	thyme	2 mL
4 tbsp	flour	60 mL
2 cups	chicken stock, heated	500 mL
	salt and pepper	

- Preheat oven to 400 °F (200 °C).

- Season cavity of turkey with salt and pepper. Fill with stuffing. Carefully peel away skin from meat on breast portions of turkey. Slide pieces of chili pepper butter between skin and meat. Truss turkey and season well. Sprinkle with lemon juice.

- Place turkey in large roasting pan. Cook 30 minutes at 400 °F (200 °C). Reduce heat to 325 °F (160 °C); continue cooking 2 hours and 30 minutes. Baste turkey every 15 minutes. Note: If breast of turkey browns too quickly, cover with sheet of aluminum foil.

- Remove cooked turkey from roasting pan and keep hot but do not carve.

- To make sauce, place roasting pan on stove over high heat. Add vegetables and seasonings; cook 7 minutes. Mix in flour and cook 4 minutes over medium heat. Pour in chicken stock and mix well. Cook 7 minutes.

- Strain sauce and serve with turkey.

1 SERVING:	564 CALORIES	50 g CARBOHYDRATE	19 g PROTEIN
	32 g FAT	1.8 g FIBER	

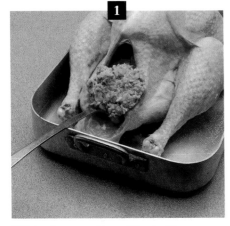

Fill turkey cavity with stuffing.

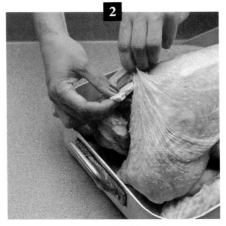

Carefully peel away skin from meat on breast portion of turkey. Slide pieces of chili pepper butter between skin and meat.

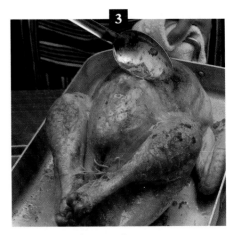

Baste roasting turkey every 15 minutes.

To make sauce, place vegetables in roasting pan and cook 7 minutes over high heat.

Mix in flour and cook 4 minutes over medium heat.

Pour in chicken stock and mix well. Cook 7 minutes.

TENDER MARINATED LAMB CHOPS
(SERVES 4)

1 cup	dry white wine	250 mL
2	garlic cloves, smashed and chopped	2
1 tbsp	chopped fresh rosemary	15 mL
1	shallot, finely chopped	1
1	fresh basil leaf, finely chopped	1
1 tsp	pepper	5 mL
1 tbsp	olive oil	15 mL
3 tbsp	ketchup	45 mL
8	lamb chops, 1 in (2.5 cm) thick, most of fat removed	8
	juice of 1 lemon	
	few drops of hot pepper sauce	

■ Mix all ingredients, except lamb, together in bowl.

■ Place lamb on large platter and cover with marinade. Marinate 1 hour. Turn chops over 2 to 3 times during this time.

■ Preheat barbecue at medium-high.

■ Oil grill and add lamb chops. Cook, uncovered, 6 to 7 minutes on each side.

■ Accompany with boiled potatoes and broccoli.

1 SERVING:	281 CALORIES	7 g CARBOHYDRATE	28 g PROTEIN
	11 g FAT	0 g FIBER	

GRILLED PEPPERS

(SERVES 4 TO 6)

Marinade

2 tbsp	olive oil	30 mL
1 tbsp	Worcestershire sauce	15 mL
2 tbsp	lemon juice	30 mL
1 tsp	thyme	5 mL
1 tsp	basil	5 mL

Peppers

| 6 to 8 | assorted bell and hot peppers | 6 to 8 |
| | salt and pepper | |

■ Mix all marinade ingredients together and set aside.

■ Wash peppers, cut in two and remove seeds. Place peppers on plate and season well. Pour marinade over and marinate 15 minutes.

■ Preheat barbecue at medium.

■ Oil grill. Place peppers on grill and cover; cook 12 minutes. Turn peppers over 4 to 5 times during cooking and baste occasionally with marinade. Avoid charring peppers.

■ Serve at once.

1 SERVING: 44 CALORIES   6 g CARBOHYDRATE   1 g PROTEIN
               2 g FAT   1.0 g FIBER

ROAST LOIN OF PORK WITH FIGS
(SERVES 4 TO 6)

Fig Compote

4	lemon slices, chopped with rind	4
½ cup	sugar	125 mL
1 lb	fresh figs, washed and halved	500 g
1 tsp	vanilla	5 mL
1 cup	water	250 mL
6 tbsp	white wine	90 mL

Roast Pork

2 lbs	pork loin	900 g
1 tbsp	olive oil	15 mL
12	small white onions, peeled	12
6	shallots, peeled	6
½ tsp	paprika	2 mL
	salt and pepper	

- Place all ingredients of fig compote in saucepan. Bring to boil over medium heat.

- Reduce heat and continue cooking 20 minutes.

- Preheat oven to 350 °F (180 °C).

- Place pork loin in roasting pan. Brush meat with oil and season with salt and pepper. Add whole onions and shallots; sprinkle with paprika. Cook 30 minutes in oven.

- Remove roasting pan from oven. Spread fig compote over meat. Return to oven and continue cooking 30 minutes. Serve.

1 SERVING:	533 CALORIES	51 g CARBOHYDRATE	35 g PROTEIN
	21 g FAT	4.9 g FIBER	

GRILLED BONELESS BREAST OF CHICKEN

(SERVES 4)

4 tbsp	olive oil	60 mL
6 tbsp	dry white wine	90 mL
1 tbsp	Dijon mustard	15 mL
½ tsp	oregano	2 mL
1 tsp	chopped fresh basil	5 mL
¼ tsp	cayenne pepper	1 mL
2 tbsp	chopped red chili pepper	30 mL
1 tsp	brown sugar	5 mL
4	boneless chicken breast halves, skinned	4
	salt and pepper	

■ Mix all ingredients, except chicken, together in bowl.

■ Place chicken breasts on plate and pour marinade over. Marinate 1 hour in refrigerator.

■ Preheat barbecue at high.

■ Oil grill and add chicken breasts. Cook 16 minutes uncovered. Turn chicken over 2 to 3 times during cooking and baste frequently. Season to taste.

■ Serve with grilled peppers (see page 131).

1 SERVING: 222 CALORIES 1 g CARBOHYDRATE 27 g PROTEIN
10 g FAT 0 g FIBER

JUICY DOUBLE BURGERS
(SERVES 4 TO 6)

1 lb	lean ground beef	500 g
¼ lb	ground veal	125 g
¼ tsp	pepper	1 mL
¼ tsp	cayenne pepper	1 mL
1 tsp	Worcestershire sauce	5 mL
1 tbsp	olive oil	15 mL
1	medium onion, finely chopped	1
3	green onions, chopped	3
½ tsp	thyme	2 mL
1 tsp	basil	5 mL
2	garlic cloves, blanched and puréed	2
1	egg	1
	salt	

■ Place both meats in bowl of mixer; blend together. Add pepper, cayenne and Worcestershire sauce. Season with salt and blend again. Set aside.

■ Heat half of oil in saucepan over medium heat. Add both onions, seasonings and garlic. Stir and cook 3 minutes over medium heat.

■ Add cooked onions to meat mixture. Blend to incorporate. Add egg and blend again.

■ Shape mixture into hamburgers and brush with oil.

■ Preheat barbecue at medium.

■ Oil grill and add hamburgers. Cover and cook 5 minutes on each side. Season to taste. Serve with condiments.

1 SERVING:	205 CALORIES	2 g CARBOHYDRATE	20 g PROTEIN
	13 g FAT	0 g FIBER	

Use good quality ground meats.

Blend both meats together in bowl of mixer.

Add pepper, cayenne and Worcestershire sauce. Season with salt and blend again.

Add cooked onions to meat mixture.

Add egg and incorporate.

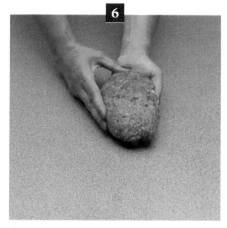

Shape mixture into hamburgers.

HOT CHILI PEPPER BUTTER
(SERVES 8 TO 10)

½ lb	unsalted butter, softened	250 g
2	green chili peppers, roasted and puréed	2
3	garlic cloves, blanched and puréed	3
1 tbsp	chopped fresh chives	15 mL
¼ tsp	cayenne pepper	1 mL
	juice of ½ lemon	
	salt and freshly ground pepper	

■ Place all ingredients in bowl of food processor; blend until well mixed.

■ Transfer butter to large sheet of aluminum foil. Shape butter into cylindrical tube and roll in foil. Twist ends shut and store in freezer.

Note: This butter will keep 3 months in freezer. Each time you wish to use some butter, simply open package and cut off appropriate number of slices. Always roll tightly in foil and twist ends shut.

1 SERVING:	205 CALORIES	1 g CARBOHYDRATE	1 g PROTEIN
	22 g FAT	0 g FIBER	

BASIL BUTTER
(SERVES 4 TO 6)

½ lb	unsalted butter, softened	250 g
15	fresh basil leaves, chopped	15
1 tbsp	chopped fresh parsley	15 mL
1	shallot, chopped	1
¼ tsp	pepper	1 mL
¼ tsp	paprika	1 mL
	few drops Tabasco sauce	
	few drops lemon juice	

■ Place all ingredients in bowl of food processor. Blend until combined.

■ Transfer butter to large sheet of aluminum foil. Shape butter into cylindrical tube, roll foil and twist ends shut. Freeze.

■ Use as needed.

1 SERVING:	375 CALORIES	2 g CARBOHYDRATE	1 g PROTEIN
	40 g FAT	0 g FIBER	

THICK BARBECUE SAUCE

(SERVES 4)

4 tbsp	ketchup	60 mL
4 tbsp	dry white wine	60 mL
1 tbsp	olive oil	15 mL
2	garlic cloves, blanched and puréed	2
1 tbsp	Worcestershire sauce	15 mL
1 tsp	horseradish	5 mL
1 tbsp	chopped fresh basil	15 mL
	few drops Tabasco sauce	
	salt and freshly ground pepper	

■ Mix all ingredients together in bowl.

■ Use sauce to brush onto steaks, chops and chicken breasts during grilling.

1 SERVING:	62 CALORIES	5 g CARBOHYDRATE	1 g PROTEIN
	3 g FAT	0 g FIBER	

GRILLED ITALIAN SAUSAGES
(SERVES 4)

2	garlic cloves, smashed and finely chopped	2
2 tbsp	teriyaki sauce	30 mL
1 tbsp	olive oil	15 mL
2 tbsp	ketchup	30 mL
4	large spicy Italian sausages	4
	juice of 1 lemon	
	few drops of hot pepper sauce	
	freshly ground pepper	

■ Mix all ingredients, except sausages, together in small bowl.

■ Place sausages on platter and cover with marinade. Let stand 15 minutes. Turn sausages over 3 times during this time.

■ Preheat barbecue at medium.

■ Oil grill and add sausages. Cover and cook 5 minutes on each side.

■ Serve with zucchini and grilled corn on the cob.

1 SERVING:	342 CALORIES	4 g CARBOHYDRATE	20 g PROTEIN
	27 g FAT	0 g FIBER	

FRESH CORN AND CHICKEN KEBABS
(SERVES 4)

1	large whole chicken breast, skinned and boned	1
2 tbsp	olive oil	30 mL
1 tbsp	lemon juice	15 mL
1 tsp	curry powder	5 mL
2	red peppers, cut in 1-in (2.5-cm) cubes	2
1	large ear of corn, husked and cut in 1-in (2.5-cm) pieces	1
	salt and pepper	

■ Cut chicken meat into 1-in (2.5-cm) pieces. Place chicken in bowl with oil, lemon juice and curry powder. Season well, stir and marinate 30 minutes.

■ Alternate pieces of chicken, red pepper and corn on skewers.

■ Preheat oven at broil.

■ Place kebabs in baking dish. Baste with marinade and season well. Broil 12 minutes. Turn kebabs over and baste with marinade during cooking process.

■ Serve on rice.

1 SERVING:	121 CALORIES	7 g CARBOHYDRATE	14 g PROTEIN
	4 g FAT	1.2 g FIBER	

BARBECUED LEG OF LAMB

(SERVES 6 TO 8)

1	leg of lamb, 5 to 6 lbs (2.3 to 2.7 kg)	1	

Barbecue Sauce #1 (see page 116)

salt and pepper

- Have butcher prepare lamb by trimming skin and removing most of fat from leg.

- Place leg in roasting pan and pour barbecue sauce over meat. Marinate 1 to 2 hours in refrigerator.

- Preheat oven to 375 °F (190 °C).

- Transfer roasting pan with lamb from refrigerator to oven. Cook 45 minutes, basting frequently. Season with salt and pepper.

- Preheat barbecue at medium.

- Oil grill and set leg on grill. Cook 20 minutes, uncovered. Baste lamb 7 to 8 times during cooking and turn leg over 2 to 3 times. Season to taste.

- Serve with sweet potatoes.

1 SERVING:	575 CALORIES	13 g CARBOHYDRATE	77 g PROTEIN
	23 g FAT	0 g FIBER	

BARBECUED LOIN OF PORK

(SERVES 6)

4-lb	pork loin	1.8-kg
1	recipe Barbecue Sauce 1, 2 or 3 (see pages 116, 117)	1
	salt and pepper	

■ Remove most of fat from pork loin. Place roast on platter and cover with barbecue sauce. Marinate 1 to 2 hours in refrigerator.

■ Preheat oven to 350 °F (180 °C).

■ Transfer pork to roasting pan. Cook 1 hour and 15 minutes in oven.

■ Preheat barbecue at low.

■ Oil grill. Remove pork from pan and transfer to barbecue grill. Baste with barbecue sauce and season well. Cover and cook 40 minutes. Turn roast over 2 to 3 times during cooking. Baste occasionally with barbecue sauce.

■ Serve with grilled zucchini.

1 SERVING:	594 CALORIES	15 g CARBOHYDRATE	54 g PROTEIN
	35 g FAT	0 g FIBER	

SHRIMP AND SPICY ITALIAN SAUSAGE KEBABS

(SERVES 4)

16	large shrimp, peeled, deveined and cleaned	16
2	spicy Italian sausages, cut on the bias ¾ in (2 cm) thick	2
2 tbsp	lemon juice	30 mL
½ cup	dry white wine	125 mL
2 tbsp	olive oil	30 mL
½ tsp	cayenne pepper	2 mL
½ tsp	pepper	2 mL
3	large shallots, blanched and puréed	3
½ tsp	paprika	2 mL

■ Place shrimp and sausages in bowl.

■ Mix remaining ingredients together, then pour over shrimp and sausages. Marinate 1 hour.

■ Preheat barbecue at medium.

■ Alternate shrimp and pieces of sausage on skewers. Brush with marinade.

■ Oil grill and add skewers. Cover and cook 3 to 4 minutes on each side. Season to taste and baste with marinade during cooking.

■ Serve.

1 SERVING: 262 CALORIES   7 g CARBOHYDRATE   17 g PROTEIN
                 16 g FAT   0 g FIBER

Peel shrimp.

Use small knife to remove small black vein located on back of shrimp.

Mix marinade ingredients together.

Begin by threading shrimp on skewer.

Follow shrimp by piece of sausage. Continue alternating to fill skewer.

Brush shrimp and sausage with marinade.

BARBECUED FROG LEGS

(SERVES 4)

24 to 32	small frog legs, (the smaller, the better the flavor)	24 to 32
1 cup	beer	250 mL
6	garlic cloves, smashed and finely chopped	6
2 tbsp	honey	30 mL
¼ cup	chili sauce	50 mL
1 tsp	Worcestershire sauce	5 mL
	few drops Tabasco sauce	
	salt and freshly ground pepper	

■ Place frog legs on large platter.

■ Mix remaining ingredients together and pour over frog legs. Marinate 2 hours in refrigerator.

■ Preheat barbecue at medium.

■ Oil grill. Remove frog legs from marinade and wrap bony ends of legs in pieces of aluminum foil to prevent charring.

■ Place frog legs on grill and cover. Cook 12 minutes or according to size. Baste frequently and turn legs over 2 to 3 times during cooking.

■ Serve with lemon slices.

1 SERVING:	135 CALORIES	8 g CARBOHYDRATE	19 g PROTEIN
	1 g FAT	0 g FIBER	

MIXED VEGETABLE GRILL

(SERVES 4 TO 6)

2 tbsp	olive oil	30 mL
2	garlic cloves, blanched and puréed	2
1 tbsp	Worcestershire sauce	15 mL
1	red pepper, cubed	1
1	green pepper, cubed	1
1	zucchini, sliced ½ in (1.2 cm) thick	1
1	yellow summer squash, halved lengthwise and sliced ½ in (1.2 cm) thick	1
4	green onions, cut in 1-in (2.5-cm) pieces	4
24	snow pea pods	24
1	leaf Chinese cabbage, in large pieces	1
2	carrots, pared, blanched and sliced on the bias ½ in (1.2 cm) thick	2
1	yellow pepper, cubed	1
1	red onion, in wedges	1
	juice of 1 lemon	
	salt and ground pepper	

■ Preheat barbecue at high.

■ Mix oil, garlic, lemon juice and Worcestershire sauce together in small bowl.

■ Place all vegetables in large bowl. Pour oil mixture over and toss to coat evenly. Season to taste.

■ Arrange vegetables in barbecue grilling basket as displayed in photograph. Place basket on barbecue grill and partly cover. Cook 9 minutes on each side. Serve.

1 SERVING:	125 CALORIES	16 g CARBOHYDRATE	3 g PROTEIN
	6 g FAT	5.9 g FIBER	

SALMON EN PAPILLOTE WITH BASIL BUTTER

(SERVES 4)

Basil Butter

15	fresh basil leaves	15
3	garlic cloves, peeled	3
¼ tsp	cayenne pepper	1 mL
¼ lb	unsalted butter	125 g
	few drops lemon juice	
	salt and white pepper	

Salmon Filets

4	salmon steaks	4
¼ lb	basil butter	125 g
8	tomato slices	8
4	lemon slices	4
4	bay leaves	4
	salt, pepper and paprika	

■ To make basil butter, mix basil and garlic together in bowl of food processor. Add remaining ingredients and season to taste. Mix again until well combined.

■ Preheat barbecue at medium.

■ Place each salmon steak on double piece of aluminum foil. Place a spoon of basil butter on each steak and top with slice of tomato. Add lemon slice and bay leaf. Season and seal packages.

■ Place foil packages on grill. Cover and cook 25 to 30 minutes.

Note: If desired, the same technique can be done in the oven at 325 °F (160 °C).

1 SERVING:	493 CALORIES	3 g CARBOHYDRATE	40 g PROTEIN
	36 g FAT	1.4 g FIBER	

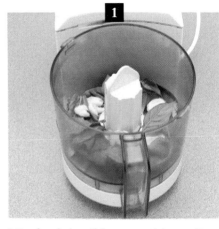

Mix fresh basil leaves with garlic cloves in food processor.

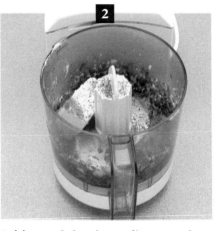

Add remaining ingredients and mix until well combined.

Choose fresh salmon steaks.

Each salmon steak will require
a double sheet of aluminum foil.
Have ready on counter.

Place ingredients on foil.

Seal packages.

HALIBUT STEAKS EN PAPILLOTE

(SERVES 4)

4	halibut steaks	4
1	large carrot, pared and sliced	1
8	lemon slices	8
1	red pepper, cut in julienne	1
4	slices of Basil Butter (see page 136)	4
	lime juice	
	salt and pepper	

■ Preheat barbecue at medium.

■ Place each halibut steak on double sheet of aluminum foil. Divide remaining ingredients between steaks and season to taste. Seal foil packages.

■ Place packages on grill. Cover and cook 20 minutes.

1 SERVING:	597 CALORIES	6 g CARBOHYDRATE	33 g PROTEIN
	49 g FAT	1.0 g FIBER	

SOLE FILETS IN CREAM SAUCE

(SERVES 4)

4	large sole filets	4	
¼ cup	dry white wine	50 mL	
1	red pepper, cut in strips	1	
1	green pepper, cut in strips	1	
½ tsp	curry powder	2 mL	
¼ cup	heavy cream	50 mL	
	juice of 1 lime		
	salt and pepper		

■ Place filets in large buttered frying pan. Season with salt and pepper.

■ Add wine, lime juice and peppers. Cover with sheet of waxed paper. Bring to boil over medium heat.

■ As soon as liquid starts to boil, remove pan from heat. Let stand 2 minutes.

■ Remove fish and vegetables from pan; keep hot.

■ Return pan to stove over high heat. Incorporate curry powder into liquid and cook 3 minutes.

■ Stir in heavy cream and continue cooking 3 minutes over high heat.

■ Pour sauce over filets and serve.

1 SERVING:	188 CALORIES	3 g CARBOHYDRATE	18 g PROTEIN
	10 g FAT	0 g FIBER	

COD AU GRATIN

(SERVES 4)

1	celery stalk, diced	1
1	carrot, pared and diced	1
1	onion, sliced	1
2	bay leaves	2
4 cups	water	1 L
2 lbs	fresh cod, cut in 4 pieces	900 g
1½ cups	white sauce, heated	375 mL
1 cup	grated Gruyère cheese	250 mL
	a few parsley sprigs	
	salt and pepper	

■ Place vegetables and seasonings in sauté pan. Add water and bring to boil over medium heat.

■ Add fish to pan. It should be covered completely by liquid. Cook 8 minutes over low heat.

■ Use slotted spoon to remove fish from pan and drain well. Transfer fish to buttered ovenproof baking dish. Pour white sauce over fish and top with grated cheese.

■ Place in oven and broil 5 minutes.

1 SERVING:	586 CALORIES	11 g CARBOHYDRATE	75 g PROTEIN
	27 g FAT	1.0 g FIBER	

SHRIMP COCKTAIL
(SERVES 4)

½ cup	chili sauce	125 mL
½ cup	ketchup	125 mL
1½ tbsp	horseradish	25 mL
1 tsp	Worcestershire sauce	5 mL
24	cooked shrimp, peeled and deveined	24
	few drops Tabasco sauce	
	lemon juice	
	salt and pepper	

■ Mix all ingredients, except shrimp, together in bowl. Season to taste with salt and pepper.

■ Serve sauce in small bowl to accompany shrimp.

| 1 SERVING: | 122 CALORIES | 19 g CARBOHYDRATE | 10 g PROTEIN |
| | 1 g FAT | 0 g FIBER | |

SAVANNAH STEAMED SHRIMP
(SERVES 4)

1¼ lbs	large shrimp, washed	625 g
1 tsp	black pepper	5 mL
½ tsp	paprika	2 mL
	pinch crushed chilies	
	salt	

■ Mix ingredients together in bowl and refrigerate 2 hours.

■ Steam shrimp 6 to 7 minutes, stirring 2 to 3 times during cooking.

■ Serve with fresh lemon.

| 1 SERVING: | 194 CALORIES | 5 g CARBOHYDRATE | 39 g PROTEIN |
| | 2 g FAT | 1.0 g FIBER | |

SHRIMP REMOULADE

(SERVES 4 TO 6)

1	small celeriac, peeled and cut in fine julienne	1	
4 tbsp	mayonnaise	60 mL	
1 tsp	Dijon mustard	5 mL	
2 tbsp	sour cream	30 mL	
1 lb	cooked shrimp, peeled, deveined and cut in two	500 g	
2 tbsp	finely chopped lemon rind	30 mL	
1	small green pepper, cut in julienne	1	
	lemon juice		
	salt, pepper, paprika		

■ Cook celeriac 3 minutes in boiling, salted water with lemon juice. Place saucepan under cold water to stop cooking process, then drain celeriac well. Squeeze out excess liquid from celeriac and blot with paper towels.

■ Place mayonnaise in bowl. Add mustard and sour cream. Mix and add salt, pepper, paprika and lemon juice to taste. Mix again.

■ Place celeriac, shrimp, lemon rind and green pepper in bowl. Add sauce and mix well. Correct seasoning and serve.

1 SERVING:	194 CALORIES	6 g CARBOHYDRATE	25 g PROTEIN
	8 g FAT	1.3 g FIBER	

Lobster à la Bretonne

LOBSTER À LA BRETONNE
(SERVES 4)

Beurre Manié (Kneaded Butter)

5 tbsp	butter	75 mL
2 tbsp	flour	30 mL

Lobster

4	live lobsters, each 1½ lbs (750 g)	4
3 tbsp	butter	45 mL
2	shallots, chopped	2
2	garlic cloves, smashed and chopped	2
2	sprigs fresh tarragon	2
3 tbsp	cognac	45 mL
½ cup	dry white wine	125 mL
1½ cups	fish stock, heated (see page 182)	375 mL
3 tbsp	beurre manié	45 mL
3 tbsp	heavy cream	45 mL
	few drops Tabasco sauce	
	salt and pepper	

■ Blend butter with flour to make beurre manié. Set aside.

■ Place lobsters in large pot filled with boiling, salted water. Boil 1 minute over high heat. Remove lobsters and drain. Set aside to cool.

■ Place lobsters right-side up on counter and hold with left hand. Spread tails flat on counter. Cut off claws.

■ Cut lobster bodies into large pieces. Discard gravel sac in head and intestinal vein in tail. Remove tomalley and reserve in bowl.

■ Heat butter in frying pan. Add shallots, garlic and tarragon. Cook 1 minute.

■ Add lobster pieces and claws. Season with salt and pepper; cook 2 minutes over high heat. Cover and continue cooking just until lobster shells become red in color.

■ Add cognac and flambé. Remove lobster pieces from pan and set aside.

■ Pour white wine into pan and cook 3 minutes over high heat. Incorporate fish stock and continue cooking 4 minutes over high heat.

■ Stir in beurre manié and continue cooking to thicken sauce. Whisk constantly.

■ Mix cream with reserved tomalley. Stir into sauce and add few drops Tabasco sauce. Cook 3 minutes over medium heat.

■ Place lobster pieces in sauce and simmer 2 minutes. Serve.

1 SERVING:	605 CALORIES	8 g CARBOHYDRATE	71 g PROTEIN
	27 g FAT	0 g FIBER	

SAUTÉ OF SHRIMP AND POTATO

(SERVES 4)

2 tbsp	olive oil	30 mL
1 lb	medium shrimp, peeled, deveined and cut in two	500 g
2	medium potatoes, peeled and diced	2
½ lb	fresh mushrooms, cleaned and quartered	250 g
2	garlic cloves, smashed and chopped	2
1 tbsp	chopped fresh parsley	15 mL
1 tsp	chopped fresh fennel leaves salt and pepper	5 mL

■ Heat 1 tbsp (15 mL) olive oil in frying pan over high heat. Add shrimp and sauté 3 minutes. Remove from pan and set aside.

■ Add remaining oil to hot pan. Add potatoes and season well; cook 4 minutes over medium heat. Mix well and cover pan; continue cooking 6 minutes or just until potatoes are almost cooked.

■ Add mushrooms, garlic, parsley and fennel. Season and cook 4 minutes over high heat.

■ Return shrimp to pan, mix and cook 2 minutes to reheat. Serve.

1 SERVING:	301 CALORIES	23 g CARBOHYDRATE	33 g PROTEIN
	9 g FAT	1.6 g FIBER	

Cut shrimp in two.

Sauté shrimp in hot oil.

Remove shrimp from pan and set aside.

Add remaining oil to hot pan. Add potatoes and season well.

When potatoes are almost cooked, add mushrooms, garlic, parsley and fennel.

Return shrimp to pan.

SALMON FILETS WITH MAÎTRE D'HÔTEL BUTTER
(SERVES 4)

Maître d'Hôtel Butter

½ lb	butter, softened	250 g
2 tbsp	chopped fresh parsley	30 mL
1 tsp	finely chopped chives	5 mL
	juice ½ lemon	
	few drops Worcestershire sauce	
	few drops Tabasco sauce	
	salt and pepper	

Filets

4	salmon filets	4
1 cup	seasoned flour	250 mL
2 tbsp	butter	30 mL
1 tsp	vegetable oil	5 mL
4	slices maître d'hôtel butter	4
	juice of 1 lemon	
	salt and pepper	

■ Mix first seven ingredients together in food processor. Position sheet of aluminum foil on counter. Spoon butter along center of foil and roll into cylindrical shape. Twist ends shut.

Note: This butter will keep 3 months in freezer.

■ Preheat oven to 375 °F (190 °C).

■ Season fish and dredge in flour; set aside.

■ Heat 2 tbsp (30 mL) butter with oil in frying pan over medium heat. When hot, add filets and cook 6 to 8 minutes depending on thickness. Turn fish over 3 to 4 times during cooking process.

■ Sprinkle fish with lemon juice, transfer to oven and finish cooking, about 6 minutes. When done, place slice of maître d'hôtel butter on each filet and serve.

1 SERVING:	434 CALORIES	14 g CARBOHYDRATE	41 g PROTEIN
	24 g FAT	0 g FIBER	

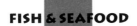

STEAMED FRESH SHRIMP

(SERVES 4)

2 cups	fish stock, heated (see page 182)	500 mL
½ tsp	fennel seed	2 mL
1 tsp	rosemary	5 mL
1½ lbs	large fresh shrimp	750 g
1 tsp	black pepper	5 mL
	lemon juice	

■ Pour fish stock into saucepan. Add fennel and rosemary; cover and bring to boil.

■ Toss shrimp with black pepper. Place shrimp in steamer basket (stainless steel, bamboo, etc.) and set in saucepan so that liquid does not touch the shrimp. Cover and cook 6 to 7 minutes. Stir shrimp in basket 2 to 3 times during cooking.

■ Remove shrimp from basket and sprinkle with lemon juice. Serve.

1 SERVING:	200 CALORIES	0 g CARBOHYDRATE	45 g PROTEIN
	2 g FAT	0 g FIBER	

MARYLAND CRAB CAKES
(SERVES 4)

2	slices white bread, crusts removed	2
¼ cup	milk	50 mL
1 lb	crab meat, fresh or frozen and thawed, flaked	500 g
3	green onions, chopped	3
¼ cup	mayonnaise	50 mL
1 tsp	Worcestershire sauce	5 mL
1 tsp	dry mustard	5 mL
¼ tsp	cayenne pepper	1 mL
	juice of ½ lemon	
	salt	
	peanut oil	

- Place bread in bowl and cover with milk. Soak 5 minutes.

- Squeeze out excess milk from bread and place in clean bowl. Add remaining ingredients to bread and mix well. Cover and refrigerate 2 hours.

- Shape mixture into thick pancakes. Cook in hot peanut oil over medium heat, about 4 to 5 minutes or until nicely browned.

- Serve with fresh lemon.

1 SERVING:	235 CALORIES	14 g CARBOHYDRATE	24 g PROTEIN
	9 g FAT	1.0 g FIBER	

GROUPER BURGERS

(SERVES 4)

4	small pieces grouper, ¼ lb (125 g) each	4
1	garlic clove, smashed and chopped	1
3 tbsp	Chinese black bean sauce	45 mL
4	onion buns	4
4	large slices mozzarella cheese	4
	few drops of Worcestershire sauce	
	juice of 1 lemon	
	lettuce leaves, washed and dried	
	salt and pepper	

■ Place pieces of grouper on large plate.

■ Mix Worcestershire sauce, lemon juice, garlic and bean sauce together in small bowl. Pour sauce over fish and marinate 10 minutes.

■ Preheat oven to broil.

■ Slice onion buns open and place under broiler. Brown 2 minutes, then remove and keep hot.

■ Remove fish from marinade and arrange in roasting pan. Place under broiler and cook 3 minutes on each side.

■ Remove fish from oven; skin and debone. Place piece of fish on each bun and brush with remaining marinade. Season with salt and pepper.

■ Top fish with cheese and place in middle of oven. Broil 2 minutes.

■ Add lettuce leaves and replace tops of buns. Serve with tomatoes and potato chips.

1 SERVING: 486 CALORIES   32 g CARBOHYDRATE   49 g PROTEIN
18 g FAT   1.7 g FIBER

SCALLOPS CHARLESTON-STYLE

(SERVES 4)

1	shallot, finely chopped	1
1 lb	fresh mushrooms, cleaned and quartered	500 g
1¼ lbs	fresh scallops, washed	625 g
1 tbsp	chopped fresh parsley	15 mL
1 cup	dry white wine	250 mL
¼ cup	water	50 mL
¼ tsp	paprika	1 mL
2 tbsp	butter	30 mL
3 tbsp	flour	45 mL
1 cup	grated Gruyère cheese	250 mL
	juice of 1 lemon	
	salt and pepper	

■ Place shallot, mushrooms, scallops and parsley in sauté pan. Do not mix. Add wine, lemon juice and water. Season with salt, pepper and paprika. Stir gently and cover with sheet of waxed paper. Bring to boil over medium heat.

■ As soon as liquid starts to boil, remove pan from heat. Let stand 2 minutes.

■ Using slotted spoon, remove scallops from pan and set aside in bowl.

■ Return pan to stove and cook mushrooms and liquid 4 minutes over high heat.

■ Melt butter in saucepan over medium heat. Add flour and mix well; cook 2 minutes over low heat.

■ Pour mushrooms and cooking liquid from scallops into flour mixture in saucepan. Mix well and cook sauce 10 minutes over low heat.

■ Stir scallops into mushroom sauce. Transfer mixture to ovenproof baking dish and top with cheese. Broil in oven 4 minutes to brown. Serve.

1 SERVING:	454 CALORIES	19 g CARBOHYDRATE	46 g PROTEIN
	17 g FAT	3.4 g FIBER	

Place shallot, mushrooms, scallops and parsley in sauté pan.

Add wine, lemon juice and water. Season with salt, pepper and paprika. Stir gently.

Cover with sheet of waxed paper and bring to boil.

Use slotted spoon to remove cooked scallops from pan.

Return pan to stove and cook mushrooms and cooking liquid 4 minutes over high heat.

Add scallops to mushroom sauce.

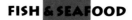

POACHED SALMON WITH JULIENNED VEGETABLES
(SERVES 4)

½	carrot, pared	½
½	stalk celery	½
½	green pepper, seeded	½
½	red pepper, seeded	½
⅓	zucchini	⅓
1 tbsp	butter	15 mL
½ tsp	fennel seed	2 mL
½ tsp	chopped fresh parsley	2 mL
3 cups	water	750 mL
½ cup	dry white wine	125 mL
4	salmon steaks	4
	lemon juice	
	salt and pepper	

■ Cut vegetables into julienne.

■ Heat butter in sauté pan. Add vegetables and seasonings. Cover and cook 3 minutes over low heat. Remove vegetables from pan and set aside.

■ Add water and wine to sauté pan. Season with salt and pepper and bring to boil. Cook 8 minutes over low heat.

■ Add salmon steaks to liquid in pan. Simmer 6 minutes over low heat. Turn salmon over once during cooking. About 2 minutes before the salmon is cooked, add vegetables to pan to reheat.

■ The salmon is cooked when the flesh feels firm to the touch.

■ Remove salmon steaks from pan and serve with julienned vegetables. Sprinkle with lemon juice.

■ If desired, top salmon steaks with a slice of herb or garlic butter.

1 SERVING:	316 CALORIES	3 g CARBOHYDRATE	40 g PROTEIN
	14 g FAT	0 g FIBER	

HOUSTON SHRIMP KEBABS

(SERVES 4)

1½ lbs	medium shrimp, peeled and deveined	750 g	
1 cup	olive oil	250 mL	
3	garlic cloves, peeled and cut in three	3	
¼ cup	ketchup	50 mL	
1 tbsp	paprika	15 mL	
	juice of 1 lemon		

■ Place all ingredients in bowl. Marinate 12 hours in refrigerator.

■ Thread shrimp on skewers. Place skewers on hot grill preheated at medium. Cook 4 to 5 minutes. Turn skewers over during cooking and baste with marinade.

■ Serve with rice.

1 SERVING:	495 CALORIES	4 g CARBOHYDRATE	46 g PROTEIN
	33 g FAT	0 g FIBER	

GROUPER BRAISED IN TOMATOES

(SERVES 4)

1 tbsp	olive oil	15 mL
2	small onions, sliced	2
1	garlic clove, smashed and chopped	1
4	small tomatoes, peeled, cored and quartered	4
4 tsp	Dijon mustard	20 mL
4	grouper steaks	4
1 cup	fish stock, heated (see page 182)	250 mL
¼ tsp	fennel seed	1 mL
	salt and pepper	

■ Preheat oven to 425 °F (220 °C).

■ Heat oil in frying pan over medium heat. Add onions and garlic; cook 5 minutes. Stir once during cooking.

■ Add tomatoes and season well. Cover and continue cooking 5 minutes.

■ Spread mustard over grouper steaks. Place fish in ovenproof baking dish and cover with tomato mixture. Pour in fish stock and sprinkle with fennel seed.

■ Cook 10 to 12 minutes in oven or adjust cooking time according to size of grouper steaks.

1 SERVING:	280 CALORIES	9 g CARBOHYDRATE	37 g PROTEIN
	11 g FAT	2.4 g FIBER	

GRILLED MARINATED RED SNAPPER

(SERVES 4)

¼ tsp	black pepper	1 mL
¼ tsp	paprika	1 mL
1 tsp	fennel seed	5 mL
2 tbsp	teriyaki sauce	30 mL
4 tbsp	olive oil	60 mL
4	medium red snapper filets	4
	juice of 2 limes	
	salt	

■ Grind pepper, salt, paprika and fennel seed in mortar. Add teriyaki sauce, oil and lime juice; mix well.

■ Place fish in large dish and cover with marinade. Refrigerate 1 hour.

■ Preheat oven to broil.

■ Remove filets from marinade and arrange, skin-side down, in roasting pan. Place in oven, 6 in (15 cm) from broiler element, and broil 8 minutes. Baste with marinade once during cooking and do not turn fish over.

■ Serve with sautéed mushrooms.

1 SERVING:	241 CALORIES	7 g CARBOHYDRATE	19g PROTEIN
	15 g FAT	0 g FIBER	

POACHED PAPRIKA SHRIMP

(SERVES 4)

3 tbsp	butter	45 mL
½ cup	water	125 mL
1½ lbs	medium shrimp, peeled and deveined	750 g
1 tbsp	lemon juice	15 mL
2 tbsp	tarragon	30 mL
1 tbsp	paprika	15 mL
	freshly ground pepper	

■ Heat butter and water in sauté pan over medium heat. Bring to boil and cook 2 minutes to melt butter completely.

■ Reduce heat to low. Add shrimp and remaining ingredients; mix well. Cover with sheet of waxed paper and cook 5 minutes. Stir twice during cooking.

■ Drain shrimp well and serve with lemon slices.

■ Serve with cocktail sauce, if desired.

1 SERVING:	280 CALORIES	0 g CARBOHYDRATE	45 g PROTEIN
	11g FAT	0 g FIBER	

SALMON SALAD

(SERVES 4)

2 cups	cooked flaked salmon	500 mL	
2	hard-boiled eggs, diced	2	
½	cucumber, peeled, seeded and diced medium	½	
1	red pepper, diced (optional)	1	
5 tbsp	light mayonnaise	75 mL	
	salt, pepper, paprika		

■ Place salmon in bowl. Add eggs and mix gently.

■ Add remaining ingredients and mix.

■ Serve on lettuce leaves.

1 SERVING:	268 CALORIES	5 g CARBOHYDRATE	23 g PROTEIN
	17 g FAT	0 g FIBER	

POACHED SCALLOPS WITH CAPERS

(SERVES 4)

1½ lbs	fresh scallops, washed	750 g
1½ cups	water	375 mL
1	celery stalk, diced	1
1	carrot, pared and sliced	1
¼ tsp	fennel seed	1 mL
1	sprig fresh tarragon	1
½ cup	dry white wine	125 mL
3 tbsp	butter	45 mL
1½ tbsp	flour	25 mL
1½ tbsp	fresh dill	25 mL
2 tbsp	capers	30 mL
	lemon juice	
	pinch of cayenne pepper	
	salt and pepper	

■ Place scallops, water, celery, carrot, lemon juice, fennel seed, tarragon, cayenne and black pepper in sauté pan.

■ Pour in wine and cover with sheet of waxed paper. Bring to boil over medium heat. As soon as liquid starts to boil, remove pan from heat. Let stand 2 minutes.

■ Use slotted spoon to remove scallops. Set aside in bowl.

■ Return sauté pan to stove over high heat. Bring to boil and cook 3 minutes. Season well, then pour sauce through sieve into bowl.

■ Pour half of strained liquid into sauté pan over low heat. Mix butter with flour. Incorporate into cooking liquid, stirring constantly with whisk. Sauce will thicken.

■ Add dill and capers. Place scallops in sauce and warm a few minutes over low heat.

■ Serve with fresh pasta.

1 SERVING:	370 CALORIES	11 g CARBOHYDRATE	44 g PROTEIN
	15 g FAT	1.0 g FIBER	

Add wine to sauté pan containing scallops and vegetables.

Cover with sheet of waxed paper and bring to boil over medium heat.

Use slotted spoon to remove cooked scallops.

Return sauté pan to stove over high heat. Bring to boil and cook 3 minutes.

Mix butter with flour.

Incorporate butter mixture into reduced cooking liquid in sauté pan. Stir constantly with whisk.

SALMON STEAKS WITH PESTO
(SERVES 4)

4	small salmon steaks	4	
½ cup	chopped fresh basil	125 mL	
2	garlic cloves, blanched, peeled and smashed	2	
3 tbsp	grated Parmesan cheese	45 mL	
3 tbsp	olive oil	45 mL	
	few drops lemon juice		
	salt and freshly ground pepper		
	oil		

■ Brush salmon steaks with oil and place on platter. Season with salt and pepper; sprinkle with lemon juice. Set aside.

■ Place basil and garlic in food processor; mix 10 seconds.

■ Add cheese and replace top. Add oil gradually while mixing. Continue mixing until mixture is well incorporated. Season to taste. Set pesto aside.

■ Place cast iron pan on stove over medium heat. When pan is hot, add oiled salmon steaks. Cook 12 minutes, turning fish over 2 to 3 times during cooking.

■ When salmon is cooked, serve with pesto sauce. Accompany with lemon slices and vegetables.

1 SERVING:	365 CALORIES	1 g CARBOHYDRATE	41 g PROTEIN
	22 g FAT	0 g FIBER	

PAN-FRIED SALMON TROUT FILETS

(SERVES 4)

1 tbsp	olive oil	15 mL
1 tsp	butter	5 mL
4	salmon trout filets	4
⅓ cup	pine nuts	75 mL
1 tbsp	chopped fresh parsley	15 mL
	juice of 1 lemon	
	salt and pepper	

■ Heat oil and butter in frying pan over medium heat. Add filets and cook 4 minutes.

■ Turn filets over and season well. Continue cooking about 3 minutes, depending on thickness of filets. Remove fish from pan and keep hot.

■ Add pine nuts and parsley to frying pan; cook 1 minute. Add lemon juice and season with pepper; cook 20 seconds.

■ Pour juices over hot fish. Serve with sautéed potatoes.

1 SERVING:	346 CALORIES	2 g CARBOHYDRATE	23 g PROTEIN
	28 g FAT	0 g FIBER	

SALMON STEAKS CUCUMBER

(SERVES 4)

Vegetable Stock

1 tsp	butter	5 mL
1	onion, sliced	1
1	large carrot, peeled and sliced	1
½	stalk celery, sliced	½
1	shallot, finely chopped	1
3	parsley sprigs	3
¼ tsp	fennel seed	1 mL
¼ tsp	tarragon	1 mL
6 cups	water	1.5 L
	salt and pepper	

■ To prepare vegetable stock, heat butter in large saucepan over medium heat. Add vegetables and seasonings. Cover and cook 5 minutes over low heat.

■ Stir in water and season well. Bring to boil and cook 20 minutes over low heat.

■ Strain liquid and set aside.

(continued)

Salmon Steaks

4	salmon steaks, ¾ in (2 cm) thick	4
1	large cucumber	1
5 cups	vegetable stock, heated	1.2 L
1 tsp	chopped fresh parsley	5 mL
	lemon wedges	
	salt and pepper	

- Place salmon steaks in sauté pan. Set aside.

- Peel cucumber and cut in half lengthwise. Seed and slice.

- Cover salmon steaks with sliced cucumber. Season with salt and pepper and pour in vegetable stock. Place on stove over medium heat and bring to boil. Reduce heat to low and simmer 5 minutes.

- Remove salmon from liquid and place on serving platter. Garnish with cucumber and sprinkle with parsley.

- Serve with fresh lemon.

1 SERVING: 306 CALORIES 9 g CARBOHYDRATE 41 g PROTEIN
12 g FAT 1.2 g FIBER

SALMON STEAKS WITH DILL HOLLANDAISE
(SERVES 4)

4	salmon steaks	4
1 tbsp	melted butter	15 mL
1 tsp	lemon juice	5 mL
1 tsp	olive oil	5 mL
2 tbsp	chopped fresh dill	30 mL
½ tsp	lemon juice	2 mL
1 cup	Hollandaise sauce	250 mL
	salt and pepper	

- Season salmon steaks.

- Mix butter with 1 tsp (5 mL) of lemon juice. Brush mixture over both sides of each salmon steak.

- Heat oil in cast iron pan over medium heat. Add salmon steaks and cook 12 minutes. Turn salmon over 3 to 4 times during cooking and season with salt and pepper.

- Stir fresh dill and lemon juice into Hollandaise sauce.

- Serve sauce with fish.

1 SERVING: 342 CALORIES 4 g CARBOHYDRATE 41 g PROTEIN
18 g FAT 0 g FIBER

LOBSTER AU GRATIN
(SERVES 4)

2	cooked lobsters, each 1½ lbs (750 g), split in half	2
2 tbsp	butter	30 mL
½ lb	cooked shrimp, shelled, deveined, and cut in three	250 g
1	shallot, chopped	1
½ tsp	paprika	2 mL
1 tsp	tarragon	5 mL
¼ cup	dry white wine (optional)	50 mL
2 cups	white sauce, heated	500 mL
½ cup	grated Gruyère cheese	125 mL
	pinch crushed chilies	
	salt and pepper	

■ Discard gravel sac and intestinal vein from lobsters. Remove meat from bodies, claws and tails. Chop in large pieces.

■ Heat butter in frying pan over medium heat. Add lobster meat, shrimp, shallot and seasonings. Cook 2 minutes. Remove seafood from pan and set aside.

■ Pour in wine and cook 2 minutes over high heat.

■ Stir in white sauce and season well. Cook 2 minutes.

■ Return seafood to pan and cook 2 minutes over low heat.

■ Spoon mixture into lobster shells and top with cheese. Broil 4 minutes until nicely browned.

1 SERVING: 512 CALORIES   13 g CARBOHYDRATE   59 g PROTEIN
              24 g FAT   0 g FIBER

Break off claws.

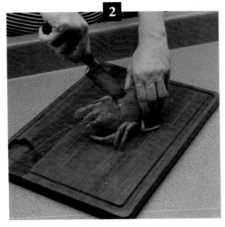

Prepare to split lobster in half by piercing shell at the head.

Cut body in half lengthwise from head to tail.

Discard gravel sac located near the head and intestinal vein in the tail.

Remove meat from body and tail.

Fill lobster shells with mixture and prepare to broil in oven.

BAKED PICKEREL
(SERVES 4)

4	medium pickerel filets	4
1 tbsp	chopped fresh parsley	15 mL
2	large tomatoes, cored and sliced thick	2
2	fennel sprigs	2
2	tarragon sprigs	2
¼ cup	dry white wine	50 mL
3	garlic cloves, smashed and chopped	3
4 tsp	butter	20 mL
	salt and pepper	

■ Preheat oven to 375 °F (190 °C).

■ Place fish, skin-side down, in roasting pan. Season with salt and pepper; sprinkle with parsley.

■ Arrange tomatoes slices on filets. Add fresh herbs. Pour in wine and add garlic.

■ Place piece of butter on each filet. Bake 15 minutes in oven.

1 SERVING:	144 CALORIES	4 g CARBOHYDRATE	20 g PROTEIN
	5 g FAT	1.0 g FIBER	

SAUTÉED MARINATED SHRIMP

(SERVES 4)

1 lb	shrimp, peeled and deveined	500 g
2	garlic cloves, smashed and chopped	2
2 tbsp	teriyaki sauce	30 mL
2 tbsp	olive oil	30 mL
1	large shallot, sliced	1
1	large zucchini, sliced with skin	1
1	green pepper, seeded and sliced	1
¼ cup	slivered almonds	50 mL
	pinch crushed chilies	
	juice of 1 lemon	
	salt and pepper	

■ Place shrimp in bowl. Add garlic, crushed chilies, teriyaki sauce and lemon juice. Marinate 30 minutes.

■ Heat half of oil in frying pan over high heat. Add vegetables and season; cook 6 minutes. Remove vegetables from pan and set aside.

■ Add remaining oil to pan and heat. Add shrimp and sauté 2 minutes on each side over high heat.

■ Return vegetables to pan with shrimp. Pour in marinade and season well. Add almonds, stir and cook 2 minutes.

■ Serve with rice.

1 SERVING:	298 CALORIES	12 g CARBOHYDRATE	34 g PROTEIN
	13 g FAT	1.4 g FIBER	

COD WITH TOMATO FONDUE

(SERVES 4 TO 6)

Tomato Fondue

1 tbsp	olive oil	15 mL
1	onion, chopped	1
1	celery stalk, diced	1
3	garlic cloves, smashed and chopped	3
28-oz	can tomatoes, drained and chopped or 4 large fresh tomatoes, peeled and chopped	796-mL
1 tsp	basil	5 mL
½ tsp	thyme	2 mL
¼ tsp	cayenne pepper	1 mL
	salt and pepper	

■ Heat oil in saucepan over medium heat. Add onion, celery and garlic. Cook 6 minutes over low heat.

■ Add remaining ingredients of fondue and mix well. Bring to boil over medium heat. Reduce heat to low and continue cooking 18 minutes. Set aside.

(continued)

Cod

1	celery stalk, diced	1
1	carrot, pared and diced	1
1	onion, peeled and diced	1
3	parsley sprigs	3
2	bay leaves	2
4 cups	water	1 L
2 lbs	fresh cod, cut in four pieces	900 g
2 cups	tomato fondue	500 mL
	salt and pepper	

■ Preheat oven to 350 °F (180 °C).

■ Place vegetables and seasonings in roasting pan. Pour in water and bring to boil over high heat.

■ Add fish and cook 6 minutes over low heat. The fish should be covered completely by the liquid.

■ Remove fish from liquid and drain well. Transfer to buttered ovenproof baking dish; season well. Cover with tomato fondue and place in oven. Bake 6 minutes. Serve.

1 SERVING: 361 CALORIES 9 g CARBOHYDRATE 53 g PROTEIN
13 g FAT 2.4 g FIBER

BROILED PICKEREL
(SERVES 4)

¼ tsp	crushed bay leaves	1 mL
¼ tsp	black pepper	1 mL
¼ tsp	paprika	1 mL
¼ tsp	celery seed	1 mL
2 tbsp	olive oil	30 mL
4	medium pickerel filets	4
	juice of 2 limes	
	salt	

■ Preheat oven to broil.

■ Grind all spices together in mortar. Add oil and lime juice; mix together.

■ Brush mixture over both sides of filets.

■ Place filets, skin-side down, on ovenproof platter. Place in oven, 6 in (15 cm) from broiler element, and broil 7 to 8 minutes. Do not turn fish over.

■ Serve with vegetables.

1 SERVING: 154 CALORIES 2 g CARBOHYDRATE 19 g PROTEIN
8 g FAT 0 g FIBER

FISH STOCK
(SERVES 6)

2 lbs	fish bones	900 g
2 tbsp	butter	30 mL
2	celery stalks with leaves, chopped	2
½	onion, quartered	½
1	carrot, cut in thick slices	1
1	thyme sprig	1
3 to 4	parsley sprigs	3 to 4
1	bay leaf	1
1 tbsp	peppercorns	15 mL
1 cup	dry white wine	250 mL
5 cups	water	1.2 L
	salt and pepper	

■ Place fish bones and butter in large saucepan. Cover and cook 6 minutes over medium heat, stirring once.

■ Add vegetables and seasonings; cover and cook 6 minutes.

■ Pour in wine and water; season well. Bring to boil over medium heat. Continue cooking 18 minutes over low heat.

■ Strain liquid and let cool. Cover stock with sheet of plastic wrap so that it touches surface. The stock will keep 4 to 5 days in refrigerator.

1 SERVING:	72 CALORIES	2 g CARBOHYDRATE	0 g PROTEIN
	4 g FAT	0 g FIBER	

FRESH MUSSELS

(SERVES 4)

9 lbs	mussels, washed and scrubbed	4 kg
1 cup	dry white wine	250 mL
2	parsley sprigs	2
2	shallots, chopped	2
1 tsp	fennel seed	5 mL
½ cup	fish stock (see page 182) or water	125 mL
1 tbsp	beurre manié (see page 155)	15 mL
1 tbsp	chopped fresh parsley salt and pepper	15 mL

■ Place mussels in large saucepan. Add wine, pepper, parsley sprigs, shallots, fennel seed and fish stock. Cover and cook 10 to 12 minutes over medium heat or just until shells open. Shake pan 2 to 3 times during cooking.

■ When mussels open, remove from pan and place in bowl. Set aside. (Discard any unopened mussels.)

■ Line sieve with cheesecloth and strain cooking liquid into clean saucepan. Season with salt and pepper. Stir in beurre manié and chopped parsley. Cook 3 minutes over high heat, whisking constantly.

■ Pour sauce over mussels and serve.

1 SERVING: 461 CALORIES   21 g CARBOHYDRATE   73 g PROTEIN
5 g FAT   0 g FIBER

RED SNAPPER WITH ROASTED PECANS

(SERVES 4)

¼ tsp	black pepper	1 mL
¼ tsp	paprika	1 mL
½ tsp	fennel seed	2 mL
4	large red snapper filets	4
3 tbsp	butter	45 mL
⅓ cup	roasted pecans	75 mL
1 tbsp	chopped fresh parsley	15 mL
	lemon juice	
	salt	

■ Grind pepper, salt, paprika and fennel seed together in mortar. Sprinkle mixture over both sides of each filet.

■ Heat 2 tbsp (30 mL) butter in large frying pan over medium heat. Add fish and cook 4 minutes.

■ Turn filets over and continue cooking 3 to 4 minutes or adjust cooking time according to size of filets. Remove cooked filets from pan and keep hot.

■ Add remaining butter to pan and melt. Add pecans and cook 1 minute. Add lemon juice and mix. Pour over fish, sprinkle with parsley and serve.

1 SERVING:	282 CALORIES	6 g CARBOHYDRATE	19 g PROTEIN
	20 g FAT	0 g FIBER	

Choose large fresh red snapper filets.

Grind spices together in mortar.

Sprinkle mixture over both sides of each filet.

Place fish in hot butter and cook 4 minutes over medium heat.

Turn filets over and continue cooking.

Remove cooked fish from pan and add remaining butter to melt. Cook pecans in butter 1 minute.

SAUTÉED HALIBUT STEAKS

(SERVES 4)

4	halibut steaks	4	
1 cup	seasoned flour	250 mL	
2 tbsp	butter	30 mL	
1 tbsp	vegetable oil	15 mL	
1	carrot, pared and thinly sliced	1	
1	green pepper, thinly sliced	1	
1	celery stalk, thinly sliced	1	
1 cup	fish stock, heated	250 mL	
½ tsp	cornstarch	2 mL	
2 tbsp	cold water	30 mL	
	salt and pepper		
	lemon juice		

■ Preheat oven to 375 °F (190 °C).

■ Season fish and dredge in flour. Heat butter and oil in large ovenproof frying pan over medium heat. Add halibut and cook about 8 minutes; adjust time depending on size of steaks. Turn fish over 2 to 3 times during cooking.

■ Transfer pan to oven and finish cooking fish 6 minutes. Remove fish from pan to serving platter and keep warm.

■ Add all vegetables to frying pan and season well. Cover and cook 4 minutes over medium heat.

■ Pour in fish stock and bring to boil. Cook 1 minute.

■ Dissolve cornstarch in cold water; stir into vegetable mixture until well blended. Cook 1 minute over reduced heat.

■ Spoon vegetables alongside fish, sprinkle with lemon juice and serve at once.

1 SERVING:	325 CALORIES	16 g CARBOHYDRATE	34 g PROTEIN
	14 g FAT	1.0 g FIBER	

FILET OF SOLE AMANDINE
(SERVES 4)

4	large sole filets	4	
1 cup	flour	250 mL	
2 tbsp	butter	30 mL	
1 tsp	vegetable oil	5 mL	
3 tbsp	slivered almonds	45 mL	
1 tbsp	chopped fresh parsley	15 mL	
	salt and pepper		
	paprika		
	juice 1 lemon		

■ Season filets with salt, pepper and paprika. Dredge in flour.

■ Heat butter and oil in large frying pan over high heat. Add fish and cook 2 minutes. Turn filets over and continue cooking 2 minutes. Transfer fish to heated serving platter.

■ Add almonds, parsley and lemon juice to frying pan; cook 1 minute over high heat. Spoon over sole and serve at once.

1 SERVING:	264 CALORIES	15 g CARBOHYDRATE	20 g PROTEIN
	14 g FAT ·	1.0 g FIBER	

SEA BASS EN PAPILLOTE
(SERVES 4)

4	whole sea bass, ¾ to 1 lb (375 to 500 g) each, cleaned	4
3 tbsp	melted butter	45 mL
2	shallots, finely chopped	2
½ lb	fresh mushrooms, cleaned and chopped	250 g
1 tbsp	chopped fresh parsley	15 mL
1	red pepper, diced	1
	juice of 1 lemon	
	salt and pepper	

- Preheat oven to 425 °F (220 °C).

- Season cavities of fish with salt, pepper and lemon juice. Place each fish on large sheet of aluminum foil. Set aside.

- Heat half of butter in frying pan over medium heat. Add shallots and cook 2 minutes.

- Add mushrooms, parsley and red pepper. Season and cook 6 minutes.

- Stuff fish with vegetable mixture and baste skin with remaining melted butter. Seal foil packages and place in roasting pan. Cook 16 to 18 minutes in oven.

- Serve with lemon juice.

1 SERVING:	646 CALORIES	30 g CARBOHYDRATE	83 g PROTEIN
	22 g FAT	2.0 g FIBER	

BLACKENED GROUPER BATON ROUGE

(SERVES 4)

1 tsp	black pepper	5 mL
1 tsp	chili powder	5 mL
1 tsp	thyme	5 mL
¼ tsp	ginger	1 mL
1 tsp	paprika	5 mL
1 tsp	cayenne pepper	5 mL
4	slices grouper	4
	olive oil	

■ Mix spices together in small bowl. Set aside.

■ Preheat oven to 350 °F (180 °C).

■ Wash and dry fish. Pour small amount of oil in plate and coat each piece of fish in oil. Set aside.

■ Pour small amount of oil in cast iron pan; use paper towel to spread evenly. Heat pan over high heat. When hot, add spices to pan and cook 2 minutes, stirring occasionally.

■ Add fish to pan. Reduce heat to medium and cook 3 to 4 minutes on each side or adjust time according to thickness.

■ Put pan in preheated oven and continue cooking in oven for 7 to 8 minutes.

1 SERVING:	212 CALORIES	0 g CARBOHYDRATE	35 g PROTEIN
	8 g FAT	0 g FIBER	

MONKFISH WITH TOMATO BASIL COULIS
(SERVES 4)

2 tbsp	olive oil	30 mL
1	onion, finely chopped	1
1	garlic clove, smashed and chopped	1
4	large tomatoes, cored and cut in six	4
3 tbsp	chopped fresh basil	45 mL
¼ cup	fish stock (see page 182)	50 mL
2 tbsp	tomato paste	30 mL
4	medium monkfish filets	4
	pinch brown sugar	
	salt and pepper	

■ Preheat oven to 350 °F (180 °C).

■ Heat 1 tbsp (15 mL) olive oil in sauté pan over medium heat. Add onion and garlic; cook 6 minutes over low heat.

■ Add tomatoes and basil. Season and cook 10 minutes over low heat, stirring occasionally.

■ Stir in fish stock, tomato paste and brown sugar. Continue cooking 6 to 7 minutes.

■ Heat remaining oil in second frying pan over medium heat. Add fish and cook 2 minutes on each side.

■ Transfer fish to roasting pan and top with tomato mixture. Cook in oven 10 minutes or adjust time according to size of filets.

■ If desired, pass tomato sauce through sieve and stir in 2 tbsp (30 mL) sour cream before serving.

1 SERVING:	342 CALORIES	9 g CARBOHYDRATE	42 g PROTEIN
	15 g FAT	2.0 g FIBER	

Choose fresh monkfish.

Cook onion and garlic in hot oil 6 minutes over low heat.

Add tomatoes and basil. Season and cook 10 minutes, stirring occasionally.

Stir in fish stock, tomato paste and brown sugar.

Sear fish 2 minutes on each side.

Transfer fish to roasting pan and top with tomato mixture. Continue cooking in oven.

SAUTÉED PICKEREL
(SERVES 4)

1 tbsp	butter	15 mL
1 tbsp	olive oil	15 mL
4	pickerel filets	4
1	red pepper, in julienne	1
1	zucchini, in julienne	1
½ cup	pine nuts	125 mL
2 tbsp	grated orange rind	30 mL
	lemon juice	
	salt and pepper	

■ Preheat oven to 375 °F (190 °C).

■ Heat butter and oil in ovenproof sauté pan over medium heat. Add fish and season well; cook 3 minutes.

■ Turn filets over. Place pan in oven and continue cooking 6 to 8 minutes or adjust time according to thickness of filets.

■ Remove fish from sauté pan and keep hot.

■ Return sauté pan to burner. Add red pepper and zucchini; cook 4 minutes over high heat.

■ Add remaining ingredients and season well. Cook 3 more minutes. Pour vegetables and juices from pan over fish and serve.

1 SERVING:	236 CALORIES	6 g CARBOHYDRATE	25 g PROTEIN
	12 g FAT	0 g FIBER	

RICHMOND SHRIMP SAUTÉ

(SERVES 4)

1 tbsp	olive oil	15 mL
1¼ lbs	fresh shrimp, shelled and deveined	625 g
2	medium beets, cooked and quartered	2
1 cup	cooked corn	250 mL
2	garlic cloves, smashed and chopped	2
1 tbsp	chopped fresh tarragon	15 mL
1	avocado, peeled, cut in wedges	1
1 tsp	chopped fresh parsley	5 mL
	juice of 1 lemon	
	salt and pepper	

■ Heat oil in frying pan over high heat. Add shrimp and season well; cook 2 minutes.

■ Turn shrimp over and continue cooking 2 to 3 minutes. Remove shrimp from pan and set aside.

■ Add vegetables and garlic to hot pan. Cook 1 minute over high heat. Return shrimp to pan and season. Add tarragon and cook 2 minutes.

■ Serve shrimp and vegetables garnished with wedges of avocado. Sprinkle with lemon juice and chopped parsley.

1 SERVING:	334 CALORIES	20 g CARBOHYDRATE	40 g PROTEIN
	10 g FAT	3.7 g FIBER	

Mussels au Gratin

MUSSELS AU GRATIN
(SERVES 4)

9 lbs	mussels, scrubbed and washed	4 kg
½ cup	dry white wine	125 mL
3	slices white bread, crusts removed	3
½ cup	milk	125 mL
2 tbsp	butter	30 mL
½ cup	chopped shallots	125 mL
4	garlic cloves, smashed and chopped	4
4 tbsp	chopped fresh parsley	60 mL
2 tbsp	chopped fresh chives	30 mL
	pinch cayenne pepper	
	salt and pepper	

■ Place mussels in very large saucepan. Add wine, cover and cook over medium heat just until shells open. Shake pan 2 to 3 times during cooking. Discard any shells that do not open.

■ Remove mussels from shells, drain well and chop. Set aside. Empty liquid from shells back into pan. Set shells aside.

■ Line sieve with cheesecloth and strain cooking liquid into saucepan. Place pan on stove and cook 5 minutes over high heat. Set aside.

■ Place bread in bowl and cover with milk; set aside to soak.

■ Heat butter in frying pan over medium heat. Add shallots and garlic; cook 4 minutes.

■ Add parsley, chives and cayenne pepper. Cook 1 minute.

■ Add chopped mussels and season well. Mix, then remove pan from heat.

■ Squeeze out excess milk from bread and incorporate bread into mussel mixture. Add reduced cooking liquid and mix well.

■ Fill shells with stuffing and broil in oven for 3 minutes. Serve.

1 SERVING:	560 CALORIES	39 g CARBOHYDRATE	76 g PROTEIN
	9 g FAT	1.0 g FIBER	

STUFFED CLAMS
(SERVES 4)

24	clams, scrubbed and washed	24
½ cup	water	125 mL
4	slices white bread, crusts removed	4
½ cup	milk	125 mL
2 tbsp	butter	30 mL
1	onion, finely chopped	1
1	garlic clove, smashed and chopped	1
1 tsp	chopped fresh parsley	5 mL
1 tsp	oregano	5 mL
	few drops Worcestershire sauce	
	salt, pepper, paprika	

■ Place clams in large saucepan. Add water, cover and bring to boil. Cook 5 minutes. Check that shells are wide open. Discard any clams that are closed.

■ Remove clams from shells and chop; place in bowl. Reserve 24 half shells.

■ Place bread in another bowl. Pour in milk and let soak 5 minutes.

■ Heat butter in frying pan over medium heat. Add onion and garlic; cook 4 minutes. Remove pan from heat.

■ Squeeze out excess milk from bread. Add bread to onion and garlic mixture in frying pan. Add chopped clams and mix well. Season with salt and pepper, then add remaining seasonings. Mix again.

■ Return pan to stove and cook 2 to 3 minutes over high heat.

■ Fill clam shells with stuffing. Spread layer of coarse salt in bottom of roasting pan for support. Position stuffed shells on salt and broil 5 minutes in oven.

1 SERVING:	238 CALORIES	24 g CARBOHYDRATE	15 g PROTEIN
	9 g FAT	1.1 g FIBER	

Only use fresh clams for this recipe. Wash and scrub shells before cooking.

Place clams in large saucepan. Add water, cover and cook.

Remove cooked clams from opened shells. Discard clams that did not open.

Chop clams.

Soak bread in milk.

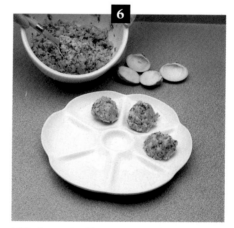

Fill clam shells with stuffing.

POACHED HALIBUT STEAKS WITH CREAMY FISH SAUCE

(SERVES 4)

4	halibut steaks, each 1 in (2.5 cm) thick	4
6 cups	fish stock, heated (see page 182)	1.5 L
2 tbsp	butter	30 mL
3 tbsp	flour	45 mL
1½ cups	fish stock, heated	375 mL
2 tbsp	heavy cream (optional)	30 mL
1 tbsp	chopped fresh parsley	15 mL
	salt and pepper	
	paprika	

■ Place halibut in large skillet and pour in 6 cups (1.5 L) fish stock. Cook over low heat at simmer 8 to 10 minutes, depending on size of halibut steaks. Turn fish over once during cooking.

■ Meanwhile, heat butter in saucepan over medium heat. Add flour and mix. Stir for 1 minute over low heat. Whisk in 1½ cups (375 mL) fish stock; continue cooking 6 minutes.

■ Add heavy cream and correct seasoning; continue cooking 2 minutes.

■ Spoon sauce over fish arranged on serving platter. Sprinkle with parsley and paprika, and serve with mushrooms, if desired.

1 SERVING:	321 CALORIES	6 g CARBOHYDRATE	33 g PROTEIN
	18 g FAT	0 g FIBER	

BRAISED BEEF

(SERVES 4 TO 6)

2 tbsp	olive oil	30 mL
4 lbs	bottom round roast, tied	1.8 kg
3	large onions, cut in 6	3
2	garlic cloves, smashed and chopped	2
1 cup	cranberry sauce	250 mL
28-oz	can tomatoes, drained and chopped	796-mL
½ cup	sherry	125 mL
3 cups	beef stock, heated	750 mL
1 tsp	basil	5 mL
½ tsp	thyme	2 mL
1 tsp	oregano	5 mL
	salt and pepper	

■ Preheat oven to 350 °F (180 °C).

■ Heat oil in ovenproof casserole over high heat. Add meat and sear on all sides. Season with salt and pepper.

■ Add onions and garlic; continue cooking 8 minutes to sear onions. Stir once or twice during cooking.

■ Add remaining ingredients. Season and bring to boil. Cover and cook 2½ to 3 hours in oven.

■ Serve with fresh vegetables.

Note: To thicken sauce at end of cooking, pour 2 cups (500 mL) of sauce into saucepan. Dissolve 1 tbsp (15 mL) cornstarch in 3 tbsp (45 mL) cold water. Stir into sauce and cook 1 minute over high heat.

1 SERVING:	634 CALORIES	17 g CARBOHYDRATE	87 g PROTEIN
	23 g FAT	2.0 g FIBER	

SHERRIED ROAST PORK

(SERVES 4)

3½ lbs	boneless pork roast, tied	1.6 kg
2	garlic cloves, peeled and cut in slivers	2
1 tbsp	olive oil	15 mL
2	large onions, cut in 6	2
2	whole garlic cloves, peeled	2
½ tsp	rosemary	2 mL
½ tsp	thyme	2 mL
½ cup	sherry	125 mL
1½ cups	chicken stock, heated	375 mL
1 tbsp	cornstarch	15 mL
3 tbsp	cold water	45 mL
	salt and pepper	

■ Preheat oven to 350 °F (180 °C).

■ Make slits in meat and insert garlic slivers. Heat oil in ovenproof casserole over high heat. Add roast and sear on all sides.

■ Add onions, garlic and seasonings. Place in oven, uncovered, and cook 1 hour and 15 minutes.

■ Remove cooked roast from casserole, cover with aluminum foil and let stand 10 minutes.

■ Place casserole on stove over high heat; cook 2 minutes. Add sherry and cook 2 minutes. Incorporate chicken stock and continue cooking 3 minutes.

■ Dissolve cornstarch in cold water. Pour into sauce and bring to boil. Do not strain sauce.

■ Slice roast and serve with sauce. Accompany with potatoes.

1 SERVING:	822 CALORIES	6 g CARBOHYDRATE	84 g PROTEIN
	49 g FAT	1.0 g FIBER	

Seafood Casserole

SEAFOOD CASSEROLE
(SERVES 4)

¾ lb	large scallops	375 g
¾ lb	shrimp, peeled and deveined	375 g
½ tsp	fennel seed	2 mL
1 tbsp	chopped fresh parsley	15 mL
½ cup	dry white wine	125 mL
1½ cups	clam juice	375 mL
4 tbsp	butter	60 mL
½ lb	fresh mushrooms, cleaned and chopped	250 g
2	dry shallots, peeled and chopped	2
3 tbsp	flour	45 mL
3 tbsp	breadcrumbs	45 mL
	salt and pepper	

■ Place scallops and shrimp in sauté pan. Add fennel, parsley, wine and clam juice. Season with salt and pepper. Place sheet of waxed paper on surface of ingredients. Place on stove and bring just to boiling point over medium heat. Do not allow liquid to boil. Remove sauté pan from heat and let stand 4 minutes.

■ Remove seafood from liquid and set aside. Place sauté pan over medium heat and cook liquid 4 minutes.

■ Heat 3 tbsp (45 mL) butter in second frying pan over medium heat. Add mushrooms and shallots. Season well and cook 4 minutes. Mix in flour and cook 1 minute.

■ Pour in reserved cooking liquid and mix well. Cook 4 minutes.

■ Slice seafood on the bias. Place seafood in baking dish and cover with mushroom sauce.

■ Preheat oven to broil.

■ Mix remaining butter with breadcrumbs; sprinkle over casserole. Broil 3 minutes in oven, then serve.

1 SERVING:	416 CALORIES	19 g CARBOHYDRATE	48 g PROTEIN
	15 g FAT	2.1 g FIBER	

BOEUF BOURGUIGNON
(SERVES 4 TO 6)

2 tbsp	olive oil	30 mL
3½ lbs	blade steak, in ¾-in (2-cm) cubes	1.6 kg
3	dry shallots, peeled and chopped	3
3	garlic cloves, smashed and chopped	3
4 tbsp	flour	60 mL
3 cups	dry red wine	750 mL
1	bay leaf	1
2 cups	beef stock, heated	500 mL
1 tsp	basil	5 mL
1 tsp	chopped fresh parsley	5 mL
3 tbsp	butter	45 mL
24	pearl onions, peeled	24
1 lb	fresh mushrooms, cleaned and halved	500 g
	salt and pepper	

■ Preheat oven to 305 °F (180 °C).

■ Heat half of oil in large ovenproof sauté pan over medium heat. Add half of meat and sear on all sides. Season well, remove meat and set aside.

■ Pour remaining oil in pan and heat. Add rest of meat, shallots and garlic. Sear on all sides, then return first batch of meat to pan. Season with salt and pepper. Sprinkle flour over meat and mix well. Cook 4 to 5 minutes over medium heat.

■ Pour wine into a saucepan, add bay leaf and bring to boil. Cook until reduced by ⅔, then pour remaining liquid into sauté pan containing meat.

■ Add beef stock and herbs; bring to boil. Cover pan and cook 2 hours in oven.

■ Thirty minutes before end of cooking, heat butter in frying pan over medium heat. Add pearl onions and season; cook 5 minutes. Add mushrooms, season to taste and cook 4 minutes.

■ Add vegetables to stew and continue cooking in oven. Serve with toasted bread.

1 SERVING:	788 CALORIES	31 g CARBOHYDRATE	78 g PROTEIN
	32 g FAT	4.7 g FIBER	

Sear meat with shallots and garlic in hot oil.

Sprinkle flour over meat, mix well and cook 4 to 5 minutes over medium heat.

Bring wine to boil in saucepan over medium heat. Cook about 4 to 5 minutes to reduce by ⅔.

Pour wine into pan containing meat.

Add beef stock and herbs.

Thirty minutes before end of cooking, sauté pearl onions and mushrooms in hot butter.

VEGETABLE CASSEROLE

(SERVES 6)

1	large eggplant, halved lengthwise	1
2 tbsp	olive oil	30 mL
½	zucchini, diced medium	½
1	green pepper, diced medium	1
2	summer squash, diced medium	2
3	dry shallots, peeled chopped	3
2	garlic cloves, smashed and chopped	2
¼ tsp	paprika	1 mL
3	tomatoes, peeled and diced	3
½ cup	sherry	125 mL
1 cup	cooked white beans	250 mL
1½ cups	grated Gruyère cheese salt and pepper	375 mL

■ Preheat oven to 400 °F (200 °C).

■ Score eggplant flesh in crisscross pattern. Brush with oil and place, skin-side up, in roasting pan. Cook 40 minutes in oven. Remove flesh from skin, chop flesh and set aside.

■ Heat remaining oil in frying pan over medium heat. Add vegetables, except tomatoes and beans. Add garlic, paprika and season well. Mix well and cook 10 minutes, stirring occasionally.

■ Add chopped eggplant and tomatoes. Mix well and season. Cover and cook 12 minutes over low heat. Incorporate sherry and beans.

■ Preheat oven to 375 °F (190 °C).

■ Transfer mixture to buttered baking dish. Sprinkle with cheese and cook 12 minutes in oven.

1 SERVING:	231 CALORIES	19 g CARBOHYDRATE	11 g PROTEIN
	12 g FAT	5.1 g FIBER	

BAKED LEEK CASSEROLE
(SERVES 4 TO 6)

1 tbsp	butter	15 mL
4	cooked leeks, white part only, drained and chopped	4
4	beaten eggs	4
⅔ cup	flour	150 mL
¼ tsp	nutmeg	1 mL
1½ cups	milk	375 mL
	pinch paprika	
	salt and pepper	

- Preheat oven to 375 °F (190 °C).

- Butter baking dish.

- Place cooked, chopped leeks in bowl with beaten eggs; mix together. Incorporate flour. Add paprika, nutmeg and milk; season well. Mix together with whisk.

- Pour mixture into baking dish and bake 40 minutes in oven. Slice and serve.

1 SERVING:	244 CALORIES	31 g CARBOHYDRATE	11 g PROTEIN
	9 g FAT	3.6 g FIBER	

BEEF GOULASH

(SERVES 4 TO 6)

2 tbsp	olive oil	30 mL
3½ lbs	blade steak, in ¾-in (2-cm) cubes	1.6 kg
3	onions, sliced	3
3 tbsp	paprika	45 mL
3	garlic cloves, smashed and chopped	3
4 tbsp	flour	60 mL
4 cups	beef stock, heated	1 L
1 tbsp	basil	15 mL
1 tsp	caraway seeds	5 mL
½ tsp	thyme	2 mL
	salt and pepper	

- Preheat oven to 325 °F (160 °C).

- Heat half of oil in ovenproof sauté pan over medium heat. Add half of meat and sear well on all sides. Season with salt and pepper. Remove meat from pan and set aside. Add remaining oil to pan and repeat searing technique for remaining meat. Place all meat aside.

- Add onions to hot pan and cook 8 minutes over medium heat, stirring occasionally. Add paprika and garlic; mix well and cook 8 minutes over medium heat.

- Return meat to sauté pan. Sprinkle in flour and mix well. Cook 4 minutes over low heat. Add remaining ingredients and season; mix well. Bring to boil, cover and cook 3 hours in oven.

- Serve with sour cream and boiled potatoes.

1 SERVING:	576 CALORIES	15 g CARBOHYDRATE	75 g PROTEIN
	24 g FAT	1.2 g FIBER	

Sear meat in hot oil.

Remove meat from sauté pan and set aside.

Add onions to hot pan and cook.

Add paprika and garlic; mix and cook 8 minutes over medium heat.

Return seared meat to pan, sprinkle with flour and mix well.

Add beef stock and remaining ingredients.

ALL-SEASON VEGETABLE CHILI

(SERVES 6 TO 8)

1 tbsp	olive oil	15 mL
1	large onion, finely chopped	1
3	garlic cloves, smashed and chopped	3
2	celery stalks, diced	2
2	carrots, peeled and diced	2
2	zucchini, diced	2
1	green pepper, diced	1
1	red pepper, diced	1
2 tbsp	chili powder	30 mL
½ tsp	ground cloves	2 mL
1½ tbsp	oregano	25 mL
1	bay leaf	1
28-oz	can tomatoes, chopped, with juice	796-mL
2 tbsp	tomato paste	30 mL
½ lb	fresh mushrooms, cleaned and halved	250 g
	pinch paprika	
	pinch sugar	
	salt and pepper	
	grated Cheddar cheese	

- Preheat oven to 325 °F (160 °C).

- Heat oil in large ovenproof sauté pan over high heat. Add onion, garlic and celery. Cook 8 minutes over medium heat, stirring occasionally.

- Add carrots, zucchini, peppers, spices and herbs; mix well. Cover and cook 8 minutes over low heat.

- Stir in tomatoes with juice, tomato paste and sugar. Cover and cook 40 minutes in oven.

- Mix in mushrooms and continue cooking 20 minutes in oven. Do not cover.

- Serve with grated cheese and toasted bread.

---

1 SERVING:	116 CALORIES	14 g CARBOHYDRATE	5 g PROTEIN
	5 g FAT	3.6 g FIBER	

GARLIC BAKED BEANS

(SERVES 4 TO 6)

1 lb	dried navy beans	500 g
1	bouquet garni*	1
12	whole garlic cloves, peeled	12
2 tbsp	chopped fresh parsley	30 mL
2 cups	dry white wine	500 mL
1 tbsp	basil	15 mL
	salt and pepper	

■ Place beans in bowl and cover completely with water. Soak 12 hours.

■ Drain beans and transfer to ovenproof casserole. Cover completely with fresh water. Season with salt and pepper. Add bouquet garni and cook over medium heat for 1½ hours. Do not cover.

■ Preheat oven to 300 °F (150 °C).

■ Drain beans well and return to same casserole. Add garlic, parsley, wine and basil; season well. Cover with water and bring to boil. Cover casserole and cook 1½ hours in oven.

■ Thirty minutes before end of cooking, remove cover.

*Tie together sprigs of parsley, thyme, basil and a bay leaf.

1 SERVING:	174 CALORIES	18 g CARBOHYDRATE	8 g PROTEIN
	0 g FAT	7.5 g FIBER	

SWEET BAKED BEANS

(SERVES 4 TO 6)

1 lb	dried navy beans	500 g	
¼ lb	salt pork, diced	125 g	
1 tbsp	dry mustard	15 mL	
1½	onions, finely chopped	1½	
⅔ cup	ketchup	150 mL	
2	garlic cloves, smashed and chopped	2	
¼ cup	molasses	50 mL	
5 cups	hot water	1.2 L	
	salt and pepper		

■ Place beans in large bowl and cover completely with cold water. Soak 12 hours.

■ Drain beans and transfer to large saucepan. Cover completely with fresh water and bring to boil. Season with salt and pepper; cook 30 minutes over medium heat.

■ Preheat oven to 300 °F (150 °C).

■ Drain beans and transfer to bean pot. Add remaining ingredients, including hot water. Season generously. Cover and cook 3 hours in oven.

■ Thirty minutes before end of cooking, remove cover.

1 SERVING:	296 CALORIES	34 g CARBOHYDRATE	8 g PROTEIN
	15 g FAT	7.7 g FIBER	

CREAMY LEEK AND POTATO AU GRATIN
(SERVES 4)

4	large leeks, white part only	4
¼ cup	sliced onions, cooked	50 mL
4	large potatoes, peeled and sliced	4
¼ tsp	nutmeg	1 mL
2 cups	light white sauce, heated	500 mL
1 cup	grated Gruyère cheese	250 mL
	pinch paprika	
	salt and white pepper	

■ Slit leeks in 4, leaving ¾ in (2 cm) uncut at base. Spread leeks apart and rinse under cold water to remove all dirt and sand. Cook 35 minutes in salted, boiling water. Drain well.

■ Preheat oven to 350 °F (180 °C).

■ Slice leeks and place in buttered baking dish. Spread cooked onions over leeks and top with sliced potatoes. Season with salt and pepper.

■ Mix nutmeg and paprika into white sauce. Pour over potatoes and top with cheese. Cook 40 minutes in oven. Serve.

1 SERVING: 481 CALORIES   64 g CARBOHYDRATE   16 g PROTEIN
18 g FAT   3.9 g FIBER

CURRIED LAMB SHOULDER STEW

(SERVES 4)

2 tbsp	olive oil	30 mL
3 lbs	lamb shoulder, in large cubes	1.4 kg
1	large onion, chopped	1
2	garlic cloves, smashed and chopped	2
3 tbsp	curry powder	45 mL
3 tbsp	flour	45 mL
3 cups	chicken stock, heated	750 mL
2	plantain bananas, sliced	2
	salt and pepper	

■ Preheat oven to 350 °F (180 °C).

■ Heat oil in ovenproof sauté pan over high heat. Add meat and sear on all sides for 6 minutes. Season with salt and pepper.

■ Add onion and garlic. Mix and cook 4 minutes over high heat. Add curry powder, mix well and cook 3 minutes.

■ Mix in flour and cook 3 minutes over medium heat.

■ Incorporate chicken stock, season well and bring to boil. Cover and cook 2 hours in oven.

■ Fifteen minutes before end of cooking, add bananas.

■ Serve with pasta.

1 SERVING:	673 CALORIES	21 g CARBOHYDRATE	73 g PROTEIN
	33 g FAT	1.2 g FIBER	

Sear meat in hot oil.

Add onion and garlic. Mix and cook 4 minutes over high heat.

Add curry powder, mix well and cook 3 minutes.

Add flour, mix well and cook 3 minutes over medium heat.

Incorporate chicken stock.

Fifteen minutes before end of cooking, add bananas.

CRÊPE BATTER

1 cup	all-purpose flour	250 mL
½ tsp	salt	2 mL
4	eggs	4
1 cup	Perrier or other mineral water	250 mL
1¼ cups	milk	300 mL
3 tbsp	melted butter, tepid	45 mL

■ Sift flour and salt into bowl. Add eggs and mix well. Add mineral water and incorporate with whisk. Pour in milk and whisk. Add melted butter and whisk.

■ Strain batter through fine sieve into bowl. Refrigerate 1 hour before using.

Note: If batter is too thick, add a bit of water. Be sure to mix very well before using.

1 RECIPE:	1273 CALORIES	122 g CARBOHYDRATE	50 g PROTEIN
	65 g FAT	4.7 g FIBER	

EGGPLANT-STUFFED CRÊPES

(SERVES 4)

1	large eggplant, halved lengthwise	1
1 tbsp	olive oil	15 mL
2 tbsp	butter	30 mL
3	dry shallots, peeled and chopped	3
2	garlic cloves, smashed and chopped	2
2	large tomatoes, peeled and chopped	2
1 tsp	basil	5 mL
1 tsp	chopped fresh parsley	5 mL
8	crêpes (see page 216)	8
2 cups	light white sauce, heated	500 mL
1¼ cups	grated Gruyère cheese	300 mL
	salt and pepper	

■ Preheat oven to 375 °F (190 °C).

■ Score eggplant flesh in crisscross pattern. Brush with oil and place, skin-side up, in roasting pan. Cook 40 minutes in oven. Remove flesh from skins, chop and set aside.

■ Reduce oven heat to 350 °F (180 °C).

■ Heat butter in saucepan over medium heat. Add shallots and garlic; cook 5 minutes over low heat.

■ Add chopped eggplant and mix well. Incorporate tomatoes and herbs; season with salt and pepper. Cook 12 minutes over low heat.

■ Spread mixture over crêpes and roll. Place in buttered baking dish. Cover with white sauce and top with cheese. Cook 12 minutes in oven and serve.

1 SERVING:	715 CALORIES	51 g CARBOHYDRATE	27 g PROTEIN
	45 g FAT	3.0 g FIBER	

LAMB CASSEROLE WITH VEGETABLES

(SERVES 4)

1 tsp	basil	5 mL
¼ tsp	thyme	1 mL
4 tbsp	flour	60 mL
2½ lbs	lamb shoulder, trimmed of fat and cut in large cubes	1.2 kg
2 tbsp	olive oil	30 mL
¼ cup	sherry	50 mL
2 cups	chicken stock, heated	500 mL
1 tbsp	butter	15 mL
24	white pearl onions, peeled	24
6	whole dry shallots, peeled	6
1	celery stalk, cut in large pieces and blanched	1
4	carrots, pared, cut in large pieces and blanched	4
1	yellow pepper, diced large	1
1	red pepper, diced large	1
	salt and pepper	

- Preheat oven to 350 °F (180 °C).

- Mix basil and thyme with flour. Dredge meat in seasoned flour and season generously with salt and pepper.

- Heat oil in ovenproof sauté pan over high heat. Add meat and sear on all sides for 8 minutes. Add sherry and cook 3 minutes.

- Incorporate chicken stock. Season, bring to boil and cover pan. Cook in oven 2 to 2½ hours or adjust time according to size of cubed meat.

- Meanwhile, heat butter in frying pan over medium heat. Add pearl onions and shallots. Cook 8 minutes, stirring occasionally.

- One and a half hours before end of cooking, add onions to meat.

- Fifteen minutes before end of cooking, add all other vegetables. Season with salt and pepper and resume cooking.

- Serve with mashed sweet potatoes.

1 SERVING: 709 CALORIES 37 g CARBOHYDRATE 66 g PROTEIN
33 g FAT 4.5 g FIBER

Dredge cubes of meat in seasoned flour.

Sear meat in hot oil.

Add sherry.

Sauté onions and shallots in hot butter.

One and a half hours before end of cooking, add onions to meat.

Fifteen minutes before end of cooking, add all other vegetables to pan.

SMOKED PORK CHOPS AND SAUERKRAUT
(SERVES 4)

1 oz	salt pork, diced	30 g
2	onions, diced	2
1	large can sauerkraut	1
1 cup	dry white wine	250 mL
1 cup	chicken stock, heated	250 mL
1	bouquet garni*	1
4	smoked pork chops	4
	salt and pepper	

■ Preheat oven to 375 °F (190 °C).

■ Heat salt pork in ovenproof casserole over medium heat. Add onions and cook 7 minutes over medium heat.

■ Rinse sauerkraut under cold water for 3 minutes. Drain and squeeze out excess liquid.

■ Add sauerkraut to casserole. Add wine, chicken stock and bouquet garni. Mix and bring to boil. Cover and cook 2 hours in oven, mixing twice during cooking.

■ Thirty minutes before end of cooking, add pork chops. Cover and resume cooking.

■ Serve with boiled potatoes and carrots.

*Tie together sprigs of parsley, thyme, basil and a bay leaf.

1 SERVING:	403 CALORIES	10 g CARBOHYDRATE	22 g PROTEIN
	26 g FAT	1.0 g FIBER	

SHORT RIBS AND VEGETABLES

(SERVES 4 TO 6)

6 lbs	beef short ribs, in 2-in (5-cm) pieces	2.7 kg
4	leeks, white part only	4
4	large carrots, pared	4
2	red onions, peeled	2
2	small white turnips, peeled	2
2	stalks of celery heart	2
2	cloves	2
1	bouquet garni *	1
1½ cups	dry white wine	375 mL
	salt and pepper	

■ Trim part of fat from meat. Place short ribs in large stock pot. Cover completely with water and bring to boil over medium heat. Add 1 cup (250 mL) cold water and bring to boil again. Skim well.

■ Cut leeks in four lengthwise, leaving ¾ in (2 cm) uncut at base. Spread leaves and rinse under cold water to remove dirt and sand.

■ Add leeks to stock pot along with remaining ingredients. Bring to boil over medium heat. Continue cooking, uncovered, for 3 hours over low heat.

■ Remove vegetables as they become cooked. Five minutes before end of cooking, return vegetables to stock pot to reheat. Serve with strong mustard.

*Tie together sprigs of parsley, thyme, basil and a bay leaf.

1 SERVING:	1003 CALORIES	29 g CARBOHYDRATE	119 g PROTEIN
	40 g FAT	8.1 g FIBER	

LAMB AND POTATO STEW

(SERVES 4)

2½ lbs	lamb shoulder, trimmed of fat and cut in 1-in (2.5-cm) cubes	1.2 kg
¼ cup	seasoned flour	50 mL
2 tbsp	olive oil	30 mL
1	large onion, sliced	1
2	garlic cloves, smashed and chopped	2
3 cups	beef stock, heated	750 mL
4	tomatoes, quartered	4
3	potatoes, peeled and quartered	3
½ cup	pitted black olives	125 mL
1	large red pepper, cubed	1
	salt and pepper	

■ Preheat oven to 350 °F (180 °C).

■ Dredge meat in flour. Set aside.

■ Heat oil in ovenproof sauté pan over high heat. Add onion and garlic; cook 6 minutes over low heat, stirring once. Remove onion with metal spatula and set aside.

■ Add meat to hot pan. Sear 6 to 8 minutes over medium heat; season well. Return onion to pan and mix well.

■ Pour in beef stock and add tomatoes. Mix well and season with salt and pepper. Bring to boil. Cover pan and cook 1 hour in oven.

■ Add potatoes and olives to stew. Cover and continue cooking 1 hour in oven.

■ Add peppers, cover and finish cooking 15 to 20 minutes. Serve.

1 SERVING:	680 CALORIES	34 g CARBOHYDRATE	65 g PROTEIN
	32 g FAT	3.9 g FIBER	

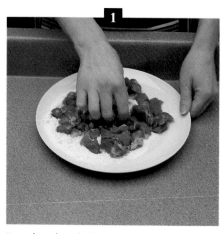

Dredge lamb in seasoned flour.

Cook onion and garlic in hot oil.

Remove onion with metal spatula.

Sear meat well.

Return cooked onion to pan.

Add beef stock.

VEAL PAUPIETTES

(SERVES 4)

3 tbsp	butter	45 mL
2	dry shallots, peeled and finely chopped	2
¼ lb	fresh mushrooms, cleaned and chopped	125 g
2	pork sausages	2
4	large veal scaloppine	4
4	large tomatoes, halved widthwise	4
½ tsp	basil	2 mL
1½ cups	dry white wine	375 mL
	salt and pepper	

■ Heat 2 tbsp (30 mL) butter in ovenproof sauté pan over medium heat. Add shallots and cook 2 minutes. Add mushrooms, season and cook 3 minutes.

■ Remove sausage meat from casing. Crumble sausage meat into sauté pan. Mix well and cook 3 minutes. Remove pan from heat.

■ Let stuffing cool, then spread over veal scaloppine. Season well, roll and tie.

■ Preheat oven to 375 °F (190 °C).

■ Place tomatoes in baking dish. Season with salt, pepper and basil. Place in oven and cook 8 minutes. Remove tomatoes from oven, drain and reserve juice; set aside. Cover tomatoes with aluminum foil to keep warm.

■ Reduce oven heat to 350 °F (180 °C).

■ Heat remaining butter in sauté pan. Add paupiettes and sear on all sides for 8 to 10 minutes.

■ Add wine and bring to boil. Add reserved juice from tomatoes, cover and cook 15 minutes in oven.

■ Serve paupiettes sliced over tomatoes with sauce.

1 SERVING:	507 CALORIES	12 g CARBOHYDRATE	36 g PROTEIN
	28 g FAT	2.7 g FIBER	

CORN AND LIMA BEANS

(SERVES 4)

1 tbsp	butter	15 mL
1	dry shallot, peeled and chopped	1
1	onion, chopped	1
2	garlic cloves, smashed and chopped	2
¼ tsp	black pepper	1 mL
1 tsp	herbes de Provence *	5 mL
1 tsp	basil	5 mL
1 cup	cooked lima beans	250 mL
1½ cups	cooked corn kernels	375 mL
¼ cup	sour cream	50 mL
	salt	

■ Heat butter in saucepan over medium heat. Add shallot, onion and garlic. Cook 4 minutes over low heat.

■ Add seasonings and mix well. Cook 2 minutes.

■ Add lima beans and corn; mix well. Cook 4 minutes over low heat. Incorporate sour cream and simmer 2 minutes. Serve.

* A mixture of thyme, rosemary, bay leaf, basil and savory.

1 SERVING:	197 CALORIES	31 g CARBOHYDRATE	6 g PROTEIN
	6 g FAT	5.3 g FIBER	

CHICKEN STEW WITH VIRGINIA HAM

(SERVES 4)

3⅓ lbs	chicken, cut in 8 pieces	1.6 kg
2 tbsp	olive oil	30 mL
3	garlic cloves, blanched, peeled and puréed	3
3	dry shallots, peeled and chopped	3
1	thick slice Virginia ham, diced large	1
½ cup	dry white wine	125 mL
2 cups	chicken stock, heated	500 mL
½ tsp	black pepper	2 mL
¼ tsp	thyme	1 mL
1 tbsp	chopped fresh basil	15 mL
½ lb	mushroom caps, cleaned	250 g
2	yellow peppers, cubed	2
2 tbsp	cornstarch	30 mL
3 tbsp	cold water	45 mL
	salt and pepper	

- Preheat oven to 325 °F (160 °C).

- Remove skin from chicken.

- Heat half of oil in ovenproof sauté pan over medium heat. Add chicken pieces and sear on all sides. Add garlic, shallots and ham. Mix and cook 6 minutes over medium heat.

- Pour in wine and cook 3 minutes. Incorporate chicken stock and seasonings. Cover and cook 30 minutes in oven.

- Heat remaining oil in frying pan over medium heat. Add mushrooms and peppers. Cook 5 minutes and season.

- Remove chicken from oven; add mushrooms and peppers to pan.

- Dissolve cornstarch in cold water. Incorporate into stew and simmer 4 minutes over low heat. Serve.

1 SERVING:	707 CALORIES	13 g CARBOHYDRATE	91 g PROTEIN
	30 g FAT	2.2 g FIBER	

Sear chicken pieces in hot oil.

Add garlic, shallots and ham. Cook 6 minutes over medium heat.

Pour in wine and cook 3 minutes.

Incorporate chicken stock and seasonings.

Sauté mushrooms and peppers in hot oil.

Dissolve cornstarch in cold water; add to stew.

PROSCIUTTO CRÊPES WITH MUSHROOM STUFFING
(SERVES 4 TO 6)

2 tbsp	butter	30 mL
2	dry shallots, peeled and chopped	2
1 tbsp	chopped fresh parsley	15 mL
½ lb	fresh mushrooms, cleaned and sliced	250 g
3 tbsp	sherry	45 mL
2 cups	light white sauce, heated	500 mL
8	thin slices prosciutto	8
8	crêpes (see page 216)	8
1¼ cups	grated Gruyère cheese salt and pepper	300 mL

- Preheat oven to 375 °F (190 °C).

- Heat butter in frying pan over medium heat. Add shallots and parsley. Cook 3 minutes. Add mushrooms, season and cook 8 minutes.

- Add sherry and ½ cup (125 mL) white sauce; mix well.

- Place slice of prosciutto on each crêpe. Add mushroom stuffing, season generously with pepper and fold crêpes in four. Arrange stuffed crêpes in buttered baking dish.

- Pour remaining white sauce over crêpes and top with cheese. Cook 12 minutes in oven.

1 SERVING:	575 CALORIES	36 g CARBOHYDRATE	23 g PROTEIN
	37 g FAT	2.4 g FIBER	

STOVE-TOP CHICKEN CASSEROLE

(SERVES 4)

3½ lbs	chicken, cut in 8 pieces	1.6 kg
3	carrots, pared and cut in half	3
2	celery stalks, in 1-in (2.5-cm) pieces	2
4	medium potatoes, peeled	4
1 tbsp	chopped fresh parsley	15 mL
1 tsp	basil	5 mL
24	fresh mushrooms, cleaned and diced (optional)	24
3 tbsp	butter	45 mL
4 tbsp	flour	60 mL
½ tsp	paprika	2 mL
	salt and pepper	

■ Remove skin from chicken pieces. Place chicken in saucepan. Cover with cold water and bring to boil. Skim off foam.

■ Add carrots, celery and potatoes. Season; add parsley and basil. Bring to boil and cook 30 minutes over medium heat.

■ Add mushrooms and continue cooking 7 minutes. Remove saucepan from heat. Remove chicken and vegetables from cooking liquid; set aside. Reserve cooking liquid.

■ Heat butter in sauté pan over medium heat. Add flour, mix and cook 3 minutes over low heat.

■ Add 3 cups (750 mL) of reserved cooking liquid to pan. Stir well and cook sauce 12 minutes over medium heat. Season well.

■ Place chicken and vegetables in sauce. Sprinkle with paprika and season to taste. Simmer 5 minutes before serving.

1 SERVING:	856 CALORIES	48 g CARBOHYDRATE	94 g PROTEIN
	32 g FAT	6.0 g FIBER	

MUSHROOM AND RICE CASSEROLE

(SERVES 4)

1	large eggplant, halved lengthwise	1
2¼ cups	water	550 mL
½ tsp	salt	2 mL
1 cup	rice, rinsed	250 mL
3 tbsp	butter	45 mL
1 lb	fresh mushrooms, cleaned and sliced	500 g
2	dry shallots, peeled and chopped	2
1	garlic clove, smashed and chopped	1
¼ tsp	black pepper	1 mL
½ tsp	basil	2 mL
1 cup	grated Gruyère cheese	250 mL
	olive oil	
	salt and pepper	

■ Preheat oven to 400 °F (200 °C).

■ Score eggplant flesh in crisscross pattern. Brush with oil and place, skin-side up, in roasting pan. Cook 40 minutes in oven. Remove flesh from skin; chop flesh and set aside.

■ Pour water into saucepan over medium heat. Add salt, cover and bring to boil. Add rice, cover and cook 12 minutes or just until liquid is completely absorbed. Mix in 1 tbsp (15 mL) butter, cover and continue cooking 15 minutes over very low heat.

■ Heat 2 tbsp (30 mL) butter in sauté pan over medium heat. Add mushrooms, shallots, garlic and seasonings. Cook 6 minutes.

■ Add chopped eggplant, mix well and season to taste. Cook 3 minutes. Add rice and incorporate well.

■ Preheat oven to broil.

■ Transfer mixture to baking dish. Sprinkle with cheese and broil 5 minutes. Serve.

1 SERVING: 325 CALORIES   34 g CARBOHYDRATE   12 g PROTEIN
16 g FAT   4.7 g FIBER

SWEET POTATO CASSEROLE
(SERVES 6)

4	large sweet potatoes, with skins	4
4	slices bacon	4
3 tbsp	butter	45 mL
½ tsp	cinnamon	2 mL
¼ tsp	nutmeg	1 mL
½ cup	light cream	125 mL
¼ cup	milk	50 mL
	salt and white pepper	

■ Cook sweet potatoes in salted, boiling water. When done, remove from water, peel and purée.

■ Preheat oven to 375 °F (190 °C).

■ Cook bacon until crisp, then chop coarsely. Set aside.

■ Incorporate all remaining ingredients, except bacon, into puréed potatoes. Mix well and correct seasoning.

■ Place mixture in baking dish and cook 18 minutes in oven. Sprinkle bacon over potatoes and continue cooking 5 minutes. Serve.

1 SERVING:	187 CALORIES	20 g CARBOHYDRATE	5 g PROTEIN
	10 g FAT	1.7 g FIBER	

CHICKEN AND PLUM TOMATOES

(SERVES 4)

3½ lbs	chicken, cut in 8 pieces	1.6 kg	
2 tbsp	olive oil	30 mL	
1	onion, sliced	1	
2	garlic cloves, smashed and chopped	2	
2	yellow peppers, cubed	2	
6	plum tomatoes, quartered	6	
¼ tsp	saffron	1 mL	
1 cup	dry white wine	250 mL	
1 tbsp	butter	15 mL	
	pinch of crushed chilies		
	salt and pepper		

■ Remove skin from chicken.

■ Heat half of oil in frying pan. Add onion and garlic; cook 4 minutes. Add peppers, tomatoes, crushed chilies and saffron. Season, mix and cook 5 minutes.

■ Pour in wine and cook 6 minutes over low heat.

■ Meanwhile, heat remaining oil with butter in sauté pan over medium heat. Add chicken pieces, season and cook 8 minutes. Turn pieces over and continue cooking 6 minutes.

■ Remove chicken breasts from pan and keep hot in oven. Continue cooking remaining pieces another 8 minutes.

■ Serve chicken with plum tomato mixture.

1 SERVING:	729 CALORIES	13 g CARBOHYDRATE	89 g PROTEIN
	33 g FAT	3.3 g FIBER	

Cook onion and garlic in hot oil.

Add peppers.

Add plum tomatoes, crushed chilies and saffron.

Pour in wine.

Sear chicken pieces for 8 minutes.

Turn chicken pieces over and continue cooking.

PASTA AND MUSHROOM CHEESE CASSEROLE
(SERVES 4)

2 tbsp	butter	30 mL
2	dry shallots, peeled and chopped	2
¾ lb	fresh mushrooms, cleaned and sliced	375 g
3 tbsp	sherry	45 mL
4 tbsp	flour	60 mL
3 cups	milk, heated	750 mL
½ tsp	white pepper	2 mL
3 cups	cooked "al dente" pasta, hot	750 mL
1 cup	grated mozzarella cheese	250 mL
	pinch nutmeg	
	salt and pepper	

■ Preheat oven to 375 °F (190 °C).

■ Heat butter in sauté pan over medium heat. Add shallots and mushrooms. Season and cook 5 minutes. Incorporate sherry and continue cooking 3 minutes.

■ Add flour, mix well and cook 2 minutes over low heat. Whisk in hot milk, season with salt, nutmeg and white pepper. Cook 12 minutes over low heat, stirring frequently.

■ Add pasta to sauce and mix well. Transfer mixture to buttered baking dish. Top with cheese and cook 10 minutes in oven.

1 SERVING:	441 CALORIES	57 g CARBOHYDRATE	20 g PROTEIN
	14 g FAT	3.1 g FIBER	

CREAMY CURRIED SALMON

(SERVES 4)

2	salmon steaks, cooked	2
3 tbsp	butter	45 mL
1	onion, finely chopped	1
1	celery stalk, sliced	1
½ lb	fresh mushrooms, cleaned and cut in 3	250 g
2 tbsp	curry powder	30 mL
3 tbsp	flour	45 mL
2½ cups	light chicken stock, heated	625 mL
3 tbsp	heavy cream	45 mL
2 tbsp	sherry	30 mL
	few drops lemon juice	
	salt and pepper	

■ Remove bones from salmon steaks. Flake salmon and set aside.

■ Heat butter in frying pan over medium heat. Add onion and celery; cook 3 minutes.

■ Add mushrooms, season and stir in curry powder. Cook 4 minutes over low heat. Add flour, mix and cook 2 minutes.

■ Pour in chicken stock and season. Cook 8 to 10 minutes over low heat. Incorporate cream and sherry. Add salmon and few drops of lemon juice. Mix and simmer 6 minutes over low heat.

■ Serve with noodles or rice.

1 SERVING:	283 CALORIES	7 g CARBOHYDRATE	22 g PROTEIN
	18 g FAT	2.0 g FIBER	

BRAISED SHORT RIBS
(SERVES 4)

5 lbs	short ribs, in 2-in (5-cm) pieces	2.3 kg
1 tbsp	olive oil	15 mL
2	onions, quartered	2
2	garlic cloves, smashed and chopped	2
3	whole dry shallots, peeled	3
1 cup	dry red wine	250 mL
1 tsp	basil	5 mL
½ tsp	thyme	2 mL
28-oz	can tomatoes, chopped, with juice	796-mL
2 cups	beef stock, heated	500 mL
1 tbsp	tomato paste	15 mL
	salt and pepper	

- Preheat oven to 350 °F (180 °C).

- Partly trim meat of fat. Heat oil in ovenproof sauté pan over high heat. Add meat and sear on all sides for 8 to 10 minutes. Season with salt and pepper.

- Add onions, garlic and shallots. Cook 5 to 6 minutes over medium heat. Pour in red wine and cook 3 minutes.

- Add remaining ingredients. Season and mix well. Bring to boil, cover and cook 3 hours in oven. If necessary, add more beef stock during cooking.

- Serve with boiled potatoes and carrots.

1 SERVING:	1049 CALORIES	20 g CARBOHYDRATE	126 g PROTEIN
	47 g FAT	2.7 g FIBER	

Sear short ribs in hot oil. Season with salt and pepper.

Add onions and garlic.

Add shallots. Cook 5 to 6 minutes over medium heat.

Pour in red wine and cook 3 minutes.

Add chopped tomatoes with juice.

Add beef stock and tomato paste.

EGGPLANT AND TOMATO CASSEROLE

(SERVES 4)

1	large eggplant, halved lengthwise	1	
2 tbsp	olive oil	30 mL	
1	onion, chopped	1	
1	garlic clove, smashed and chopped	1	
2	large tomatoes, peeled and diced	2	
1	small zucchini, halved lengthwise and sliced	1	
½ tsp	basil	2 mL	
½ cup	grated Gruyère cheese	125 mL	
	pinch sugar		
	salt and pepper		

■ Preheat oven to 400 °F (200 °C).

■ Score flesh of eggplant in crisscross pattern. Brush with oil and place, skin-side up, in roasting pan. Cook 40 minutes in oven.

■ Remove flesh from skin, chop flesh and set aside.

■ Heat remaining oil in frying pan over high heat. Add onion and garlic; mix and cook 6 minutes. Add tomatoes, zucchini and basil. Season and cook 20 minutes over medium heat, stirring occasionally.

■ Add chopped eggplant and mix well. Add half of cheese and pinch of sugar. Mix and season to taste.

■ Reduce oven heat to 375 °F (190 °C).

■ Transfer mixture to baking dish. Top with remaining cheese and cook 20 minutes in oven. Serve.

1 SERVING:	138 CALORIES	7 g CARBOHYDRATE	4 g PROTEIN
	10 g FAT	2.5 g FIBER	

BRAISED CHICKEN AND TOMATO

(SERVES 4)

3½-4 lb	chicken, washed	1.6-1.8 kg
½ cup	flour	125 mL
3 tbsp	butter	45 mL
2	dry shallots, peeled and chopped	2
2	garlic cloves, smashed and chopped	2
½ lb	fresh mushrooms, cleaned and halved	250 g
3	plum tomatoes, quartered	3
1 cup	dry white wine	250 mL
½ cup	chicken stock, heated	125 mL
1½ tsp	basil	7 mL
	salt and pepper	

■ Preheat oven to 350 °F (180 °C).

■ Cut chicken into 8 pieces and remove skin. Dredge pieces in flour.

■ Heat butter in ovenproof sauté pan over medium heat. Add chicken pieces and sear on all sides for 8 to 10 minutes.

■ Add shallots, garlic, mushrooms and tomatoes. Season and cook 6 minutes over medium heat.

■ Incorporate wine, chicken stock and basil. Bring to boil, cover and cook 25 minutes in oven.

1 SERVING:	706 CALORIES	25 g CARBOHYDRATE	96 g PROTEIN
	20 g FAT	3.6 g FIBER	

Braised Veal Shoulder

BRAISED VEAL SHOULDER
(SERVES 4 TO 6)

Veal Stock

3 lbs	veal bones, cut in pieces by butcher	1.4 kg
2	unpeeled onions, quartered	2
2	carrots, pared and sliced thick	2
½ cup	dry white wine	125 mL
2	bay leaves	2
1 tsp	thyme	5 mL
2	whole cloves	2
6	peppercorns	6
2	garlic cloves, smashed and chopped	2
	salt and pepper	

Veal Shoulder

2 tbsp	butter	30 mL
3½-4 lb	boneless veal shoulder, rolled and tied	1.6-1.8 kg
1	large onion, cubed	1
4	whole carrots, pared	4
2	garlic cloves, smashed and chopped	2
½ cup	dry white wine	125 mL
½	green cabbage, halved	½
1	bouquet garni*	1
1 tbsp	cornstarch	15 mL
3 tbsp	cold water	45 mL
	salt and pepper	

- Preheat oven to 425 °F (220 °C).

- Place bones and vegetables in roasting pan. Cook in oven 30 minutes.

- Place roasting pan with contents on stove over medium heat. Pour in 1½ cups (375 mL) water and cook 6 minutes. Transfer contents to large saucepan.

- Add wine, herbs, spices and garlic. Cover bones completely with cold water. Add salt and bring to boil. As soon as liquid starts to boil, skim liquid. Continue cooking 1½ hours over low heat.

- Remove saucepan from heat. Strain stock into clean bowl and let cool. Stock will keep up to 3 or 4 days in refrigerator.

- Preheat oven to 300 °F (150 °C).

- Choose an ovenproof casserole a bit larger than the veal shoulder. Heat butter in casserole over medium heat. Add meat and sear on all sides. Season with salt and pepper.

- Remove veal from casserole and set aside.

- Place vegetables, except cabbage, in hot casserole. Add garlic and cook 7 minutes over medium heat.

- Return veal to casserole. Add wine and cabbage; continue cooking 4 minutes. Completely cover meat with veal stock. Add bouquet garni and bring to boil. Cover and cook 1½ hours in oven.

- Remove braised veal and vegetables from casserole. Strain cooking liquid and pour half into saucepan.

- Dissolve cornstarch in cold water. Incorporate into cooking liquid in saucepan and cook 2 minutes over medium heat.

- Serve sauce with braised veal and vegetables.

*Tie together sprigs of parsley, thyme, basil and a bay leaf.

1 SERVING:	700 CALORIES	14 g CARBOHYDRATE	69 g PROTEIN
	36 g FAT	3.2 g FIBER	

BEEF MIROTON
(SERVES 4)

¾ lb	leftover boiled beef	375 g
2 tbsp	butter	30 mL
2	onions, chopped	2
2 tbsp	flour	30 mL
1 cup	dry white wine	250 mL
1 cup	light beef stock, heated	250 mL
1 tbsp	chopped fresh parsley	15 mL
4 cups	mashed potatoes	1 L
	melted butter	
	salt and pepper	

■ Preheat oven to 375 °F (190 °C).

■ Chop meat and set aside.

■ Heat butter in frying pan over medium heat. Add onions and cook 4 minutes.

■ Add meat and season well. Cook 4 minutes over medium heat. Add flour and mix well; cook 1 minute.

■ Add wine, beef stock and parsley. Mix and cook 15 minutes over low heat.

■ Transfer mixture to baking dish. Cover with mashed potatoes and sprinkle lightly with melted butter. Cook 20 minutes in oven.

1 SERVING:	520 CALORIES	40 g CARBOHYDRATE	35 g PROTEIN
	20 g FAT	2.9 g FIBER	

BEEF AND TOMATO TOPPED WITH MASHED POTATOES

(SERVES 4)

1 tbsp	oil	15 mL
1	onion, finely chopped	1
1	celery stalk, chopped	1
1	green pepper, chopped	1
3	garlic cloves, smashed and chopped	3
1 tsp	basil	5 mL
½ tsp	thyme	2 mL
1 lb	lean ground beef	500 g
1 tsp	dry mustard	5 mL
28-oz	can tomatoes, drained and chopped	796-mL
¾ cup	tomato juice	175 mL
3 cups	mashed potatoes	750 mL
	melted butter	
	salt and pepper	

■ Preheat oven to 375 °F (190 °C).

■ Heat oil in frying pan over medium heat. Add onion, celery, pepper and garlic. Cook 3 minutes.

■ Add herbs, beef and mustard. Season with salt and pepper; cook 8 minutes over medium heat.

■ Incorporate tomatoes and tomato juice. Continue cooking 3 minutes.

■ Transfer mixture to baking dish. Cover with mashed potatoes and sprinkle lightly with melted butter. Cook 20 minutes in oven.

1 SERVING:	456 CALORIES	36 g CARBOHYDRATE	32 g PROTEIN
	21 g FAT	3.8 g FIBER	

COQ AU VIN
(SERVES 4)

3½-4 lb	chicken, washed	1.6-1.8 kg
3 tbsp	flour	45 mL
¼ lb	salt pork, diced	125 g
24	pearl onions, peeled	24
½ lb	mushroom caps, cleaned	250 g
3	dry shallots, peeled and chopped	3
2	garlic cloves, smashed and chopped	2
3 tbsp	butter	45 mL
4 cups	dry red wine	1 L
1	bouquet garni *	1
	salt and pepper	

- Preheat oven to 350 °F (180 °C).

- Cut chicken into 8 pieces and remove skin. Dredge chicken pieces in flour and set aside.

- Heat salt pork in ovenproof sauté pan over medium heat. Add onions and season; cook 5 minutes. Remove onions from pan and set aside.

- Add mushrooms, shallots and garlic to hot pan. Season and cook 5 minutes over medium heat. Remove vegetables from pan and set aside.

- Add butter to pan and melt. Add chicken pieces and sear on all sides for 8 to 10 minutes.

- Add wine and bouquet garni. Season to taste and bring to boil. Cover and cook 30 minutes in oven.

- Add pearl onions and mushrooms. Return to oven, uncovered, and finish cooking 15 to 18 minutes.

*Tie together sprigs of parsley, thyme, basil and a bay leaf.

1 SERVING:	957 CALORIES	30 g CARBOHYDRATE	99 g PROTEIN
	29 g FAT	4.0 g FIBER	

Cut chicken into pieces and remove skin.

Dredge chicken in flour.

Sauté pearl onions with salt pork. Remove and set aside.

Place mushrooms, shallots and garlic in hot pan. Cook, then remove from pan and set aside.

Sear chicken in hot butter.

Turn chicken pieces over and sear other side.

Mont-Blanc Casserole

MONT-BLANC CASSEROLE
(SERVES 6)

10 oz	dry kidney beans	300 g
8 cups	water	2 L
1	meaty ham bone	1
2	bay leaves	2
½ tsp	thyme	2 mL
2	garlic cloves, halved	2
1 tsp	basil	5 mL
2 tbsp	olive oil	30 mL
1	onion, chopped	1
1	celery stalk, diced	1
1	green pepper, diced	1
2	spicy sausages, cut in ½-in (1.2-cm) pieces	2
3 tbsp	wine vinegar	45 mL
2 cups	cooked white or brown rice, hot	500 mL
	few drops hot pepper sauce	
	salt and pepper	

■ Soak beans in cold water for 8 hours. Drain.

■ Place beans in large saucepan. Add enough water to cover beans by 1 in (2.5 cm). Bring to boil, then skim off foam.

■ Add meaty ham bone, bay leaves, thyme, garlic and basil. Season with salt and pepper. Cover and cook 1 hour over medium heat.

■ Heat half of oil in frying pan over medium heat. Add onion, celery and green pepper. Season and cook 4 minutes. Add mixture to beans in saucepan. Mix and cook 15 minutes uncovered.

■ Heat remaining oil in frying pan over medium heat. Add sausages and cook 7 minutes, turning over once.

■ Add sausages to beans in saucepan. Add hot pepper sauce and mix well. Continue cooking 15 minutes or until beans are completely cooked.

■ Five minutes before end of cooking, stir in vinegar.

■ Serve over hot rice.

1 SERVING:	284 CALORIES	28 g CARBOHYDRATE	12 g PROTEIN
	14 g FAT	5.3 g FIBER	

Vegetable Lasagne

VEGETABLE LASAGNE

(SERVES 4 TO 6)

2 tbsp	olive oil	30 mL
2	onions, finely chopped	2
3	dry shallots, peeled and finely chopped	3
3	garlic cloves, smashed and chopped	3
½ cup	dry white wine	125 mL
2	celery stalks, sliced	2
2	zucchini, diced with skin	2
3	carrots, pared and sliced	3
2 tbsp	chopped fresh tarragon	30 mL
2 tbsp	basil	30 mL
2 tbsp	chopped fresh parsley	30 mL
1 tsp	ground cloves	5 mL
½ tsp	marjoram	2 mL
½ tsp	chili powder	2 mL
2	green peppers, sliced	2
1	red pepper, sliced	1
1 lb	fresh mushrooms, cleaned and sliced	500 g
3	tomatoes, peeled and diced	3
½ cup	grated Romano cheese	125 mL
1 cup	grated Parmesan cheese	250 mL
5 cups	white sauce	1.2 L
1 cup	grated Gruyère cheese	250 mL
	lasagne noodles, in sheets or strips, cooked	
	salt and pepper	

■ Preheat oven to 350 °F (180 °C).

■ Heat oil in large sauté pan over medium heat. Add onions, shallots and garlic; cook 6 minutes.

■ Add wine, stir and cook 3 minutes over high heat.

■ Add celery, zucchini and carrots; season with salt and pepper. Add all seasonings, mix and cover. Cook 10 minutes over medium heat.

■ Add remaining vegetables, season and mix. Cook 15 minutes, uncovered, over medium heat to evaporate most of the liquid.

■ Butter lasagne baking dish. Cover bottom with layer of noodles. Add layer of vegetables and sprinkle with Romano and Parmesan cheeses. Top with layer of white sauce.

■ Repeat layering procedure to fill dish. End with layer of noodles and cover with white sauce. Top with Gruyère cheese.

■ Bake 40 minutes in oven.

1 SERVING:	887 CALORIES	87 g CARBOHYDRATE	37 g PROTEIN
	42 g FAT	6.8 g FIBER	

APPLE CASSEROLE
(SERVES 4 TO 6)

4	whole eggs	4
½ cup	flour	125 mL
1 tsp	baking powder	5 mL
¼ tsp	salt	1 mL
½ cup	milk	125 mL
2 tbsp	rum	30 mL
2 tbsp	melted butter	30 mL
3	apples, peeled, cored and sliced	3
2 tbsp	granulated sugar	30 mL
1 tbsp	cinnamon	15 mL
2	egg whites, beaten firm	2
1 tbsp	brown sugar	15 mL

■ Place whole eggs in bowl and mix with whisk.

■ Sift flour, baking powder and salt together. Add to beaten whole eggs and mix well. Incorporate milk and rum. Refrigerate 1 hour.

■ Preheat oven to 375 °F (190 °C).

■ Heat butter in frying pan over medium heat. Add apples, granulated sugar and cinnamon; cook 12 minutes.

■ Remove batter from refrigerator and incorporate beaten egg whites using spatula. Pour mixture into round buttered baking dish. Arrange apple slices in center of dish. Sprinkle with brown sugar and bake 45 minutes in oven.

1 SERVING:	255 CALORIES	30 g CARBOHYDRATE	9 g PROTEIN
	10 g FAT	2.2 g FIBER	

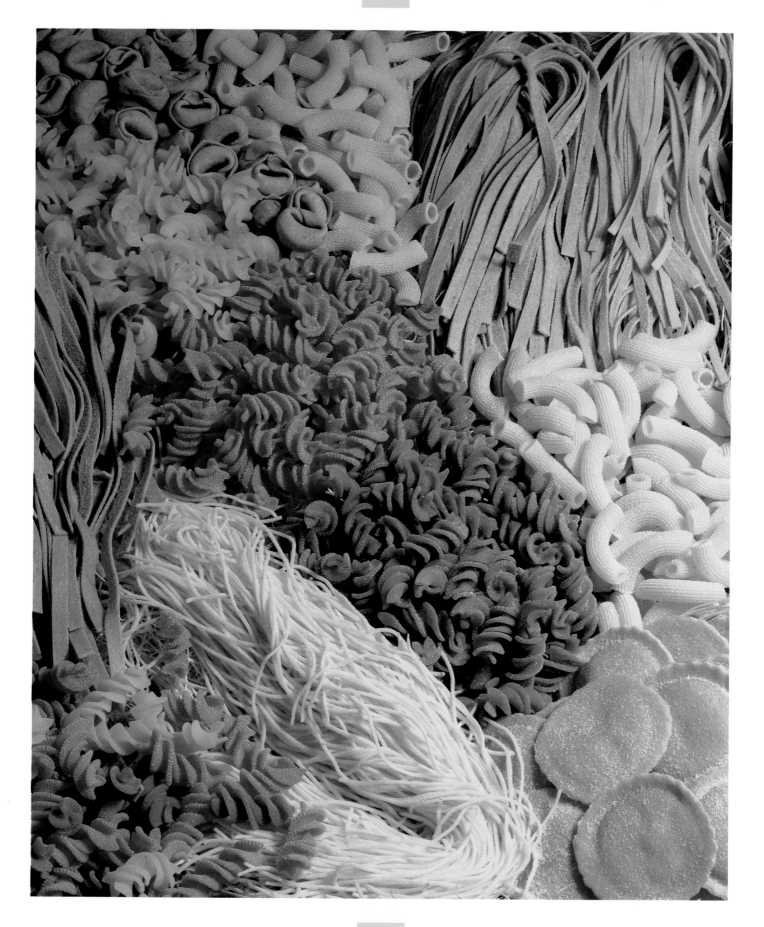

MIXED GRAIN RICE WITH GREEN ONION

(SERVES 4)

2½ cups	vegetable stock, heated	625 mL
1 cup	mixture of long grain and wild rice	250 mL
1 tbsp	butter	15 mL
4	green onions, diced	4
	salt and pepper	

■ Pour vegetable stock in saucepan. Bring to boil over medium heat. Add rice and season with salt and pepper. Cover and cook 45 minutes over low heat.

■ Remove from heat and let stand 6 minutes.

■ Melt butter in frying pan over medium heat. Add green onions and cook 4 minutes.

■ Stir onions into rice. Serve.

1 SERVING:	131 CALORIES	23 g CARBONHYDRATE	3 g PROTEIN
	3 g FAT	1.1 g FIBER	

CHEESE TORTELLINI SALAD WITH CREAMY DRESSING
(SERVES 4)

Creamy Dressing

½ tsp	salt	2 mL
½ tsp	pepper	2 mL
2 tbsp	wine vinegar	30 mL
6 tbsp	olive oil	90 mL
3 tbsp	sour cream	45 mL

Salad

1 lb	cheese tortellini, cooked	500 g
½ cup	black olives, pitted and sliced	125 mL
3	green onions, chopped	3
1	yellow pepper, sliced	1
1	red pepper, sliced	1
¼ cup	walnuts or pecans, halved	50 mL
⅓ cup	Creamy Dressing	75 mL
	salt, pepper and paprika	

■ To prepare dressing, place salt and pepper in bowl. Add vinegar and mix well. Beat in oil. Add sour cream, mix and set dressing aside.

■ Place all salad ingredients, except dressing, in bowl. Season to taste and mix.

■ Pour in dressing and mix again. Serve.

1 SERVING:	285 CALORIES	20 g CARBOHYDRATE	6 g PROTEIN
	20 g FAT	1.7 g FIBER	

Tortellini Primavera

TORTELLINI PRIMAVERA
(SERVES 4)

1 tbsp	olive oil	15 mL
1	carrot, pared and sliced	1
4	green onions, in 1-in (2.5-cm) pieces	4
1	celery stalk, sliced	1
½ lb	fresh mushrooms, cleaned and sliced	250 g
1	yellow pepper, sliced	1
2	garlic cloves, smashed and chopped	2
1 tbsp	chopped fresh basil	15 mL
1½ cups	chicken stock, heated	375 mL
1 tbsp	cornstarch	15 mL
3 tbsp	cold water	45 mL
4	portions cooked veal tortellini, hot	4
¾ cup	cooked green peas	175 mL
2 tbsp	grated Parmesan cheese	30 mL
2 tbsp	grated Romano cheese salt and pepper	30 mL

■ Heat oil in sauté pan over medium heat. Add carrot, onions and celery. Cover and cook 4 minutes.

■ Add remaining vegetables, except green peas. Season with salt and pepper. Add garlic and basil. Stir, cover and cook 3 minutes over medium heat.

■ Incorporate chicken stock and bring to boil.

■ Dissolve cornstarch in cold water and incorporate into sauce. Cook 1 minute.

■ Add pasta and mix. Add peas and cheeses. Mix again and simmer 1 minute before serving.

---

1 SERVING: 330 CALORIES   33 g CARBOHYDRATE   14 g PROTEIN
16 g FAT   4.1 g FIBER

EGG FRIED RICE WITH HAM
(SERVES 4)

1 tsp	butter	5 mL
2	eggs, beaten	2
1 tbsp	olive oil	15 mL
1	stalk Chinese cabbage (bok choy), sliced	1
1	garlic clove, smashed and chopped	1
1	yellow pepper, sliced	1
1	slice Virginia ham or prosciutto, cut in julienne	1
3 cups	cooked rice	750 mL
1 tbsp	chopped fresh parsley salt and pepper	15 mL

■ Heat butter in frying pan over medium heat. Add beaten eggs and cook 15 seconds. Stir rapidly. Continue cooking 30 seconds.

■ Flip omelet over and continue cooking 30 seconds. Remove pan from heat and let omelet cool.

■ Slice cold omelet into julienne. Set aside.

■ Heat oil in large frying pan. Add cabbage, garlic and yellow pepper. Cook 4 minutes over medium heat.

■ Add ham, stir and continue cooking 4 minutes.

■ Add rice and parsley. Season with salt and pepper; cook 8 minutes or just until rice starts to brown.

■ Add sliced omelet, mix well and cook 3 minutes. Serve.

1 SERVING: 239 CALORIES   34 g CARBOHYDRATE   8 g PROTEIN
            8 g FAT   1.7 g FIBER

Add beaten eggs to hot butter in pan and cook 15 seconds.

Stir rapidly and continue cooking 30 seconds.

Flip omelet over and cook underside 30 seconds.

Slice cold omelet into julienne.

Cook cabbage, garlic and yellow pepper in hot oil.

Add ham, mix and continue cooking 4 minutes. Add rice.

FRESH TOMATO SAUCE
(SERVES 6 TO 8)

2 tbsp	olive oil	30 mL
1	large onion, chopped	1
1	carrot, pared and diced	1
1	celery stalk, diced	1
3	garlic cloves, smashed and chopped	3
12	large ripe tomatoes, peeled and chopped	12
2 tbsp	tomato paste	30 mL
1 tbsp	chopped fresh basil	15 mL
½ tsp	thyme	2 mL
1 tbsp	chopped fresh parsley	15 mL
1 tbsp	oregano	15 mL
1	bay leaf	1
	salt and pepper	

■ Heat oil in sauté pan over medium heat. Add onion, carrot and celery. Cook 8 minutes over low heat.

■ Mix in garlic and continue cooking 3 minutes.

■ Add remaining ingredients and bring to boil. Cook 70 minutes, partly covered, over low heat. Stir 3 to 4 times during cooking.

■ Serve over hot pasta.

1 SERVING:	101 CALORIES	12 g CARBOHYDRATE	2 g PROTEIN
	5 g FAT	3.4 g FIBER	

AGNOLOTTI WITH ANCHOVY PESTO

(SERVES 4)

5	garlic cloves, peeled	5
¾ cup	pine nuts	175 mL
6 to 8	anchovy filets, drained	6 to 8
1 cup	fresh basil	250 mL
¼ cup	olive oil	50 mL
½ cup	grated Parmesan cheese	125 mL
4	portions cooked agnolotti pasta, hot	4
	freshly ground pepper	

■ Place garlic, pine nuts, anchovies and basil in food processor. Blend for 30 seconds.

■ Add oil and cheese; blend to incorporate.

■ Pour sauce over hot pasta and season with pepper. Mix and serve.

1 SERVING: 382 CALORIES   38 g CARBOHYDRATE   13 g PROTEIN
20 g FAT   1.4 g FIBER

SPAGHETTI WITH WHITE WINE MEAT SAUCE

(SERVES 4)

2 tbsp	olive oil	30 mL
1	garlic clove, smashed and chopped	1
1	medium onion, chopped	1
1	celery stalk, diced	1
1 lb	lean ground beef	500 g
1 cup	dry white wine	250 mL
2½ cups	tomato sauce	625 mL
½ tsp	basil	2 mL
½ tsp	thyme	2 mL
1 tbsp	chopped fresh parsley	15 mL
4	portions cooked spaghetti, hot	4
	salt and pepper	

■ Heat oil in sauté pan over medium heat. Add garlic, onion and celery. Cook 3 minutes over medium heat.

■ Add meat. Season with salt and pepper. Mix and cook 4 minutes over medium heat. Stir twice during cooking.

■ Pour in wine, stir and cook 4 minutes.

■ Incorporate tomato sauce and seasonings. Mix and cook 6 minutes over low heat.

■ Serve over hot spaghetti.

1 SERVING: 527 CALORIES   48 g CARBOHYDRATE   33 g PROTEIN
18 g FAT   0 g FIBER

SEAFOOD LINGUINE WITH FRESH VEGETABLES
(SERVES 4)

32	fresh clams, scrubbed and washed	32
1 cup	water	250 mL
1 tbsp	olive oil	15 mL
3	dry shallots, peeled and chopped	3
2	garlic cloves, smashed and chopped	2
2	green onions, chopped	2
1	red pepper, diced	1
2	large tomatoes, peeled and chopped	2
1 tbsp	chopped fresh tarragon	15 mL
4	portions cooked linguine, hot	4
	juice of 1 lemon	
	salt and pepper	

■ Place clams in saucepan. Pour in water and add lemon juice. Cover and cook 5 minutes, stirring once during cooking. Remove saucepan from heat. All clam shells should be fully opened. Discard unopened clams. Let clams stand in cooking liquid to keep warm.

■ Heat oil in sauté pan over medium heat. Add shallots, garlic and green onions. Mix and cook 4 minutes over low heat.

■ Add red pepper and tomatoes. Season, add tarragon and cook 12 minutes over medium heat.

■ Place linguine on plates. Arrange clams still in their shells on pasta. Ladle sauce over and serve.

---

1 SERVING: 308 CALORIES   47 g CARBOHYDRATE   17 g PROTEIN
6 g FAT   1.5 g FIBER

DOUBLE MEAT TOMATO SAUCE

(SERVES 4 TO 6)

2 tbsp	olive oil	30 mL
1	onion, chopped	1
1	celery stalk, diced	1
2	garlic cloves, smashed and chopped	2
3	green onions, chopped	3
2 lbs	large tomatoes, peeled, seeded and cubed	900 g
2 tbsp	tomato paste	30 mL
1 tbsp	chopped fresh parsley	15 mL
1 tbsp	chopped fresh thyme	15 mL
2 tbsp	chopped fresh basil	30 mL
1 tsp	chopped fresh oregano	5 mL
½ lb	lean ground beef	250 g
½ lb	ground veal	250 g
1 cup	tomato sauce	250 mL
4 to 6	portions cooked pasta, hot	4 to 6
	few drops Tabasco sauce	
	few crushed red chilies	
	pinch sugar	
	salt and pepper	

■ Heat half of oil in sauté pan over medium heat. Add onion, celery, garlic and green onions. Cook 4 minutes over low heat.

■ Add tomatoes, tomato paste, all seasonings and sugar. Mix well and bring to boil. Cook 18 minutes over low heat, stirring occasionally.

■ Heat remaining oil in frying pan over high heat. Add both ground meats and season well. Cook 7 minutes over medium heat.

■ Drain fat from cooked meat, then stir meat into tomato mixture. Add tomato sauce and season; mix well. Continue cooking sauce 35 minutes over low heat. Stir occasionally.

■ Serve over hot pasta.

1 SERVING:	454 CALORIES	50 g CARBOHYDRATE	26 g PROTEIN
	17 g FAT	3.6 g FIBER	

Cook onion, celery, garlic and green onions in hot oil.

Add tomatoes.

Add tomato paste.

Add all seasonings and sugar.

Cook meat separately in frying pan.

Drain off fat from meat before adding to tomato mixture.

RIGATONI WITH SHRIMP

(SERVES 4)

1 tbsp	olive oil	15 mL
¾ lb	shrimp, shelled, deveined, washed and halved	375 g
3	dry shallots, peeled and chopped	3
½ lb	fresh mushrooms, cleaned and halved	250 g
1 tbsp	chopped fresh ginger	15 mL
3	tomatoes, peeled and chopped	3
1 tbsp	chopped fresh basil	15 mL
4	portions cooked rigatoni, hot few crushed chilies salt and pepper	4

■ Heat oil in frying pan over medium heat. Add shrimp and cook 2 minutes over high heat. Turn shrimp over and continue cooking 1 minute. Remove shrimp from pan and set aside.

■ Add shallots, mushrooms and ginger to pan. Season and cook 5 minutes over high heat.

■ Add tomatoes, basil and crushed chilies. Season and cook 8 minutes over medium heat.

■ Return shrimp to pan and simmer 3 minutes over low heat.

■ Add hot pasta, mix and simmer another 3 minutes. Serve.

---

1 SERVING: 357 CALORIES   48 g CARBOHYDRATE   31 g PROTEIN
5 g FAT   3.0 g FIBER

PASTA WITH EGGPLANT AND TOMATOES
(SERVES 4)

1	eggplant, halved lengthwise	1
1 tbsp	olive oil	15 mL
1½	onions, finely chopped	1½
2	garlic cloves, smashed and chopped	2
½ lb	fresh mushrooms, cleaned and diced	250 g
½ tsp	basil	2 mL
¼ tsp	thyme	1 mL
1 cup	dry white wine	250 mL
2	large tomatoes, peeled and diced	2
2	portions cooked penne, hot	2
2	portions cooked tortellini, hot	2
	grated Parmesan cheese	
	salt and pepper	

■ Sprinkle cut side of eggplant with salt. Let stand at room temperature for 1 hour. Rinse under cold water, dry and peel. Dice flesh and set aside.

■ Heat oil in sauté pan over medium heat. Add onions and garlic; cook 6 minutes over low heat.

■ Add mushrooms, eggplant and seasonings. Cook 8 minutes over medium heat.

■ Pour in wine and cook 3 minutes over high heat. Mix in tomatoes and season well. Cook 12 minutes over medium heat.

■ Place both kinds of hot pasta in bowl. Pour sauce over and mix well. Serve with grated cheese.

1 SERVING:	310 CALORIES	45 g CARBOHYDRATE	9 g PROTEIN
	6 g FAT	3.5 g FIBER	

Fettuccine with Fresh Mussels

FETTUCCINE WITH FRESH MUSSELS

(SERVES 4)

2 lbs	fresh mussels, scrubbed and washed	900 g
¼ cup	water	50 mL
1 tbsp	olive oil	15 mL
2	garlic cloves, smashed and chopped	2
¼ cup	dry white wine	50 mL
2 tbsp	beurre manié (see page 155)	30 mL
1 tbsp	chopped fresh parsley	15 mL
4	portions cooked fettuccine, hot	4
	juice of 1 lemon	
	cooking liquid from mussels	
	salt and pepper	

■ Place mussels in large saucepan. Add lemon juice, water and pepper. Cover and cook over medium heat until shells open.

■ Remove saucepan from heat. Discard unopened mussels. Remove mussels from shells, place in bowl and set aside. Pour any juices left in shells back into saucepan.

■ Strain cooking liquid from mussels through sieve lined with cheesecloth. Set aside.

■ Heat oil in frying pan over medium heat. Add garlic and cook 2 minutes.

■ Pour in wine and cook 2 minutes over high heat.

■ Stir in cooking liquid from mussels and season well. Cook 2 minutes, then remove pan from heat.

■ Incorporate beurre manié using whisk. Sprinkle with chopped parsley and season with pepper. Add hot pasta and mussels to sauce, mix and serve.

1 SERVING:	358 CALORIES	39 g CARBOHYDRATE	21 g PROTEIN
	12 g FAT	0 g FIBER	

SPAGHETTI OMELET
(SERVES 4)

4	portions cooked spaghetti, hot	4
1 tbsp	chopped fresh parsley	15 mL
3 tbsp	butter	45 mL
1 cup	grated Parmesan cheese	250 mL
4	eggs, beaten well	4
	salt and pepper	

■ Place hot spaghetti in mixing bowl. Season with salt, pepper and parsley. Add 2 tbsp (30 mL) of butter and mix. Add cheese and mix again.

■ Set spaghetti aside to cool. Stir twice during cooling.

■ Season beaten eggs, then pour over spaghetti. Mix well.

■ Heat remaining butter in large frying pan. Stir spaghetti in bowl, then pour into pan. Cook 2 to 3 minutes over medium heat.

■ Flip omelet over. Continue cooking 3 minutes. Serve.

1 SERVING:	413 CALORIES	35 g CARBOHYDRATE	20 g PROTEIN
	21 g FAT	0 g FIBER	

Place hot spaghetti in mixing bowl. Season with salt, pepper and parsley.

Add 2 tbsp (30 mL) butter and stir.

Add cheese and stir again.

Pour beaten eggs over cool spaghetti. Mix well.

Pour spaghetti mixture into frying pan containing hot butter.

Flip omelet over to cook underside.

SAUTÉ OF CHICKEN WITH SOY SAUCE
(SERVES 4)

1 tbsp	olive oil	15 mL
1	whole chicken breast, skinned, boned and cut in strips	1
4	green onions, cut in 1-in (2.5-cm) sticks	4
1	celery stalk, in sticks	1
1	red pepper, roasted and cut in large pieces	1
2 tbsp	soy sauce	30 mL
1½ cups	chicken stock, heated	375 mL
1 tsp	cornstarch	5 mL
2 tsp	cold water	10 mL
4	portions cooked pasta shells, hot	4
	salt and pepper	
	grated Romano cheese	

■ Heat oil in frying pan over medium heat. Add chicken, season, and cook 3 minutes. Add green onions, celery and red pepper. Season again and continue cooking 4 minutes.

■ Stir in soy sauce and cook 2 minutes.

■ Incorporate chicken stock and simmer 2 minutes over low heat.

■ Dissolve cornstarch in cold water; stir into mixture and bring to boil for 1 minute.

■ Pour sauce over hot pasta, sprinkle with cheese and serve.

1 SERVING:	292 CALORIES	37 g CARBOHYDRATE	21 g PROTEIN
	7 g FAT	0 g FIBER	

CHICKPEA AND RICE DINNER
(SERVES 4)

1 tbsp	olive oil	15 mL
1	onion, finely chopped	1
1	garlic clove, smashed and chopped	1
½	stalk celery, diced	½
1	green pepper, diced	1
3	tomatoes, peeled and diced	3
½ tsp	basil	2 mL
¼ tsp	thyme	1 mL
1 tbsp	chopped fresh parsley	15 mL
19-oz	can chickpeas, drained	540-mL
4	portions cooked rice	4
	salt and pepper	

■ Heat oil in sauté pan over medium heat. Add onion, garlic and celery. Cook 5 minutes over low heat.

■ Add green pepper, tomatoes and seasonings. Cook 12 minutes over medium heat.

■ Add chickpeas, mix and simmer 4 minutes.

■ Serve with rice.

1 SERVING:	350 CALORIES	61 g CARBOHYDRATE	14 g PROTEIN
	6 g FAT	10.5 g FIBER	

RAVIOLI IN FRESH SPINACH SAUCE

(SERVES 4)

2	bunches fresh spinach	2	
1 cup	water	250 mL	
1 tbsp	butter	15 mL	
1	garlic clove, smashed and chopped	1	
2½ cups	white sauce, heated	625 mL	
4	portions cooked ravioli grated Parmesan cheese salt and pepper	4	

■ Trim off stems from spinach. Wash leaves carefully in plenty of cold water.

■ Place spinach in saucepan and pour in cold water. Add salt, cover and cook 3 to 4 minutes over medium-high heat. Remove saucepan from heat.

■ Drain spinach and squeeze out excess liquid using hands. Chop spinach and set aside.

■ Heat butter in frying pan over medium heat. Add spinach and garlic; sauté 3 minutes.

■ Season with salt and pepper. Stir in white sauce and continue cooking 3 minutes.

■ Place pasta in pan with spinach sauce. Mix and simmer 3 minutes.

■ Sprinkle with cheese and serve.

1 SERVING: 417 CALORIES 49 g CARBOHYDRATE 15 g PROTEIN
18 g FAT 2.9 g FIBER

SPAGHETTINI WITH FRESH BASIL AND TOMATOES

(SERVES 4)

1 tbsp	olive oil	15 mL
1	medium onion, chopped	1
2	garlic cloves, smashed and chopped	2
3 tbsp	chopped fresh basil	45 mL
4	tomatoes, peeled, seeded and chopped	4
1 tbsp	chopped hot chili pepper	15 mL
¼ tsp	thyme	1 mL
¼ cup	grated Sardo cheese	50 mL
4	portions cooked spaghettini, hot	4
	pinch sugar	
	salt and freshly ground pepper	

■ Heat oil in sauté pan. Add onion and garlic; cook 4 minutes over low heat.

■ Add basil, tomatoes, sugar, chili pepper and thyme. Season with salt and pepper. Mix and cook 25 to 30 minutes over low heat. Do not cover, but stir occasionally.

■ Stir in cheese. Add hot pasta to sauce and mix. Serve.

1 SERVING:	245 CALORIES	42 g CARBOHYDRATE	8 g PROTEIN
	5 g FAT	2.2 g FIBER	

FETTUCCINE CARBONARA
(SERVES 4)

1 tbsp	olive oil	15 mL
2	garlic cloves, smashed and chopped	2
5	slices prosciutto, cut in strips	5
½ cup	dry white wine	125 mL
2	eggs	2
¼ cup	grated Pecorino cheese	50 mL
⅔ cup	grated Parmesan cheese	150 mL
4	portions cooked fettuccine, hot	4
	chopped fresh parsley	
	freshly ground pepper	

■ Heat oil in sauté pan over medium heat. Add garlic and prosciutto; cook 3 minutes over low heat.

■ Add wine and continue cooking 2 to 3 minutes. Remove sauté pan from heat and set aside.

■ Place eggs in bowl and whisk. Add pepper, both cheeses and mix well. Pour mixture over drained, hot pasta; mix rapidly. Season again with pepper.

■ Add prosciutto mixture, sprinkle with parsley and mix well. Serve.

1 SERVING:	351 CALORIES	36 g CARBOHYDRATE	15 g PROTEIN
	14 g FAT	0 g FIBER	

Cook garlic and prosciutto in hot oil.

Add wine and continue cooking.

Beat eggs.

Add both cheeses and mix well.

Pour egg mixture over hot pasta.

Add prosciutto and mix well.

CURRIED EGG NOODLES

(SERVES 4)

1 tbsp	olive oil	15 mL
1	medium onion, chopped	1
1	garlic clove, smashed and chopped	1
1	celery stalk, diced	1
2 tbsp	curry powder	30 mL
3 tbsp	flour	45 mL
2 cups	chicken stock, heated	500 mL
1 tbsp	tomato paste	15 mL
1	apple, cored, peeled and diced	1
4	portions cooked extra-broad egg noodles, hot	4
	salt and pepper	

■ Heat oil in frying pan over medium heat. Add onion, garlic and celery; cook 3 to 4 minutes. Mix in curry powder and cook 3 to 4 minutes over low heat.

■ Mix in flour until well incorporated; cover and cook 3 minutes over low heat.

■ Pour in chicken stock, mix well and season. Add tomato paste and apple; mix and cook sauce 6 to 7 minutes, uncovered, over medium heat.

■ Pour over pasta and serve.

1 SERVING:	271 CALORIES	52 g CARBOHYDRATE	7 g PROTEIN
	4 g FAT	1.5 g FIBER	

NEW-STYLE FETTUCCINE

(SERVES 4)

1 tbsp	olive oil	15 mL
1	zucchini, thinly sliced	1
1	yellow pepper, thinly sliced	1
3 tbsp	flour	45 mL
2 cups	chicken stock, heated	500 mL
¼ cup	heavy cream, whipped	50 mL
1 cup	grated Gruyère cheese	250 mL
4	portions cooked fettuccine, hot	4
	salt and pepper	

- Heat oil in skillet over medium heat. Add zucchini and yellow pepper; season and cook 4 minutes.

- Mix in flour until well incorporated. Cover and cook 3 to 4 minutes over low heat.

- Pour in chicken stock, season and mix very well. Stir in whipped cream. Cook 2 to 3 minutes, uncovered, over medium heat.

- Stir in cheese and cook 2 more minutes.

- Add pasta, stir and cook 1 minute to reheat. Serve.

1 SERVING:	356 CALORIES	47 g CARBOHYDRATE	13 g PROTEIN
	13 g FAT	1.2 g FIBER	

WHITE RICE FOR SEAFOOD OR VEGETABLES
(SERVES 4)

2 cups	cold water	500 mL
1 cup	rice, rinsed and drained	250 mL
1 tbsp	butter	15 mL
	salt	

■ Pour water into saucepan. Add salt and rice. Stir, cover and bring to boil.

■ Reduce heat to low and continue cooking 16 minutes.

■ Mix in butter with fork. Replace cover and cook 3 minutes over low heat.

■ Serve with seafood or vegetables.

1 SERVING:	124 CALORIES	22 g CARBOHYDRATE	2 g PROTEIN
	3 g FAT	1.0 g FIBER	

PECORINO SPAGHETTI
(SERVES 4)

4	portions spaghetti	4
1 cup	grated Pecorino cheese	250 mL
	salt and freshly ground pepper	

■ Cook pasta in plenty of salted, boiling water. Drain cooked spaghetti well, reserving ½ cup (125 mL) of cooking liquid.

■ Place pasta in large saucepan. Add cheese and pepper. Pour in reserved cooking liquid and mix well. Serve immediately.

1 SERVING:	257 CALORIES	35 g CARBOHYDRATE	14 g PROTEIN
	7 g FAT	0 g FIBER	

RISOTTO
(SERVES 4)

2 tbsp	butter	30 mL
½	onion, finely chopped	½
½ cup	dry white wine	125 mL
4 cups	water	1 L
1 cup	Italian rice	250 mL
¼ cup	grated Parmesan cheese	50 mL
	salt and pepper	

■ Melt half of butter in saucepan over medium heat. Add onion and cook 3 minutes over low heat.

■ Add wine and cook 3 minutes over medium heat.

■ Pour in half of water and season. Bring to boil.

■ Add rice, stir and cook over medium heat until liquid is completely absorbed.

■ Add remaining water, stir and cook over low heat until liquid is completely absorbed.

■ Add cheese and mix with fork. Add remaining butter, mix and season. Cover and let stand 5 minutes before serving.

1 SERVING:	194 CALORIES	23 g CARBOHYDRATE	4 g PROTEIN
	7 g FAT	1.0 g FIBER	

PESTO PARSLEY SAUCE FOR PASTA

(SERVES 4)

1 cup	fresh parsley, washed and dried	250 mL
1 cup	fresh basil, washed and dried	250 mL
3	garlic cloves, peeled	3
¼ cup	olive oil	50 mL
⅓ cup	grated Parmesan cheese	75 mL
4	portions cooked pasta, hot	4
¼ cup	pine nuts	50 mL
	salt and pepper	

- Place parsley and basil in food processor; blend together.

- Add garlic and blend again.

- Add oil and cheese. Season with salt and pepper. Process until mixture is well blended.

- Mix sauce with hot pasta. Sprinkle with pine nuts and serve.

1 SERVING:	313 CALORIES	38 g CARBOHYDRATE	8 g PROTEIN
	15 g FAT	2.5 g FIBER	

Place parsley and basil in food processor.

Blend well.

Add garlic and blend again.

Add oil and cheese.

Season with salt and pepper. Process until mixture is well blended.

Mix sauce with hot pasta.

SPAGHETTI AND MEATBALLS

(SERVES 4)

¾ lb	lean ground beef	375 g
1	egg	1
3 tbsp	chopped onion, cooked	45 mL
1 tbsp	chopped fresh parsley	15 mL
2 tbsp	olive oil	30 mL
1	yellow pepper, diced	1
2 cups	spicy tomato sauce	500 mL
4	portions cooked spaghetti, hot	4
½ cup	grated Romano or Parmesan cheese	125 mL
	salt, pepper and paprika	

■ Place beef, egg, onion and parsley in bowl. Season with salt and pepper; sprinkle with paprika. Mix until well combined. Shape into meatballs and set aside.

■ Heat oil in sauté pan over medium heat. Add meatballs and cook 6 minutes, browning all sides.

■ Add yellow pepper and continue cooking 3 minutes.

■ Pour in tomato sauce, season and stir. Simmer 8 minutes over low heat.

■ Place hot spaghetti on dinner plates. Divide meatballs between servings and top with sauce.

■ Serve with grated cheese.

1 SERVING: 480 CALORIES 45 g CARBOHYDRATE 31 g PROTEIN
20 g FAT 0 g FIBER

TORTELLINI AU GRATIN
(SERVES 4)

2 tbsp	butter	30 mL
1	onion, finely chopped	1
2½ tbsp	flour	40 mL
2 cups	hot milk	500 mL
1 cup	grated Gruyère cheese	250 mL
4	portions cooked tortellini, hot	4
	pinch of nutmeg	
	salt and white pepper	

■ Preheat oven to 400 °F (200 °C).

■ Melt butter in saucepan over medium heat. Add onion and cook 5 minutes over low heat.

■ Add flour, mix well and cook 1 minute over low heat.

■ Incorporate milk using whisk. Sprinkle in nutmeg and season with salt and pepper. Cook sauce 10 minutes over low heat. Whisk 2 to 3 times during cooking.

■ Add half of cheese and mix well. Cook 1 minute. Add hot pasta, mix and remove pan from heat.

■ Transfer pasta to buttered ovenproof baking dish. Sprinkle with remaining cheese. Cook 8 minutes in oven.

1 SERVING:	409 CALORIES	50 g CARBOHYDRATE	17 g PROTEIN
	16 g FAT	1.0 g FIBER	

PASTA WITH SPRING VEGETABLES

(SERVES 4)

1 tbsp	olive oil	15 mL
3	green onions, chopped	3
2	carrots, pared and sliced on the bias	2
1 tbsp	chopped fresh ginger	15 mL
½ tsp	basil	2 mL
1	green pepper, diced	1
½ cup	dry white wine	125 mL
1½ cups	chicken stock, heated	375 mL
1	head broccoli, washed and in florets	1
1 tbsp	cornstarch	15 mL
3 tbsp	cold water	45 mL
4	portions cooked pasta, hot	4
	salt and pepper	

■ Heat oil in frying pan over medium heat. Add green onions and carrots; cook 3 minutes.

■ Add ginger, basil, green pepper and wine. Mix and cook 3 minutes.

■ Add chicken stock and broccoli. Season and cook 4 minutes.

■ Dissolve cornstarch in cold water; incorporate into sauce and cook 1 minute. Correct seasoning.

■ Serve over hot pasta.

1 SERVING: 250 CALORIES   42 g CARBOHYDRATE   7 g PROTEIN
4 g FAT   2.2 g FIBER

ROTINI ARTICHOKE SALAD
(SERVES 4 TO 6)

2 cups	cooked rotini (spiral pasta)	500 mL
4	artichoke hearts, quartered	4
½ cup	black olives, pitted and sliced	125 mL
½	red pimento, chopped	½
½	stalk celery, chopped	½
1 tsp	Dijon mustard	5 mL
¼ cup	mayonnaise	50 mL
2 tbsp	chili sauce	30 mL
	salt and pepper	

■ Place all ingredients in bowl and mix well. Season with salt and pepper. Marinate salad 2 hours in refrigerator.

■ Mix again before serving.

1 SERVING:	182 CALORIES	20 g CARBOHYDRATE	3 g PROTEIN
	10 g FAT	1.0 g FIBER	

RICE PILAF
(SERVES 4)

1 tbsp	butter	15 mL	■ Preheat oven to 350 °F (180 °C).
2	dry shallots, peeled and chopped	2	■ Heat butter in ovenproof casserole over medium heat. Add shallots, celery and seasonings. Cook 3 minutes over medium heat.
½	stalk celery, chopped	½	
1 tbsp	chopped fresh basil	15 mL	■ Add rice and mix well. Season with salt and pepper. Cook 3 minutes over medium heat or until rice starts to stick to bottom of casserole.
1 tbsp	chopped fresh parsley	15 mL	
¼ tsp	cayenne pepper	1 mL	
1 cup	long grain rice, rinsed	250 mL	■ Pour in chicken stock, stir and bring to boil. Cover and cook 18 minutes in oven.
1½ cups	chicken stock, heated	375 mL	
	salt and pepper		

1 SERVING: 145 CALORIES 26 g CARBOHYDRATE 3 g PROTEIN
3 g FAT 1.0 g FIBER

Place shallots and celery in casserole containing hot butter.

Add seasonings and cook 3 minutes over medium heat.

Add rice and mix well. Season with salt and pepper.

Cook 3 minutes or until rice starts to stick to bottom of casserole.

Pour in chicken stock and stir.

Bring to boil, then finish cooking in oven.

SPAGHETTI TOSSED IN HOT OLIVE OIL

(SERVES 4)

3 tbsp	olive oil	45 mL
3	garlic cloves, smashed and chopped	3
¼ tsp	chili powder	1 mL
4	portions cooked spaghetti, hot	4
	salt and pepper	

■ Heat oil in frying pan over medium heat. Add garlic and chili powder. Stir and cook 2 minutes over very low heat.

■ Place hot spaghetti in large bowl. Pour in hot oil with garlic and chili and season well. Toss to evenly coat.

■ If desired, add julienned vegetables sautéed in oil.

■ Serve with cheese.

1 SERVING:	252 CALORIES	35 g CARBOHYDRATE	5 g PROTEIN
	11 g FAT	0 g FIBER	

PENNE À LA PROVENÇALE

(SERVES 4)

2 tbsp	olive oil	30 mL
2	garlic cloves, smashed and chopped	2
1	red pepper, chopped	1
2 tbsp	chopped fresh parsley	30 mL
12	whole Greek olives	12
1 tbsp	capers	15 mL
2	anchovy filets, chopped	2
2	large tomatoes, peeled and diced	2
¼ tsp	cayenne pepper	1 mL
4	portions cooked penne, hot	4
½ cup	grated Parmesan cheese	125 mL
	salt and pepper	

■ Heat oil in sauté pan over medium heat. Add garlic, red pepper and parsley. Cook 2 minutes.

■ Add olives, capers and anchovies; mix and cook 2 minutes.

■ Incorporate tomatoes and cayenne pepper. Season and cook 6 minutes over medium heat.

■ Add hot pasta and cheese; mix and serve.

1 SERVING:	314 CALORIES	39 g CARBOHYDRATE	11 g PROTEIN
	13 g FAT	2.0 g FIBER	

Fresh Scallops in White Wine over Pasta

FRESH SCALLOPS IN WHITE WINE OVER PASTA
(SERVES 4)

2	dry shallots, peeled and chopped	2
½ lb	fresh mushrooms, cleaned and cut in 3	250 g
1 lb	fresh scallops, washed	500 g
1 tbsp	chopped fresh parsley	15 mL
½ cup	dry white wine	125 mL
1½ cups	clam juice	375 mL
2 tbsp	butter	30 mL
2 tbsp	flour	30 mL
½ cup	grated Gruyère cheese	125 mL
4	portions cooked rotini (spiral pasta), hot	4
	salt and pepper	
	grated Parmesan cheese	

■ Place shallots, mushrooms, scallops, parsley, wine and clam juice in sauté pan. Season with salt and pepper. Cover with sheet of waxed paper touching surface of food. Bring to boil over medium heat, then remove immediately from stove. Let stand 3 minutes.

■ Use slotted spoon to remove scallops and transfer to bowl. Set scallops aside.

■ Return sauté pan to stove. Cook contents of pan 7 minutes over medium heat. Set aside.

■ Heat butter in saucepan over medium heat. Add flour, mix with wooden spoon and cook 2 minutes over low heat.

■ Add cooking liquid and mushrooms to flour mixture. Mix well and cook 5 minutes over low heat.

■ Add Gruyère and scallops. Mix and simmer 3 minutes over very low heat.

■ Add hot pasta, mix and simmer another 3 minutes. Serve with grated Parmesan cheese.

1 SERVING:	493 CALORIES	51 g CARBOHYDRATE	41 g PROTEIN
	12 g FAT	2.0 g FIBER	

VEAL LASAGNE
(SERVES 4 TO 6)

1 tbsp	olive oil	15 mL
1	medium onion, diced	1
1	green pepper, diced	1
1	yellow pepper, diced	1
1	celery stalk, diced	1
1	zucchini, diced medium	1
1 tsp	butter	5 mL
1 lb	lean ground veal	500 g
4 cups	white sauce, heated	1 L
2½ cups	grated mozzarella cheese	625 mL
	pinch ground cloves	
	salt, pepper and paprika	
	lasagne noodles, cooked	

■ Preheat oven to 375 °F (190 °C).

■ Heat olive oil in sauté pan over medium heat. Add onion, both peppers, celery and zucchini. Season with salt and pepper. Cook 8 to 10 minutes over low heat.

■ Melt butter in frying pan. Add ground veal and sauté until meat browns. Drain meat, then incorporate into vegetable mixture.

■ Stir in 1 cup (250 mL) of white sauce. Add seasonings and simmer 3 to 4 minutes over low heat.

■ Butter lasagne dish. To assemble lasagne, begin with layer of noodles. Follow with layer of vegetable/meat mixture, layer of grated cheese, and layer of white sauce.

■ Repeat layers, ending with noodles. Top with white sauce and remaining cheese. Season with pepper.

■ Bake 20 to 30 minutes in oven until nicely browned. Serve.

1 SERVING:	835 CALORIES	62 g CARBOHYDRATE	45 g PROTEIN
	45 g FAT	1.0 g FIBER	

Cook vegetables in hot oil.

Sauté ground veal in frying pan.

Add drained meat to vegetables and stir in 1 cup (250 mL) of white sauce. Add seasonings.

Spread layer of vegetable/meat mixture over bottom layer of lasagne noodles.

Follow with layer of grated cheese.

Cover with layer of white sauce.

LINGUINE SICILY

(SERVES 4)

1 tbsp	olive oil	15 mL
2	green onions, sliced	2
1	yellow pepper, sliced	1
1	dry shallot, peeled and sliced	1
2 tbsp	chopped fresh basil	30 mL
1	cooked Italian sausage, sliced	1
½ lb	fresh mushrooms, cleaned and sliced	250 g
1½ cups	chicken stock, heated	375 mL
1 tbsp	cornstarch	15 mL
3 tbsp	cold water	45 mL
4	portions cooked linguine, hot	4
	salt and pepper	

■ Heat oil in sauté pan. Add green onions, yellow pepper, shallot, basil and sausage. Cook 3 minutes over medium-high heat.

■ Add mushrooms. Season and cook 3 minutes over medium heat.

■ Incorporate chicken stock and bring to boil.

■ Dissolve cornstarch in cold water. Stir into sauce and cook 2 minutes over low heat.

■ Pour sauce over hot pasta in bowl, mix and serve.

1 SERVING: 295 CALORIES   43 g CARBOHYDRATE   11 g PROTEIN
                   9 g FAT   2.2 g FIBER

ROTINI IN RICH MEAT SAUCE
(SERVES 4)

1 tbsp	olive oil	15 mL
1	onion, finely chopped	1
2	garlic cloves, smashed and chopped	2
1	celery stalk, diced	1
1 tbsp	chopped fresh basil	15 mL
1 tbsp	chopped fresh parsley	15 mL
½ cup	dry white wine	125 mL
½ lb	lean ground pork	250 g
1½ lb	lean ground veal	750 g
5	large tomatoes, peeled and chopped	5
2 tbsp	tomato paste	30 mL
½ tsp	thyme	2 mL
4	portions cooked rotini (spiral pasta), hot	4
	pinch of sugar	
	salt and pepper	
	grated Parmesan cheese	

■ Heat oil in sauté pan over medium heat. Add onion, garlic and celery. Cook 6 minutes over medium heat.

■ Add basil, parsley and wine. Cook 3 minutes.

■ Add both meats and season. Cook 6 minutes over medium heat. Stir twice during cooking.

■ Add tomatoes, tomato paste, sugar and thyme. Season and cook 18 minutes over low heat.

■ Mix in hot pasta and serve with grated cheese.

1 SERVING:	687 CALORIES	45 g CARBOHYDRATE	57 g PROTEIN
	29 g FAT	2.5 g FIBER	

STRIPS OF CHICKEN WITH LEEKS OVER PASTA

(SERVES 4)

1 tbsp	butter	15 mL
2	leeks, white part only, cleaned, cooked and sliced	2
1	whole chicken breast, skinned, boned and cut in strips	1
½ cup	dry white wine	125 mL
1 tbsp	chopped fresh tarragon	15 mL
1½ cups	chicken stock, heated	375 mL
1 tbsp	cornstarch	15 mL
3 tbsp	cold water	45 mL
1 tbsp	chopped fresh parsley	15 mL
4	portions cooked penne or rigatoni, hot	4
	salt and pepper	

■ Melt butter in sauté pan over medium heat. Add leeks and chicken. Season, cover and cook 5 minutes over low heat.

■ Remove cover and add wine and tarragon; cook 3 minutes over low heat.

■ Add chicken stock and correct seasoning. Simmer 3 minutes.

■ Dissolve cornstarch in cold water. Incorporate into sauce and bring to boil for 1 minute. Pour sauce into bowl; add parsley and hot pasta. Mix well and serve.

1 SERVING:	309 CALORIES	41 g CARBOHYDRATE	19 g PROTEIN
	5 g FAT	0 g FIBER	

SAUTÉED VEGETABLE MEDLEY WITH STUFFED PASTA

(SERVES 4)

1 tbsp	olive oil	15 mL
4	pork cutlets, cut in strips *or* 2 whole skinned chicken breasts cut in strips	4
1	celery stalk, in 1-in (2.5-cm) sticks	1
1	red pepper, sliced	1
20	snow peas, strings removed	20
6	canned artichoke hearts, quartered	6
2 tbsp	teriyaki sauce	30 mL
1½ cups	chicken stock, heated	375 mL
1 tsp	cornstarch	5 mL
2 tbsp	cold water	30 mL
4	portions cooked stuffed pasta medallions, hot	4
	salt and pepper	

■ Heat oil in frying pan over medium heat. Add meat and cook 3 minutes. Season, remove meat and set aside.

■ Add all vegetables to hot pan. Mix and cook 3 minutes over medium heat. Add teriyaki sauce and chicken stock. Season with pepper and bring to boil.

■ Dissolve cornstarch in cold water. Incorporate into vegetables and cook 1 minute over medium heat.

■ Return meat to pan and simmer 1 minute.

■ Serve over hot pasta.

1 SERVING:	458 CALORIES	34 g CARBOHYDRATE	40 g PROTEIN
	18 g FAT	4.1 g FIBER	

RIGATONI WITH FRESH CLAMS AND TOMATOES

(SERVES 4 TO 6)

3 lbs	fresh clams, scrubbed and washed	1.4 kg
½ cup	water	125 mL
2 tbsp	olive oil	30 mL
1	onion, chopped	1
1	dry shallot, peeled and chopped	1
3	garlic cloves, smashed and chopped	3
2 lbs	tomatoes, peeled, seeded and cubed	900 g
3 tbsp	tomato paste	45 mL
1 tsp	basil	5 mL
1 tsp	oregano	5 mL
4 to 6	portions cooked rigatoni, hot	4 to 6
	juice of 1 lemon	
	few drops hot pepper sauce	
	salt and pepper	

■ Place clams in large saucepan. Add water and lemon juice. Cover and cook over medium heat until shells open. Discard any unopened shells.

■ Remove clams from shells, chop and set aside.

■ Strain cooking liquid from clams through sieve lined with cheesecloth. Set liquid aside.

■ Heat oil in sauté pan over medium heat. Add onion, shallot and garlic. Cook 3 minutes over low heat.

■ Add tomatoes, tomato paste and seasonings; bring to boil. Reduce heat to low and cook 45 minutes. Stir a few times during cooking.

■ Pour reserved cooking liquid from clams into small saucepan. Cook 6 minutes over high heat.

■ Incorporate ½ cup (125 mL) of reduced cooking liquid into tomato sauce. Continue cooking sauce 15 minutes over medium heat.

■ Place chopped clams in tomato sauce and mix well. Simmer 3 minutes over low heat.

■ Add pasta to sauce, mix and serve.

1 SERVING: 377 CALORIES   50 g CARBOHYDRATE   25 g PROTEIN
          9 g FAT   3.0 g FIBER

Place clams in large saucepan. Add water and lemon juice.

Cover and cook over medium heat until shells open. Discard unopened shells.

Remove clams from shells.

Cook onion, shallot and garlic in hot oil.

Add tomatoes, tomato paste and seasonings. Continue cooking.

Add chopped clams to tomato sauce.

ROTINI WITH WHITE MUSHROOM SAUCE

(SERVES 4)

3 tbsp	butter	45 mL
1	dry shallot, peeled and finely chopped	1
1 lb	fresh mushrooms, cleaned and sliced in 3	500 g
3 tbsp	flour	45 mL
2 cups	chicken stock, heated	500 mL
1 cup	hot milk	250 mL
¼ tsp	nutmeg	1 mL
1 tbsp	chopped fresh parsley	15 mL
4	portions cooked rotini, hot	4
	salt and pepper	
	paprika	
	grated Parmesan cheese	

■ Heat butter in saucepan over medium heat. When hot, add shallot and cook 2 minutes. Add mushrooms, season and cook 5 minutes.

■ Mix in flour until well incorporated and cook 2 minutes over reduced heat.

■ Season well and pour in chicken stock; mix well and bring to boil. Pour in milk, add nutmeg, parsley and paprika. Mix well and cook 7 minutes over low heat, stirring occasionally.

■ Serve sauce over hot pasta and accompany with cheese.

1 SERVING:	380 CALORIES	55 g CARBOHYDRATE	13 g PROTEIN
	12 g FAT	3.6 g FIBER	

ARTICHOKES WITH VINAIGRETTE

(SERVES 4)

4	large artichokes, washed	4
4	slices lemon	4
1½ cups	vinaigrette	375 mL

■ Cut off artichoke stems and snap off leaves near bottom end. Cover base with lemon slice and secure with kitchen string.

■ Place artichokes in large pot containing at least 8 cups (2 L) salted boiling water. Partly cover and cook 40 to 50 minutes over medium heat, depending on size.

■ When cooked (center leaves should pull free easily), drain well and squeeze out excess water. Separate leaves on platter and remove and discard fuzzy choke. Place artichoke bottoms with leaves.

■ Serve with vinaigrette for dipping.

1 SERVING:	662 CALORIES	17 g CARBOHYDRATE	3 g PROTEIN
	65 g FAT	0 g FIBER	

PARMESAN LEEKS

(SERVES 4)

6	leeks	6
3 tbsp	honey	45 mL
3 tbsp	grated Parmesan cheese	45 mL
	juice of ½ lemon	
	pinch of nutmeg	
	salt and pepper	
	lemon slices	

■ Preheat oven to 400 °F (200 °C).

■ Discard dark green leaves from leeks. Cut light green and white part of stalks into 1½-in (4-cm) pieces. Place pieces of leek into bowl of cold water; let stand 20 minutes.

■ Remove leeks from water and transfer to shallow ovenproof baking dish. Add cold water so that it barely covers leeks. Add honey, lemon juice, nutmeg, salt and pepper.

■ Place over medium heat and bring to boil. Continue boiling 5 minutes. Do not cover.

■ Place baking dish in oven and cook 30 minutes, uncovered. Turn leeks over and continue cooking another 30 minutes.

■ Transfer leeks to serving platter and sprinkle with cheese. Serve with lemon slices.

1 SERVING:	114 CALORIES	26 g CARBOHYDRATE	2 g PROTEIN
	0 g FAT	1.0 g FIBER	

BRAISED RED CABBAGE

(SERVES 4 TO 6)

1	medium red cabbage	1
1 oz	diced salt pork	30 g
2	slices bacon, diced	2
1	large onion, in narrow wedges	1
2	garlic cloves, peeled and halved	2
1 tbsp	chopped green chili pepper	15 mL
2 cups	dry red wine	500 mL
	salt and pepper	

■ Preheat oven to 325 °F (160 °C).

■ Core cabbage. Cut in quarters and slice thinly. Place cabbage in bowl with cold water for 30 minutes. Drain and set aside.

■ Place salt pork in deep ovenproof sauté pan. Cook 3 minutes over medium heat. Discard salt pork and add bacon to hot pan. Cook 3 minutes.

■ Add cabbage, onion, garlic and chili pepper. Season with salt and pepper; cook 12 minutes over low heat.

■ Pour in wine and bring to boil over high heat. Cover pan and braise 2 hours in oven.

Note: If necessary, add water during cooking.

1 SERVING: 150 CALORIES   5 g CARBOHYDRATE   2 g PROTEIN
6 g FAT   1.3 g FIBER

FRESH VEGETABLE STIR-FRY

(SERVES 4 TO 6)

1 tbsp	olive oil	15 mL
½	yellow onion, sliced	½
3	baby carrots, pared and sliced on the bias	3
½	red pepper, cubed	½
½	white Holland pepper, cubed	½
1	sweet banana pepper, cubed	1
½	zucchini, halved lengthwise and sliced on the bias	½
⅓	yellow summer squash, halved lengthwise and sliced on the bias	⅓
2 tbsp	pine nuts	30 mL
1 tbsp	chopped fresh ginger	15 mL
2	garlic cloves, smashed and chopped	2
	salt and pepper	

■ Heat olive oil in frying pan over medium-high heat. Add onion and carrots; cook 2 minutes. Cover and continue cooking 2 minutes.

■ Add remaining ingredients and mix well. Season with salt and pepper. Cook, uncovered, 5 to 6 minutes over high heat.

■ If desired, add lemon juice before serving.

1 SERVING:	68 CALORIES	7 g CARBOHYDRATE	1 g PROTEIN
	4 g FAT	1.7 g FIBER	

VIRGINIA-STYLE BAKED CORN ON THE COB
(SERVES 4 TO 6)

10 to 12	ears of corn
	butter
	salt

- Preheat oven to 350 °F (180 °C).

- Peel back husk, leaving it attached, and remove silk. Replace husk and soak corn cobs in cold water for 12 minutes.

- Remove from water and drain. Arrange corn cobs in roasting pan and pour in 1½ cups (375 mL) water. Cook 35 to 40 minutes in oven.

- Husk corn, season with salt and serve with butter.

| 1 SERVING: | 273 CALORIES | 42 g CARBOHYDRATE | 6 g PROTEIN |
| | 9 g FAT | 7.8 g FIBER | |

CAROLINA CORN ON THE COB
(SERVES 4)

8	ears of corn
	pinch of sugar
	butter
	salt

- Husk ears and add to boiling water. Do not salt. Add pinch of sugar and cover pan. Boil about 5 minutes, depending on size.

- Season with salt and serve with butter.

| 1 SERVING: | 255 CALORIES | 39 g CARBOHYDRATE | 5 g PROTEIN |
| | 9 g FAT | 7.2 g FIBER | |

Virginia-Style Baked Corn on the Cob

CHINESE CABBAGE WITH GINGER

(SERVES 4)

1	Chinese cabbage (bok choy)	1	
1 tbsp	olive oil	15 mL	
1 tbsp	chopped fresh ginger	15 mL	
1	garlic clove, smashed and chopped	1	
2	tomatoes, cored and cut in wedges	2	
1 tbsp	teriyaki sauce	15 mL	
	salt and pepper		

■ Slice off white base from cabbage. Separate stalks and wash well in cold water. Use only the leafy part of the stalks, and cut in thick slices on the bias.

■ Heat oil in frying pan over medium heat. Add cabbage and cover; cook 3 minutes.

■ Add ginger and garlic; season well. Add tomatoes and cook 5 minutes over high heat, uncovered.

■ Stir in teriyaki sauce and serve.

1 SERVING:	49 CALORIES	4 g CARBOHYDRATE	1 g PROTEIN
	3 g FAT	1.8 g FIBER	

CRISP POTATO MEDALLIONS

(SERVES 4 TO 6)

2	eggs, lightly beaten	2
1 tsp	chopped fresh parsley	5 mL
¼ tsp	paprika	1 mL
¼ tsp	white pepper	1 mL
⅓ cup	flour	75 mL
4	large potatoes, peeled and placed in bowl of cold water	4
2	garlic cloves, peeled	2
	vegetable oil	
	salt and pepper	

■ Place eggs and parsley in bowl. Add paprika, white pepper and flour; mix well.

■ Remove potatoes from water and dry with clean cloth. Grate potatoes, then rinse under cold water. Drain well.

■ Squeeze out excess liquid from potatoes. Dry again on clean cloth.

■ Place potatoes in bowl containing egg mixture. Season and mix well. Cover and refrigerate 15 minutes.

■ Heat 2 tbsp (30 mL) vegetable oil in cast iron frying pan over high heat. Add garlic cloves and cook 2 minutes. Discard garlic.

■ Using spoon, drop small scoops of potato mixture into hot pan, well spaced. Use spatula to flatten mounds into medallions. Cook 3 minutes over medium heat.

■ Turn medallions over and continue cooking 3 minutes. Remove medallions and place on paper towels to drain. Keep hot in oven.

■ Repeat cooking procedure for remaining potato mixture.

■ Serve with sour cream.

1 SERVING:	228 CALORIES	33 g CARBOHYDRATE	6 g PROTEIN
	8 g FAT	1.6 g FIBER	

Place eggs and parsley in bowl.

Add paprika, white pepper and flour; mix well.

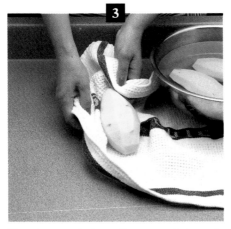

Remove potatoes from water and dry with clean cloth.

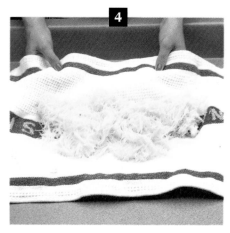

Squeeze out excess liquid from grated potatoes, then dry on clean cloth.

Place potatoes in bowl containing egg mixture.

Use spatula to flatten mounds of potato into medallions. Cook in hot oil.

TRADITIONAL MASHED POTATOES

(SERVES 4)

5	large potatoes, peeled, washed and quartered	5	
3 tbsp	butter	45 mL	
¼ cup	hot milk	50 mL	
	pinch of nutmeg		
	salt and white pepper		

■ Place potatoes in saucepan and cover with cold water. Add salt and cover pan. Bring to boil and cook over medium heat.

■ When potatoes are cooked, drain water from saucepan. Leave potatoes in saucepan and cook over very low heat for 2 minutes.

■ Remove saucepan from heat. Force potatoes, one by one, through fine sieve into bowl.

■ Return puréed potatoes to saucepan. Add butter and hot milk. Season with salt, pepper and nutmeg. Mix well and serve.

1 SERVING: 229 CALORIES   34 g CARBOHYDRATE   3 g PROTEIN
9 g FAT   1.7 g FIBER

OVEN GRATIN POTATOES
(SERVES 4)

3	large potatoes, peeled, sliced and placed in cold water	3
¼ tsp	savory	1 mL
¼ tsp	cayenne pepper	1 mL
¼ tsp	white pepper	1 mL
1 tbsp	chopped fresh parsley	15 mL
1	garlic clove, peeled	1
2	eggs, beaten	2
¾ cup	milk	175 mL
½ cup	heavy cream	125 mL
	salt	
	butter	

■ Preheat oven to 350 °F (180 °C).

■ Drain potatoes and dry slices well. Place in bowl.

■ Mix savory, cayenne pepper, white pepper and parsley together. Add to potatoes and mix.

■ Rub baking dish with garlic clove. Butter dish generously and arrange potato slices in layers. Season with salt.

■ Mix eggs, milk and cream together. Pour over potatoes. Bake in oven 40 to 50 minutes. Serve.

1 SERVING:	259 CALORIES	24 g CARBOHYDRATE	7 g PROTEIN
	15 g FAT	1.1 g FIBER	

FLAGEOLETS PROVENÇALE

(SERVES 8)

2 cups	dried white pea beans	500 mL
1	onion, studded with 3 cloves	1
1 tbsp	olive oil	15 mL
1	onion, chopped	1
3	garlic cloves, smashed and chopped	3
28-oz	can tomatoes, drained and chopped	796-mL
¼ cup	tomato paste	50 mL
2 tsp	chopped fresh basil	10 mL
2 tsp	chopped fresh parsley	10 mL
	salt and pepper	

■ Place dried beans in salted, boiling water. Cook, partly covered,10 minutes over medium heat. Remove saucepan from stove and let stand 1 hour, uncovered.

■ Drain beans and transfer to clean saucepan. Cover with cold water and drop in clove-studded onion. Season with salt and pepper. Cover and cook 3 hours over low heat. Replenish water during cooking, if necessary.

■ Heat oil in frying pan over medium heat. Add chopped onion and garlic; cook 3 minutes over low heat.

■ Mix in tomatoes and tomato paste. Add fresh herbs and season well. Cook 10 minutes over low heat.

■ Drain beans and reserve stock. Return beans to saucepan and stir in tomato mixture. Mix in 1 cup (250 mL) of reserved stock and correct seasoning. Continue cooking 35 minutes over low heat. Serve with roasts.

1 SERVING:	170 CALORIES	29 g CARBOHYDRATE	9 g PROTEIN
	2 g FAT	8.6 g FIBER	

BAKED ONIONS

(SERVES 4 TO 6)

6	large onions
	water
	salt

■ Preheat oven to 375 °F (190 °C).

■ Do not peel onions, but remove stem ends.

■ Place onions in baking dish and pour in enough water to cover bottom of dish. Add salt and cook about 70 minutes in oven, depending on size. Do not cover.

■ When cooked, remove from oven and peel before serving.

1 SERVING:	41 CALORIES	9 g CARBOHYDRATE	1 g PROTEIN
	0 g FAT	1.5 g FIBER	

SPANISH ONION PURÉE

(SERVES 4 TO 6)

4	Spanish onions, peeled and quartered	4
1 tbsp	butter	15 mL
2 tbsp	heavy cream	30 mL
1½ cups	mashed potatoes	375 mL
	pinch of nutmeg	
	pinch of ground cloves	
	breadcrumbs	
	salt and pepper	
	butter	

■ Add onions to saucepan filled with salted, boiling water. Cook 40 minutes or until tender.

■ Remove from heat and drain onions well. Purée onions in food processor.

■ Return puréed onions to saucepan. Cook 3 to 4 minutes over high heat, stirring occasionally.

■ Add 1 tbsp (15 mL) butter and cream; mix well. Continue cooking 3 to 4 minutes.

■ Incorporate mashed potatoes and all seasonings. Cook 3 to 4 minutes over low heat.

■ Spoon mixture into baking dish. Sprinkle with breadcrumbs and dot top with bits of butter. Broil 3 minutes.

1 SERVING:	267 CALORIES	36 g CARBOHYDRATE	4 g PROTEIN
	12 g FAT	2.5 g FIBER	

BRAISED ENDIVES WITH CHEESE

(SERVES 4 TO 6)

8	endives	8
⅓ cup	cold water	75 mL
3 tbsp	butter	45 mL
2 cups	cheese sauce, heated	500 mL
½ cup	grated Gruyère cheese	125 mL
	juice of 1 lemon	
	salt and white pepper	

■ Remove and discard outer leaves from endives. Cut away hard core. Rinse endives under cold water but do not soak: endives turn dark if left in water too long.

■ Butter sauté pan and add endives. Add lemon juice and cold water. Add butter in small pieces and place sheet of waxed paper on endives. Cover pan and cook 40 minutes over low heat or, if prefered, in oven at 300 °F (150 °C).

■ Transfer endives to baking dish. Season and cover with cheese sauce. Sprinkle with grated cheese. Brown 15 minutes in preheated oven at 375 °F (190 °C). Serve.

1 SERVING: 275 CALORIES   18 g CARBOHYDRATE   10 g PROTEIN
18 g FAT   1.8 g FIBER

FRESH SPINACH WITH ROASTED GARLIC PURÉE
(SERVES 4)

4	bunches fresh spinach	4
1 tbsp	butter	15 mL
1 tbsp	Roasted Garlic Purée (see page 346)	15 mL
1	apple, cored, peeled and sliced	1
2 tbsp	chopped green chili pepper	30 mL
4 tbsp	slivered almonds	60 mL
	salt and pepper	

■ Trim stems from spinach leaves. Wash spinach 3 to 4 times in cold water to remove all dirt and sand. Drain. Steam spinach or cook in salted, boiling water. Drain well and set aside.

■ Heat butter in sauté pan over medium heat. Add garlic purée, apple, chili pepper and almonds. Mix and cook 2 minutes.

■ Add spinach and season well. Cover and cook 3 minutes over low heat. Serve.

1 SERVING:	170 CALORIES	12 g CARBOHYDRATE	6 g PROTEIN
	11 g FAT	6.3 g FIBER	

BRAISED CELERY HEARTS
(SERVES 4 TO 6)

6	celery hearts, white inner stalks only, trimmed to 5 in (13 cm) in length	6
1 tbsp	butter	15 mL
1	onion, diced small	1
1	carrot, pared and diced small	1
1	garlic clove, smashed and chopped	1
1	bay leaf	1
1 cup	chicken stock, heated	250 mL
1 tbsp	chopped fresh parsley	15 mL
	salt and pepper	

■ Preheat oven to 350 °F (180 °C).

■ Place celery hearts in saucepan filled with salted, boiling water. Partly cover and cook 8 minutes. Drain well and set aside.

■ Heat butter in ovenproof sauté pan over medium heat. Add onion, carrot and garlic; cook 4 minutes.

■ Place cooked celery hearts on top of vegetables in sauté pan. Season with salt and pepper; drop in bay leaf. Pour chicken stock into pan and cook 5 minutes over medium heat. Turn celery hearts over once during cooking.

■ Cover and cook 1 hour in oven. Drain, sprinkle with parsley and serve.

1 SERVING:	62 CALORIES	10 g CARBOHYDRATE	2 g PROTEIN
	2 g FAT	3.9 g FIBER	

ATLANTA'S HOMETOWN CORN PUDDING

(SERVES 4 TO 6)

2 cups	fresh corn kernels	500 mL
2 cups	milk, heated to boiling point	500 mL
1 tsp	butter	5 mL
3	eggs, beaten	3
2 tbsp	chopped green chili pepper	30 mL
1	red pepper, chopped	1
1	small onion, chopped and cooked	1
	salt and pepper	

■ Preheat oven to 325 °F (160 °C).

■ Place corn in food processor with steel blade attachment. Pulse several times to chop corn kernels. Transfer contents to saucepan.

■ Add 1 cup (250 mL) of hot milk and butter. Season and cook 12 minutes over low heat.

■ Pour beaten eggs into bowl and add remaining milk; mix together with whisk.

■ Incorporate corn mixture into eggs, then stir in remaining ingredients. Correct seasoning.

■ Pour pudding into 4-cup (1-L) soufflé mold. Place mold in roasting pan and pour in enough hot water to measure 1 in (2.5 cm) deep.

■ Cook 60 to 70 minutes in oven.

1 SERVING:	211 CALORIES	26 g CARBOHYDRATE	11 g PROTEIN
	7 g FAT	3.7 g FIBER	

Chop corn kernels in food processor.

Place chopped corn in saucepan. Add 1 cup (250 mL) of hot milk and butter. Season and cook 12 minutes over low heat.

Mix remaining milk with beaten eggs using whisk.

Incorporate corn mixture into eggs.

Add remaining ingredients.

Pour pudding into 4-cup (1-L) soufflé mold set in roasting pan containing 1 in (2.5 cm) of hot water.

ASPARAGUS AU GRATIN
(SERVES 4)

2	bunches fresh asparagus	2	
½	lemon	½	
2 cups	cheese sauce, heated	500 mL	
½ cup	grated Gruyère cheese	125 mL	
	salt, pepper, paprika		

■ Pare asparagus if needed and trim off tough ends. Wash asparagus, then place in saucepan with salted, boiling water. Drop in half lemon and cook 12 to 18 minutes, depending on size. Do not overcook!

■ Test if asparagus are cooked by pricking stalk with sharp knife. Stalk should be tender, not soft.

■ Preheat oven to 400 °F (200 °C).

■ Drain asparagus well and cut stalks into two. Place in buttered baking dish and cover with cheese sauce. Top with grated cheese and season to taste.

■ Brown in oven for 12 minutes. Serve.

1 SERVING:	275 CALORIES	22 g CARBOHYDRATE	14 g PROTEIN
	15 g FAT	3.1 g FIBER	

SHALLOTS AND MUSHROOMS WITH TARRAGON

(SERVES 4)

½ lb	dry shallots, peeled	250 g
1 tbsp	butter	15 mL
½ lb	fresh mushrooms, cleaned and halved	250 g
1 tbsp	chopped lemon rind	15 mL
1 tsp	tarragon	5 mL
¼ tsp	saffron	1 mL
	salt and pepper	

■ Cook shallots 10 minutes in salted, boiling water. Remove from heat and drain well.

■ Heat butter in saucepan over medium heat. Add shallots and remaining ingredients. Season with salt and pepper. Cover and cook 6 minutes over low heat.

■ Serve with a roast or grilled meat.

1 SERVING:	95 CALORIES	14 g CARBOHYDRATE	3 g PROTEIN
	3 g FAT	1.5 g FIBER	

GRATED POTATO CRÊPE

(SERVES 4 TO 6)

5	large potatoes, peeled and placed in bowl with cold water	5
¼ cup	butter	50 mL
1	garlic clove, peeled	1
	salt, pepper, paprika	

■ Remove potatoes from water and dry with clean cloth. Grate potatoes finely, then rinse under cold water. Drain well. Squeeze out excess liquid from potatoes, then dry again on clean cloth.

■ Melt half of butter in frying pan. Add garlic clove and cook 1 minute. Discard garlic.

■ Add grated potatoes to hot butter. Season with salt and pepper and flatten with spatula. Scatter remaining butter in small pieces over potatoes. Season to taste. Cover and cook 17 minutes over medium heat.

■ Remove cover 2 to 3 times during cooking to allow the steam to escape.

■ Remove pan from heat. Secure cover and carefully turn pan upside-down. With potatoes resting on inside of cover, turn pan right-side-up and slide potatoes back into pan. The cooked side should be facing up. Continue cooking 17 minutes over medium heat. Season with salt and pepper.

■ Serve with a roast.

1 SERVING: 185 CALORIES 27 g CARBOHYDRATE 2 g PROTEIN
8 g FAT 1.4 g FIBER

FARMER'S VEGETABLE SPECIAL

(SERVES 6)

½ lb	green beans, pared and cut in half	250 g
1	carrot, pared and sliced	1
½ cup	fresh green peas	125 mL
1	small yellow summer squash, split in two lengthwise and diced medium	1
1	yellow pepper, diced medium	1
1 tbsp	butter	15 mL
1	garlic clove, smashed and chopped	1
1 tsp	tarragon	5 mL
	few drops of lemon juice	
	salt and pepper	

■ Bring 1 cup (250 mL) water to boil in saucepan over medium heat. Add beans and carrot; season with salt and cook 10 minutes.

■ Remove pan from heat and place under cold running water for 3 minutes. Drain vegetables and set aside.

■ Bring ½ cup (125 mL) salted water to boil in saucepan over medium heat. Add peas and cook 4 minutes.

■ Add yellow summer squash and pepper; continue cooking. As soon as vegetables are cooked, place saucepan under cold running water for 3 minutes. Drain well.

■ Heat butter in saucepan over medium heat. Add garlic, tarragon and all vegetables. Mix and season with salt, pepper and lemon juice. Simmer 4 minutes, then serve.

1 SERVING:	52 CALORIES	7 g CARBOHYDRATE	2 g PROTEIN
	2 g FAT	4.4 g FIBER	

OVEN-BAKED EGGPLANT AND POTATO CASSEROLE
(SERVES 4 TO 6)

1	large eggplant, peeled and diced	1
3	large potatoes, peeled, each cut in 3 and boiled	3
¼ cup	milk, heated	50 mL
1 tbsp	butter	15 mL
1 tbsp	olive oil	15 mL
1	onion, finely chopped	1
1	garlic clove, smashed and chopped	1
28-oz	can tomatoes, drained and chopped	796-mL
½ tsp	oregano	2 mL
4 tbsp	grated Gruyère cheese	60 mL
	pinch of nutmeg	
	salt and white pepper	
	coarse sea salt	

■ Place diced eggplant in bowl and sprinkle with coarse sea salt. Let stand 1 hour at room temperature. Rinse eggplant, drain very well and set aside.

■ Force boiled potatoes through fine sieve into bowl. Add milk, butter, salt, white pepper and nutmeg. Mix well and keep hot.

■ Heat oil in frying pan over medium heat. Add onion and cook 3 minutes. Stir in garlic and cook 2 minutes.

■ Add eggplant and season with salt and pepper. Cook 20 minutes over medium heat.

■ Mix in tomatoes and oregano; continue cooking 20 minutes. Season to taste.

■ Preheat oven to 350 °F (180 °C).

■ Spread eggplant mixture in bottom of buttered baking dish. Cover with layer of mashed potatoes. If desired, use a pastry bag with a star nozzle.

■ Top with cheese and cook 25 minutes in oven.

1 SERVING:	178 CALORIES	26 g CARBOHYDRATE	5 g PROTEIN
	6 g FAT	3.0 g FIBER	

Oven-Baked Eggplant
and Potato Casserole

SWEET POTATOES FROM THE CAROLINAS
(SERVES 4)

1 tbsp	olive oil	15 mL
12	dry shallots, peeled	12
4	sweet potatoes, peeled and cubed	4
1 tbsp	chopped fresh parsley	15 mL
	salt and pepper	

■ Heat oil in saucepan over medium heat. Add shallots and sweet potatoes; season well. Cover and cook 18 to 30 minutes, stirring 3 to 4 times.

■ When vegetables are cooked, sprinkle with parsley and serve.

Note: The sweet potatoes will stick to the bottom of the saucepan if not stirred frequently.

1 SERVING:	193 CALORIES	38 g CARBOHYDRATE	4 g PROTEIN
	3 g FAT	2.6 g FIBER	

SCALLOPED POTATOES WITH WHITE SAUCE

(SERVES 4)

4	large potatoes, peeled and placed in cold water for 1 hour	4
2½ cups	light white sauce	625 mL
	salt and freshly ground pepper	

■ Preheat oven to 350 °F (180 °C).

■ Dry off potatoes and slice ⅓ in (0.75 cm) thick. Arrange potato slices in layers in buttered baking dish. Season generously between each layer.

■ Pour white sauce over potatoes. Cook 1 hour 30 minutes in oven. Do not cover.

1 SERVING: 316 CALORIES 39 g CARBOHYDRATE 8 g PROTEIN
14 g FAT 1.4 g FIBER

VEGETABLE-STUFFED BAKED EGGPLANT
(SERVES 4)

2	large eggplants	2
2 tbsp	olive oil	30 mL
2	red onions, chopped	2
2	garlic cloves, smashed and chopped	2
1	yellow summer squash, chopped	1
1 tbsp	chopped fresh parsley	15 mL
1 tsp	thyme	5 mL
1 tbsp	oregano	15 mL
1 tbsp	chopped green chili pepper	15 mL
28-oz	can tomatoes, drained and chopped	796-mL
1 cup	grated Gruyère cheese	250 mL
	coarse sea salt	
	salt and pepper	

■ Slice eggplants in half lengthwise. Sprinkle coarse salt over cut sides and let stand 2 hours at room temperature. Rinse under cold water, drain well and pat dry.

■ Use spoon to remove eggplant flesh, leaving enough to support shell. Chop flesh.

■ Heat oil in sauté pan over medium heat. Add onions and garlic; cook 4 minutes.

■ Add chopped eggplant flesh. Season with salt and pepper; continue cooking 15 minutes.

■ Add summer squash, all seasonings and chili pepper. Cook 15 minutes, still over medium heat.

■ Mix in tomatoes and correct seasoning. Cook 5 minutes.

■ Add 4 tbsp (60 mL) of cheese and cook 5 minutes.

■ Preheat oven to 375 °F (190 °C).

■ Fill eggplant shells with stuffing. Cook 20 minutes in oven. Divide remaining cheese over eggplant halves and continue baking 10 minutes.

1 SERVING:	228 CALORIES	17 g CARBOHYDRATE	9 g PROTEIN
	14 g FAT	4.5 g FIBER	

Sprinkle coarse salt over cut sides of eggplant halves and let stand 2 hours at room temperature.

Use spoon to remove most of eggplant flesh. Leave enough flesh to support shell.

Add chopped eggplant to cooking onions and garlic. Cook 15 minutes.

Add summer squash, all seasonings and chili pepper. Continue cooking 15 minutes.

Mix in tomatoes, correct seasoning and cook 5 minutes.

Fill eggplant shells with stuffing.

PURÉE OF CAULIFLOWER

(SERVES 4 TO 6)

1	small cauliflower	1	
1½ cups	mashed potatoes, hot	375 mL	
3 tbsp	butter	45 mL	
2 tbsp	heavy cream	30 mL	
	salt and pepper		

■ Remove and discard outer leaves from cauliflower. Wash cauliflower and cook whole, core-side-down, in salted, boiling water. Cook about 15 minutes, depending on size.

■ Remove cauliflower from saucepan and drain well. Divide into large florets and force through sieve into bowl.

■ Return puréed cauliflower to saucepan and cook 3 minutes over very low heat.

■ Add mashed potatoes, butter and cream. Season well and mix. Serve.

1 SERVING: 272 CALORIES   29 g CARBOHYDRATE   3 g PROTEIN
16 g FAT   2.0 g FIBER

PEAS, MUSHROOMS AND SHALLOTS
(SERVES 4)

3 lbs	fresh green peas	1.4 kg
1 tbsp	butter	15 mL
½ lb	dry shallots, peeled and quartered	250 g
½ lb	mushroom caps, quartered	250 g
1 tbsp	chopped fresh parsley	15 mL
1 tsp	chopped fresh basil	5 mL
	salt and pepper	

■ Cook peas in salted, boiling water 8 minutes. Do not cover. Drain and place peas under cold, running water. Drain again and set aside.

■ Melt butter in sauté pan. Add shallots and cook 4 minutes over medium heat.

■ Add mushrooms and season well. Continue cooking 4 minutes.

■ Mix in parsley, basil, salt and pepper. Add green peas and cook 4 minutes over low heat.

■ Serve with a roast or grilled meat.

1 SERVING:	243 CALORIES	40 g CARBOHYDRATE	12 g PROTEIN
	4 g FAT	19.8 g FIBER	

FRESH GREEN BEANS WITH SOUR CREAM SAUCE
(SERVES 4)

1 lb	fresh green beans, washed and pared	500 g
2 tbsp	butter	30 mL
3 tbsp	chopped onion	45 mL
1 tsp	vinegar	5 mL
1 tsp	sugar	5 mL
2 tbsp	flour	30 mL
1 cup	cooking liquid from beans	250 mL
½ cup	sour cream	125 mL
	salt, pepper, paprika	

■ Cook beans 10 to 12 minutes in salted, boiling water. Do not cover. When cooked, remove 1 cup (250 mL) of cooking liquid and set aside. Cool saucepan under cold running water, then drain beans and set aside.

■ Heat butter in saucepan over medium heat. Add onion and cook 3 minutes over low heat.

■ Add vinegar and sugar; cook 1 minute over medium heat.

■ Mix in flour and continue cooking 1 minute.

■ Add reserved cooking liquid. Season with salt and pepper and cook 7 minutes over low heat.

■ Remove pan from heat and stir in sour cream. Sprinkle with paprika. Add beans, mix gently and let simmer 3 minutes over low heat. Serve.

1 SERVING: 171 CALORIES   18 g CARBOHYDRATE   4 g PROTEIN
9 g FAT   9.1 g FIBER

BRAISED ENDIVES

(SERVES 4)

8	endives, washed	8	
3 tbsp	butter	45 mL	
1 tsp	brown sugar	5 mL	
½ cup	dry white wine	125 mL	
2 tbsp	chopped fresh parsley	30 mL	
	juice 1 lemon		
	salt and pepper		

■ Preheat oven to 350 °F (180 °C).

■ Slit endives lengthwise leaving about 1 in (2.5 cm) uncut at base. Wash in plenty of cold water and dry well.

■ Grease baking dish with a bit of the butter. Add endives and sprinkle with brown sugar; season well. Squeeze in lemon juice, add wine and cover with foil; bake 45 minutes.

■ Remove cover and continue cooking endives 15 minutes.

■ Transfer endives to heated serving platter. Set aside 3 tbsp (45 mL) of endive cooking liquid.

■ Melt remaining butter in small saucepan. Add parsley and reserved cooking liquid. Mix well, pour over endives and serve.

1 SERVING:	156 CALORIES	10 g CARBOHYDRATE	4 g PROTEIN
	9 g FAT	2.0 g FIBER	

POTATOES ANNA
(SERVES 4 TO 6)

5	large potatoes, peeled and sliced	5
¼ cup	clarified butter*	50 mL
	salt and pepper	

■ Soak potato slices in cold water for 18 minutes. Drain and dry slices using clean cloth.

■ Preheat oven to 400 °F (200 °C).

■ Generously butter a cast iron frying pan. Beginning at outside edge of pan, arrange potato slices in an overlapping circle until bottom is covered. Brush slices with clarified butter and season.

■ Make a second circle of potatoes using same technique. Be sure that slices also overlap those of first circle. Brush with clarified butter and season.

■ Repeat to use all potato slices. Be sure to brush with butter and season between circles.

■ Use a spatula to press potatoes down. Place sheet of waxed paper on potatoes and cover pan. Cook 3 minutes over medium heat.

■ Transfer pan to oven and cook 40 minutes.

■ Unmold upside-down and serve. Garnish with chopped fresh parsley, if desired.

*To clarify butter, melt over low heat, skim off foam and pour off liquid butter. Discard sediments.

1 SERVING:	178 CALORIES	27 g CARBOHYDRATE	2 g PROTEIN
	7 g FAT	1.4 g FIBER	

CHEESE SAUCE

(SERVES 4 TO 6)

4 tbsp	butter	60 mL
1	small onion, chopped	1
4 tbsp	flour	60 mL
3 cups	milk, heated	750 mL
¼ tsp	nutmeg	1 mL
⅓ cup	grated Gruyère or Parmesan cheese	75 mL
	pinch cayenne pepper	
	salt and white pepper	

■ Heat butter in heavy-bottomed saucepan over medium heat. Add onion and cook 2 minutes.

■ Add flour and mix well. Cook 2 minutes over low heat.

■ Pour in half of milk and mix well to incorporate. Add remaining milk and mix again. Add all seasonings and cook sauce 12 minutes over low heat, whisking occasionally.

■ Mix in cheese and correct seasoning. Cook 3 minutes over low heat.

1 SERVING: 231 CALORIES   18 g CARBOHYDRATE   8 g PROTEIN
14 g FAT   0 g FIBER

MUSHROOM-STUFFED ZUCCHINI BOATS

(SERVES 4)

4	large zucchini, halved lengthwise	4
4	slices French bread, crusts removed	4
¼ cup	milk	50 mL
2 tbsp	olive oil	30 mL
½ lb	fresh mushrooms, cleaned and chopped	250 g
1	garlic clove, smashed and chopped	1
1	large onion, sliced and cooked	1
¼ cup	grated Gruyère cheese salt and pepper	50 mL

■ Preheat oven to 375 °F (190 °C).

■ Use spoon to hollow out zucchini shells. Chop zucchini flesh and set aside.

■ Place zucchini shells in saucepan containing salted, boiling water. Cook 4 minutes. Place saucepan under cold, running water to stop cooking process. Drain and dry zucchini shells. Arrange in greased baking dish.

■ Soak bread in milk for 3 minutes. Remove bread from bowl and squeeze out excess milk. Set bread aside.

■ Heat olive oil in frying pan over high heat. Add chopped zucchini flesh and season well. Cook 6 minutes over medium heat.

■ Add mushrooms and garlic; season and cook 7 minutes.

■ Mix in bread, then add cooked onion. Mix again and cook 3 minutes.

■ Divide mixture between zucchini shells and sprinkle with cheese. Cook 18 minutes in oven. Serve.

1 SERVING: 184 CALORIES 20 g CARBOHYDRATE 6 g PROTEIN
9 g FAT 4.7 g FIBER

CELERY HEARTS WITH FRENCH VINAIGRETTE

(SERVES 4 TO 6)

8	celery hearts, white stalks only	8
3 tbsp	wine vinegar	45 mL
1 tbsp	Dijon mustard	15 mL
2 tbsp	dry shallot, peeled and chopped	30 mL
9 tbsp	olive oil	135 mL
1 tbsp	chopped fresh parsley	15 mL
	juice of 1 lemon	
	salt and pepper	

■ Cook celery hearts in salted, boiling water for 20 minutes. Drain well and transfer to serving platter.

■ Place vinegar, mustard and shallot in bowl. Season with salt and pepper. Add oil in thin stream, mixing constantly with whisk.

■ Season celery hearts and sprinkle with lemon juice.

■ Pour vinaigrette over celery hearts while still warm. Sprinkle with parsley and serve.

1 SERVING:	275 CALORIES	11 g CARBOHYDRATE	2 g PROTEIN
	25 g FAT	4.4 g FIBER	

BAKED LEEKS AND MASHED POTATOES
(SERVES 4 TO 6)

5	leeks, white part only	5
¼ tsp	cayenne pepper	1 mL
1 tbsp	chopped fresh parsley	15 mL
5	large cooked potatoes, mashed	5
3 tbsp	melted butter	45 mL
¼ cup	grated Gruyère cheese (optional)	50 mL
	juice of ½ lemon	
	salt and white pepper	

■ Refer to the technique for the preparation of the leeks. Rinse under plenty of cold water, parting leaves to release dirt and sand.

■ Add leeks to saucepan containing boiling water. Add lemon juice and pinch of salt; cook 30 minutes over medium heat.

■ Preheat oven to 375 °F (190 °C).

■ Remove saucepan from heat and briefly place under cold, running water to stop cooking process. Drain leeks well, drying off excess water with paper towel. Squeeze out any remaining liquid from leeks.

■ Slice leeks and place in bottom of medium-size buttered baking dish. Season with salt and pepper.

■ Stir cayenne pepper and parsley into mashed potatoes. Spread potatoes over leeks and top with melted butter. Sprinkle with cheese.

■ Cook 30 minutes in oven. Change oven setting to broil and brown several minutes before serving.

1 SERVING:	233 CALORIES	37 g CARBOHYDRATE	4 g PROTEIN
	8 g FAT	1.4 g FIBER	

Trim off green leaves and use white part of leek. Cut stalk in half lengthwise to within 1 in (2.5 cm) of base.

Turn leek a quarter turn and repeat cut. This technique allows leaves to be spread for washing.

Cook washed leeks in salted, boiling water with lemon juice.

Slice hot leeks.

Place leeks in buttered baking dish and season well.

Spread mashed potatoes over leeks and top with melted butter. Sprinkle with cheese.

FANCY BAKED POTATOES
(SERVES 4)

7	large baking potatoes	7
3 tbsp	butter	45 mL
1	egg yolk	1
4 tbsp	whipped cream	60 mL
	grated Gruyère cheese	
	salt, pepper, nutmeg	

■ Preheat oven to 400 °F (200 °C).

■ Prick potatoes with fork to allow steam to escape during cooking. Bake about 1 hour in oven, depending on size.

■ When cooked, remove potatoes from oven. Cutting lengthwise, slice off thin top from each potato. Spoon out potato flesh, leaving enough to support shell. Set 4 shells aside.

■ Force potato flesh through fine sieve into bowl. Add butter, egg and nutmeg; season well. Mix until combined.

■ Incorporate whipped cream and stuff 4 potato shells using pastry bag. Sprinkle tops with cheese. Broil 5 minutes in oven.

1 SERVING:	338 CALORIES	47 g CARBOHYDRATE	6 g PROTEIN
	14 g FAT	2.4 g FIBER	

WHITE RADISH WITH HONEY

(SERVES 4)

1	Chinese white radish, peeled	1	
1 tbsp	butter	15 mL	
2 tbsp	chopped fresh ginger	30 mL	
½ cup	chicken stock, heated	125 mL	
1 tbsp	honey	15 mL	
1 tbsp	chopped fresh parsley	15 mL	
½ tsp	cornstarch	2 mL	
2 tbsp	cold water	30 mL	
	salt and pepper		

■ Slice radish into 1-in (2.5-cm) thick rings. Cut rings into quarters. Place radish in saucepan containing salted, boiling water. Cover and cook 18 to 20 minutes. Drain and set aside.

■ Heat butter in sauté pan over medium heat. Add radish and ginger; season well. Cook 4 minutes.

■ Pour in chicken stock and bring to boil. Cook 3 to 4 minutes.

■ Mix in honey and parsley; cook 3 minutes.

■ Dissolve cornstarch in cold water; stir into radish mixture. Cook 2 minutes, then serve.

1 SERVING:	60 CALORIES	8 g CARBOHYDRATE	0 g PROTEIN
	3 g FAT	0 g FIBER	

TOMATO STEW FOR STUFFING
(SERVES 6 TO 8)

1 tbsp	olive oil	15 mL
1	onion, finely chopped	1
2	garlic cloves, smashed and chopped	2
1	red pepper, seeded and finely chopped	1
2 tsp	finely chopped hot green chili pepper	10 mL
28-oz	can tomatoes, drained and chopped	796-mL
2 tbsp	tomato paste	30 mL
½ tsp	basil	2 mL
½ tsp	oregano	2 mL
	few drops Worcestershire sauce	
	salt and pepper	

■ Heat oil in sauté pan over medium heat. Add onion and garlic; cook 2 minutes over low heat.

■ Add red pepper, chili pepper, tomatoes, tomato paste and herbs. Add Worcestershire sauce, mix well and season with salt and pepper. Bring to boil and cook 30 minutes over low heat. Stir 2 to 3 times during cooking process.

■ Transfer contents of pan to bowl. Let cool, then cover with sheet of plastic wrap. Will keep up to 3 days in refrigerator.

■ Use tomato stew to stuff summer squash or other vegetables.

1 SERVING:	53 CALORIES	8 g CARBOHYDRATE	1 g PROTEIN
	2 g FAT	1.3 g FIBER	

MUSHROOM-STUFFED ARTICHOKE BOTTOMS

(SERVES 4)

2 tbsp	butter	30 mL
2	dry shallots, peeled and chopped	2
¾ lb	fresh mushrooms, cleaned and chopped	375 g
3 tbsp	chopped pimento	45 mL
½ tsp	curry powder	2 mL
¼ cup	heavy cream	50 mL
1 tbsp	chopped fresh parsley	15 mL
1 cup	grated Gruyère cheese	250 mL
8	canned artichoke bottoms, heated	8
	salt and pepper	

■ Preheat oven to 400 °F (200 °C).

■ Heat butter in ovenproof sauté pan over medium heat. Add shallots and mushrooms; season well. Cook 8 minutes over high heat.

■ Stir in pimento and curry powder; continue cooking 3 minutes.

■ Incorporate cream and parsley; cook 3 minutes. Add half of cheese, mix well and cook 1 minute.

■ Stuff artichoke bottoms with mixture and top with remaining cheese. Brown 12 minutes in oven.

1 SERVING:	251 CALORIES	18 g CARBOHYDRATE	11 g PROTEIN
	15 g FAT	2.7 g FIBER	

BAKED TOMATOES WITH SAVORY STUFFING

(SERVES 4)

2	slices white bread, crusts removed	2
⅓ cup	milk	75 mL
4	medium tomatoes	4
1 tbsp	olive oil	15 mL
2	dry shallots, peeled and finely chopped	2
2	garlic cloves, smashed and chopped	2
20	mushroom caps, cleaned and chopped	20
1 tbsp	chopped fresh parsley	15 mL
1 tbsp	chopped green chili pepper	15 mL
½ tsp	oregano	2 mL
½ tsp	thyme	2 mL
4 tbsp	grated Parmesan cheese	60 mL
	salt and pepper	

■ Place bread in bowl, add milk and soak 15 minutes.

■ Preheat oven to 350 °F (180 °C).

■ Meanwhile, core tomatoes. Turn tomatoes upside-down. Use paring knife to cut out stem, angling knife towards bottom of tomato. Remove stem and scoop out ¾ of flesh using small spoon. Be careful not to pierce skin.

■ Chop flesh and season insides of tomatoes. Set aside.

■ Heat oil in sauté pan over high heat. Add shallots, garlic, mushrooms, parsley and chili pepper. Cook 4 minutes.

■ Add chopped tomato flesh and season well. Add oregano and thyme; mix and cook 4 minutes.

■ Squeeze bread to remove excess milk. Add bread to mixture in sauté pan. Cook 2 minutes, stirring constantly.

■ Stuff tomatoes set in muffin tins, and cook 15 minutes in oven.

■ Sprinkle stuffing with cheese and cook another 5 minutes in oven.

1 SERVING:	167 CALORIES	22 g CARBOHYDRATE	7 g PROTEIN
	6 g FAT	5.0 g FIBER	

Place bread in bowl, add milk and soak 15 minutes.

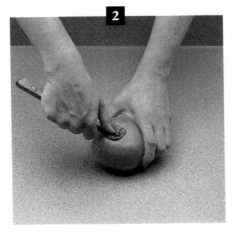

Core tomatoes.

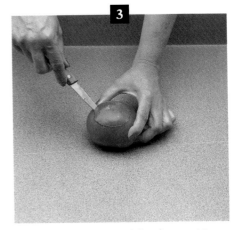

Turn tomatoes upside-down. Use paring knife to cut out stem, angling knife towards bottom of tomato.

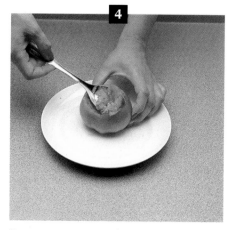

Remove stem and scoop out ¾ of flesh using small spoon. Be careful not to pierce skin.

Place hollowed tomato shells in muffin pan.

Stuff, then bake tomatoes.

ROASTED GARLIC PURÉE
(SERVES 4 TO 6)

10	garlic cloves, unpeeled	10
2 tbsp	olive oil	30 mL

■ Preheat oven to 375 °F (190 °C).

■ Wrap garlic cloves in aluminum foil package and cook 1 hour in oven.

■ Remove cloves from foil and peel.

■ Purée garlic in food processor. Add oil and blend until incorporated.

■ Store garlic purée in glass jar with tight-fitting lid. Refrigerate.

■ Use in the preparation of sauces or with meats.

1 SERVING:	53 CALORIES	2 g CARBOHYDRATE	0 g PROTEIN
	5 g FAT	0 g FIBER	

KIDNEY BEANS NEW ORLEANS
(SERVES 4 TO 6)

¾ lb	dried kidney beans	375 g
4	smoked ham hocks	4
1 tsp	thyme	5 mL
3	bay leaves	3
2 tsp	black pepper	10 mL
1 tsp	paprika	5 mL
½ tsp	oregano	2 mL
½ tsp	basil	2 mL
½ tsp	cayenne pepper	2 mL
2	garlic cloves, blanched, peeled and puréed	2
2	celery stalks, diced large	2
2	onions, diced	2
1 lb	Italian sausage, cut on the bias in 1-in (2.5-cm) pieces	500 g
1	green pepper, cubed	1
	few drops Tabasco sauce	
	salt	

■ Place beans in large bowl and cover completely with water. Let stand overnight.

■ Place smoked ham hocks in large saucepan and cover with water. Bring to boil. Add seasonings and garlic. Partly cover and cook 1½ hours over low heat. The ham hocks should be well cooked. Remove from saucepan and set aside. Leave water in pan.

■ Drain beans and add to hot water in saucepan. Add celery and onions. Add more water if liquid does not cover beans completely. Mix and partly cover; cook 1 hour over medium heat, stirring occasionally.

■ Add sausages, Tabasco sauce and green pepper to saucepan. Mix, partly cover and continue cooking 15 minutes.

■ Return ham hocks to saucepan with beans. At this point most of the water should be evaporated. Partly cover and cook 15 minutes.

■ Serve over rice.

1 SERVING:	488 CALORIES	22 g CARBOHYDRATE	32 g PROTEIN
	30 g FAT	7.4 g FIBER	

Place smoked ham hocks in large saucepan and cover with water. Bring to boil.

Add seasonings and garlic. Partly cover and cook over low heat.

Remove ham hocks from saucepan and set aside.

Add drained kidney beans, celery and onions to ham cooking liquid in saucepan. Cook 1 hour.

Add sausages, Tabasco sauce and green pepper to saucepan. Continue cooking.

Return ham hocks to saucepan.

PORK BRAISED WITH ZUCCHINI
(SERVES 4 TO 6)

½ tsp	white pepper	2 mL
½ tsp	black pepper	2 mL
1 tsp	oregano	5 mL
½ tsp	thyme	2 mL
½ tsp	cayenne pepper	2 mL
½ tsp	garlic powder	2 mL
4 tbsp	flour	60 mL
2 lbs	lean boneless pork, cubed	900 g
3 tbsp	butter	45 mL
2	onions, diced	2
1	celery stalk, diced	1
3 cups	chicken stock, heated	750 mL
1	zucchini, diced	1
1 cup	cooked kidney beans	250 mL
	salt	

■ Preheat oven to 325 °F (160 °C).

■ Mix spices and herbs together; stir into flour. Dredge cubes of pork in flour mixture.

■ Heat butter in ovenproof casserole over medium heat. Add pork and sear on all sides for 10 minutes or just until flour sticks to bottom of casserole. Season with salt.

■ Add onions and celery; mix well. Cook 8 minutes over medium heat.

■ Incorporate chicken stock. Season with salt and bring to boil. Cover and cook 2 hours in oven.

■ Fifteen minutes before end of cooking, add zucchini and beans. Mix, cover and resume cooking.

■ Serve with mashed potatoes.

1 SERVING:	491 CALORIES	18 g CARBOHYDRATE	42 g PROTEIN
	28 g FAT	4.6 g FIBER	

LOUISVILLE LENTILS

(SERVES 4)

1 tsp	olive oil	5 mL
2	carrots, pared and diced	2
1	celery stalk, diced	1
4	dry shallots, peeled and halved	4
1	onion, chopped	1
1½ cups	dried lentils, washed and drained	375 mL
1 tsp	Cajun seasoning for beans and rice	5 mL
¼ tsp	cayenne pepper	1 mL
1	chorizo sausage, sliced	1
	salt and pepper	

■ Heat oil in sauté pan over medium heat. Add vegetables and cook 6 minutes over low heat.

■ Add lentils and spices. Mix and cover with water. Bring to boil and partly cover. Cook 1 hour 15 minutes over low heat.

■ Add sausage. Season with salt and pepper. Partly cover and continue cooking 15 minutes. Serve.

1 SERVING:	159 CALORIES	14 g CARBOHYDRATE	8 g PROTEIN
	8 g FAT	3.8 g FIBER	

CHICKEN WINGS BATON ROUGE

(SERVES 4 TO 6)

Marinade

24	chicken wings	24
1 cup	beer	250 mL
1 cup	chicken stock	250 mL
1 tbsp	olive oil	15 mL
4	garlic cloves, blanched, peeled and puréed	4
2 tsp	Worcestershire sauce	10 mL
1 tsp	hot pepper sauce	5 mL

Seasoning

4 tbsp	butter	60 mL
1 tsp	cayenne pepper	5 mL
1 tsp	black pepper	5 mL
1 tsp	oregano	5 mL
1 tsp	basil	5 mL
1 tsp	thyme	5 mL
1 tsp	rosemary	5 mL
	salt	

■ Remove tips from chicken wings. Place wings in bowl and mix in marinade ingredients. Marinate 2 hours in refrigerator.

■ Preheat oven to 450 °F (230 °C).

■ Remove wings from marinade.

■ Melt butter in cast iron pan over medium heat. Add seasonings and chicken wings. Mix well and cook 7 minutes over medium heat. Stir frequently.

■ Transfer pan to oven and finish cooking 10 minutes. Serve.

1 SERVING:	342 CALORIES	4 g CARBOHYDRATE	32 g PROTEIN
	20 g FAT	0 g FIBER	

Cut off tips from chicken wings.

Place wings in bowl.

Add marinade ingredients and refrigerate.

Melt butter in cast iron pan.

Add spices and herbs.

Add chicken wings.

NAVY BEANS CAJUN-STYLE

(SERVES 4 TO 6)

1 tsp	olive oil	5 mL
3	dry shallots, peeled and diced	3
1	celery stalk, diced	1
2	carrots, pared and diced	2
2	garlic cloves, smashed and chopped	2
1¼ cups	dried navy beans, soaked 8 hours in cold water	300 mL
2 tsp	Cajun bean seasoning	10 mL
¼ tsp	cayenne pepper	1 mL
½ tsp	sage	2 mL
½ tsp	thyme	2 mL
1 tsp	oregano	5 mL
	salt and pepper	

■ Heat oil in saucepan over medium heat. Add vegetables and garlic; stir, cover and cook 6 minutes.

■ Add drained beans and mix. Incorporate remaining ingredients. Gradually pour in enough cold water to cover beans by 2½ in (6.5 cm). Season generously with salt and pepper.

■ Cook, partly covered, 2½ hours over medium heat. Stir several times, adding more water as needed.

■ Serve with fresh bread.

1 SERVING:	65 CALORIES	11 g CARBOHYDRATE	3 g PROTEIN
	1 g FAT	2.4 g FIBER	

BEANS FROM THE LATIN QUARTER

(SERVES 4 TO 6)

1½ cups	dried navy beans	375 mL
2 tbsp	butter	30 mL
2	onions, diced	2
1	celery stalk, diced	1
3	garlic cloves, smashed and chopped	3
½ tsp	black pepper	2 mL
¼ tsp	cayenne pepper	1 mL
1 tsp	taco seasoning	5 mL
1 tsp	basil	5 mL
½ tsp	thyme	2 mL
	salt	

■ Soak beans in cold water for 8 hours. Drain and set aside.

■ Heat butter in large saucepan over medium heat. Add onions and celery. Mix and cook 6 minutes. Add garlic and cook 2 minutes.

■ Add seasonings and beans. Mix well and correct seasoning with salt. Add enough water to cover beans by 2 in (5 cm). Bring to boil. Partly cover and cook beans 2½ hours over medium heat. Stir occasionally and add more water if needed.

■ Serve with fresh bread or garlic bread.

1 SERVING:	98 CALORIES	10 g CARBOHYDRATE	4 g PROTEIN
	5 g FAT	2.7 g FIBER	

PEPPER MEAT LOAF

(SERVES 6 TO 8)

1 tbsp	olive oil	15 mL
1	onion, finely chopped	1
½	celery stalk, diced	½
3	dry shallots, peeled and chopped	3
1½	red peppers, chopped	1½
2	garlic cloves, smashed and chopped	2
2 tbsp	grated lemon rind	30 mL
1 tsp	Worcestershire sauce	5 mL
1 lb	lean ground beef	500 g
¾ lb	ground veal	375 g
½ lb	lean ground pork	250 g
2	eggs	2
½ tsp	thyme	2 mL
1 tsp	basil	5 mL
¼ tsp	cayenne pepper	1 mL
½ tsp	black pepper	2 mL
¼ tsp	ground cloves	1 mL
¼ tsp	chili powder	1 mL
½ cup	fine white breadcrumbs	125 mL
3 tbsp	evaporated milk	45 mL
3 tbsp	chili sauce	45 mL
	salt	

■ Heat oil in sauté pan over medium heat. Add vegetables and garlic; mix and cook 6 minutes over low heat. Stir in lemon rind and Worcestershire sauce; continue cooking 2 minutes. Remove vegetables from pan and set aside.

■ Preheat oven to 350 °F (180 °C).

■ Place all ground meats in food processor. Season with salt and blend 15 seconds. Add eggs and blend 1 minute.

■ Mix seasonings together and add to meat in food processor. Add breadcrumbs, evaporated milk and chili sauce. Blend 15 seconds.

■ Transfer mixture to bowl. Add cooked vegetables and mix with spoon. Press mixture into meat loaf baking pan.

■ Set mold in roasting pan containing 1 in (2.5 cm) of water. Place in oven and cook 50 minutes, uncovered.

■ Increase heat to 400 °F (200 °C) and continue cooking 6 minutes.

■ Slice and serve with fresh vegetables and a spicy sauce.

1 SERVING:	381 CALORIES	11 g CARBOHYDRATE	37 g PROTEIN
	21 g FAT	1.0 g FIBER	

Pepper Meat Loaf

PORK TENDERLOIN WITH APPLE STUFFING

(SERVES 4)

2	medium pork tenderloins, trimmed of fat	2
2	garlic cloves, blanched, peeled and puréed	2
⅓ tsp	nutmeg	1.5 mL
½ tsp	black pepper	2 mL
¼ tsp	dry mustard	1 mL
¼ tsp	thyme	1 mL
⅓ tsp	cayenne pepper	1.5 mL
1½ tbsp	olive oil	25 mL
1	small onion, chopped	1
2	green onions, chopped	2
½	yellow pepper, chopped	½
¼ lb	lean ground pork	125 g

■ Preheat oven to 350 °F (180 °C).

■ Slice pork tenderloins open lengthwise without cutting all the way through. Place open tenderloins between 2 sheets of waxed paper. Flatten with mallet and set tenderloins aside.

■ Mix garlic with dry spices in small bowl; set aside.

■ Heat half of oil in cast iron pan over medium heat. Add onions and yellow pepper; cook 4 minutes over low heat.

■ Add ground pork and half of dry spice mixture. Mix well and cook 5 minutes over low heat.

(continued)

Slice pork tenderloins open lengthwise without cutting all the way through: about ¾ of their width.

Cook onions and yellow pepper in hot oil.

Add ground pork and half of dry spice mixture. Cook 5 minutes.

1	apple, peeled and chopped	1	
2 tbsp	honey	30 mL	
3	slices white bread, crusts removed and bread soaked in milk	3	
1½ cups	chicken stock, heated	375 g	
1 tsp	cornstarch	5 mL	
2 tbsp	cold water	30 mL	
1 tbsp	chopped fresh parsley salt and pepper	15 mL	

■ Add apple and honey. Stir and continue cooking 5 minutes.

■ Squeeze excess liquid from bread. Add bread to pan and mix well; cook 2 minutes.

■ Spread stuffing over flattened tenderloins; roll and tie.

■ Heat remaining oil in cast iron pan over medium heat. Add stuffed tenderloins and sear on all sides. Sprinkle in remaining dry spice mixture. Transfer pan to oven and finish cooking 25 to 30 minutes.

■ When cooked, remove pork from pan and set aside on hot serving platter. Place cast iron pan on stove over high heat. Pour in chicken stock; stir and cook 3 minutes.

■ Dissolve cornstarch in cold water; incorporate into sauce and cook 1 minute. Sprinkle in chopped parsley.

■ Slice tenderloins and serve with sauce.

1 SERVING:	463 CALORIES	29 g CARBOHYDRATE	49 g PROTEIN
	17 g FAT	2.0 g FIBER	

Add apple and honey. Continue cooking 5 minutes.

Add bread. Cook 2 minutes.

Stuff tenderloins.

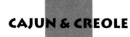

CURRY-FLAVORED CHICKEN
(SERVES 4)

3½-lb	chicken, cleaned	1.6-kg	
2 tbsp	butter	30 mL	
1	large onion, diced small	1	
1	garlic clove, smashed and chopped	1	
2 tbsp	curry powder	30 mL	
1 cup	evaporated milk	250 mL	
1 tbsp	tomato paste	15 mL	
¼ cup	chicken stock, heated	50 mL	
	salt and pepper		

- Preheat oven to 350 °F (180 °C).

- Cut chicken into 8 pieces. Remove skin. Set chicken aside.

- Heat butter in ovenproof sauté pan over medium heat. Add onion and garlic; cook 4 minutes over low heat. Add curry powder, mix and cook 5 minutes over low heat.

- Add chicken pieces. Season with salt and pepper. Cook 12 minutes to brown chicken, turning pieces over twice during cooking. If needed, add more butter.

- Add remaining ingredients, mix and cover pan. Cook 20 minutes in oven.

- If desired, serve with fresh vegetables.

1 SERVING:	507 CALORIES	10 g CARBOHYDRATE	66 g PROTEIN
	23 g FAT	0 g FIBER	

VEGETABLE CHILI

(SERVES 4 TO 6)

1 tbsp	olive oil	15 mL
2	onions, chopped	2
1	celery stalk, sliced	1
3	green onions, chopped	3
3	garlic cloves, smashed and chopped	3
1	eggplant, peeled and diced large	1
1	carrot, peeled and sliced	1
1	zucchini, diced with skin	1
28-oz	can tomatoes, chopped with liquid	796-mL
2½ tbsp	chili powder	40 mL
1 tsp	cumin	5 mL
1 tbsp	oregano	15 mL
1 tbsp	basil	15 mL
½ tsp	black pepper	2 mL
½ tsp	cayenne pepper	2 mL
2½ cups	cooked kidney beans	625 mL
1	yellow pepper, diced large	1
1	red pepper, diced large	1
	pinch sugar	
	salt	

■ Heat oil in large saucepan over medium heat. Add onions, celery, green onions and garlic. Mix and cook 5 minutes.

■ Add eggplant. Season with salt and mix well. Cover and cook 15 minutes over medium heat, stirring occasionally.

■ Add carrot, zucchini and tomatoes with juice; mix well. Incorporate spices, herbs, pinch sugar and beans. Season with salt, partly cover and bring to boil. Cook 30 minutes over medium heat, stirring occasionally.

■ Mix in peppers, partly cover and continue cooking 20 minutes over medium heat.

---

1 SERVING: 207 CALORIES   35 g CARBOHYDRATE   10 g PROTEIN
            3 g FAT   12.2 g FIBER

CAJUN VEAL SHANKS
(SERVES 4)

½ tsp	black pepper	2 mL
½ tsp	paprika	2 mL
½ tsp	cayenne pepper	2 mL
1 tsp	basil	5 mL
½ tsp	thyme	2 mL
½ cup	flour	125 mL
6 lbs	veal shanks, cut crosswise 1 in (2.5 cm) thick	2.7 kg
3 tbsp	butter	45 mL
1	large onion, chopped	1
½	green pepper, diced	½
1	celery stalk, diced	1
3	garlic cloves, blanched, peeled and puréed	3
3 cups	veal or chicken stock, heated	750 mL
	salt and pepper	

- Preheat oven to 300 °F (150 °C).

- Mix dry spices and herbs together in small bowl.

- In separate bowl, place half of flour. Add half of spice mixture; mix together. Dredge veal shanks in flour mixture and set aside.

- Heat butter in cast iron pan over medium heat. Add veal shanks and sear both sides of meat.

- Add onion, green pepper, celery and garlic. Season with salt and pepper, mix and cook 5 minutes.

- Sprinkle remaining flour over veal and vegetables. Mix and turn shanks over. Cook another 5 minutes.

- Sprinkle in remaining spice mixture. Pour in veal stock, season with salt and bring to boil. Cover and cook 2 hours in oven or until veal shanks are very tender.

- If desired, serve over rice.

1 SERVING: 1201 CALORIES 17 g CARBOHYDRATE 146 g PROTEIN
61 g FAT 1.0 g FIBER

1

Add half of spice mixture to half of flour.

2

Dredge veal shanks in flour mixture.

3

Sear shanks in hot butter on both sides.

Add onion, green pepper, celery and garlic to pan.

Sprinkle in remaining flour.

Pour in stock.

CAJUN PORK CUTLETS

(SERVES 4)

¼ tsp	black pepper	1 mL
¼ tsp	paprika	1 mL
¼ tsp	cayenne pepper	1 mL
¼ tsp	powdered oregano	1 mL
¼ tsp	powdered thyme	1 mL
¼ tsp	ground ginger	1 mL
8	pork cutlets	8
2 tbsp	butter	30 mL
1	onion, sliced	1
1	green pepper, in thick strips	1
1	red pepper, in thick strips	1
2 tbsp	flour	30 mL
1½ cups	chicken stock, heated	375 mL
1 tsp	honey	5 mL
	salt	

■ Mix herbs and spices together. Rub half of mixture into meat.

■ Heat butter in large frying pan over medium heat. Add pork and cook 3 minutes on each side. Season with salt and remove from pan; set aside.

■ Add onion to hot pan and cook 3 minutes over medium heat. Add peppers and remaining spice mixture. Mix and cook 7 minutes.

■ Sprinkle in flour, mix well and cook 3 minutes.

■ Incorporate chicken stock and honey. Cook 5 minutes over low heat. Return pork to pan and simmer 2 minutes.

■ If desired, serve with steamed rice and broccoli.

1 SERVING:	597 CALORIES	9 g CARBOHYDRATE	57 g PROTEIN
	37 g FAT	1.0 g FIBER	

CHICKEN BREASTS WITH SOUR CREAM
(SERVES 4)

¼ tsp	cayenne pepper	1 mL
¼ tsp	black pepper	1 mL
¼ tsp	white pepper	1 mL
¼ tsp	paprika	1 mL
½ tsp	basil	2 mL
½ tsp	garlic powder	2 mL
¼ tsp	dry mustard	1 mL
4	boneless, skinless chicken breasts	4
2 tbsp	butter	30 mL
2	green onions, chopped	2
1½ cups	chicken stock, heated	375 mL
1 tbsp	cornstarch	15 mL
3 tbsp	cold water	45 mL
2 tbsp	sour cream	30 mL
	flour	
	salt	

■ Mix spices and herbs together. Dust chicken breasts in spice mixture and dredge with flour.

■ Heat butter in sauté pan over medium heat. Add chicken and cook 3 minutes. Season with salt, turn pieces over and cook 3 minutes.

■ Add green onions to pan and cook 1 minute. Pour in chicken stock and cook 6 minutes over low heat. Do not cover.

■ Remove chicken breasts and set aside on hot serving platter.

■ Place sauté pan over high heat and cook sauce 3 minutes.

■ Dissolve cornstarch in cold water; stir into sauce. Continue cooking 1 minute. Remove pan from heat and let stand 2 minutes.

■ Stir in sour cream. Serve chicken with sauce and potatoes.

1 SERVING:	246 CALORIES	9 g CARBOHYDRATE	30 g PROTEIN
	10 g FAT	0 g FIBER	

ROASTED LOIN OF PORK

(SERVES 4 TO 6)

2 tbsp	butter	30 mL
½ tsp	black pepper	2 mL
½ tsp	cayenne pepper	2 mL
½ tsp	thyme	2 mL
1 tsp	oregano	5 mL
½ tsp	dry mustard	2 mL
2	garlic cloves, blanched, peeled and puréed	2
4-lb	pork loin	1.8-kg
1 tbsp	olive oil	15 mL
1	celery stalk, diced medium	1
2	carrots, pared, diced medium	2
1	large onion, diced medium	1
1	red pepper, diced medium	1
3 tbsp	flour	45 mL
½ cup	pork or chicken stock, heated	125 mL
	salt and pepper	

- Preheat oven to 300 °F (150 °C).

- Heat butter in frying pan over medium heat. Add spices, herbs, mustard and garlic. Cook 1 minute.

- Using paring knife, make several small incisions in roast. Stuff slits in meat with spice mixture and spread the rest over surface of roast. Season meat with salt.

- Heat oil in roasting pan over medium heat. Add roast and surround with diced vegetables. Season with salt and pepper. Place in oven and cook 2 hours.

- Fifteen minutes before the end of cooking, increase oven heat to 425 °F (220 °C) to finish browning meat.

- Remove roast from pan and let stand 10 minutes.

- Meanwhile, place roasting pan on stove over medium heat. Sprinkle in flour, mix and cook 3 minutes. Incorporate stock and continue cooking 6 minutes. Strain sauce and serve with roast.

1 SERVING:	752 CALORIES	8 g CARBOHYDRATE	76 g PROTEIN
	46 g FAT	1.1 g FIBER	

Cook seasonings in hot butter.

Make small incisions in roast.

Stuff incisions with spice mixture and spread the rest over surface of roast.

Place meat in roasting pan surrounded with diced vegetables.

To make sauce, place roasting pan over medium heat. Sprinkle in flour.

Incorporate stock.

BROILED SWORDFISH
(SERVES 4)

4	swordfish steaks	4
1 tbsp	olive oil	15 mL
4	slices Cajun Butter (see page 193)	4
	lemon juice	
	salt and pepper	

■ Preheat oven to broil.

■ Brush both sides of each swordfish steak with oil. Place in oven and broil 4 minutes on each side. The time may vary depending on thickness of the steaks. Season during cooking.

■ To serve, place slice of Cajun Butter on each hot swordfish steak and sprinkle with lemon juice.

---

1 SERVING: 317 CALORIES   0 g CARBOHYDRATE   41 g PROTEIN
               17 g FAT   0 g FIBER

CARAMELIZED SWEET POTATOES
(SERVES 4 TO 6)

5	medium sweet potatoes	5
1 cup	brown sugar	250 mL
1 cup	water	250 mL
1 tsp	cinnamon	5 mL
3 tsbp	melted butter	45 mL
	juice of 1 lemon	
	salt and pepper	

■ Preheat oven to 350 °F (180 °C).

■ Peel potatoes. Cut in slices ½ in (1.2 cm) thick. Place in buttered baking dish; set aside.

■ Place sugar, water, cinnamon, and lemon juice in saucepan. Bring to boil; cook 4 minutes.

■ Add butter and continue cooking 2 minutes. Season with salt and pepper. Pour syrup over potatoes and cover baking dish with aluminum foil. Cook 35 to 45 minutes in oven.

---

1 SERVING: 425 CALORIES   84 g CARBOHYDRATE   2 g PROTEIN
               9 g FAT   2.6 g FIBER

RICE AND CHICKEN CASSEROLE

(SERVES 4)

4-lb	chicken, cleaned	1.8-kg
1 tbsp	olive oil	15 mL
1	large Spanish onion, cubed	1
2	garlic cloves, smashed and chopped	2
1 tbsp	chopped jalapeño pepper	15 mL
2 tbsp	chopped pimento	30 mL
28-oz	can tomatoes, drained and chopped	796-mL
1 cup	chicken stock, heated	250 mL
1 cup	rice, rinsed	250 mL
1	green pepper, sliced	1
	pinch cayenne pepper	
	salt and pepper	

■ Preheat oven to 350 °F (180 °C).

■ Cut chicken into 8 pieces and remove skin. Set chicken aside.

■ Heat oil in large ovenproof sauté pan over medium heat. Add chicken pieces and brown on all sides. Season with salt and pepper.

■ Add onion, garlic, jalapeño pepper and pimento. Mix and cook 3 minutes over medium heat. Add tomatoes and chicken stock. Sprinkle in cayenne pepper, season with salt and bring to boil.

■ Add rice, mix and bring to boil. Cover and cook 25 minutes in oven.

■ Remove cover and add green pepper. Season to taste. Continue cooking 3 minutes. Serve.

1 SERVING:	616 CALORIES	34 g CARBOHYDRATE	72 g PROTEIN
	21 g FAT	3.2 g FIBER	

JAMBALAYA
(SERVES 4 TO 6)

4	slices bacon, diced large	4
1	large onion, diced small	1
2	garlic cloves, smashed and chopped	2
4	tomatoes, peeled and chopped	4
½ tsp	fennel seed	2 mL
½ tsp	thyme	2 mL
1 cup	cooked rice	250 mL
1 cup	chicken stock, heated	250 mL
½ lb	cooked ham, in small pieces, ½ in (1.2 cm) thick	250 g
¾ lb	fresh shrimp, shelled and deveined	375 g
1	yellow pepper, cut in strips	1
1	green pepper, cut in strips	1
	few drops hot pepper sauce	
	salt and pepper	

- Preheat oven to 350 °F (180 °C).

- Cook bacon in large pan over medium heat. When cooked, remove bacon using slotted spoon and set aside.

- Add onion and garlic to hot pan. Cook 8 minutes over low heat, stirring occasionally. Stir in tomatoes, fennel and thyme. Cook 5 minutes.

- Add rice, chicken stock, ham and cooked bacon. Mix well and bring to boil. Cover and cook 15 minutes in oven.

- Add shrimp and peppers to pan. Mix and add hot pepper sauce. Cover and return to oven; continue cooking 8 to 10 minutes.

---

1 SERVING:	260 CALORIES	18 g CARBOHYDRATE	33 g PROTEIN
	6 g FAT	2.2 g FIBER	

Cook bacon.

Remove bacon using slotted spoon.

Add onion and garlic to pan and cook in hot bacon fat.

Stir in tomatoes, fennel and thyme. Cook 5 minutes.

Add rice, chicken stock, ham and cooked bacon. Cover and cook in oven.

Add shrimp and peppers.

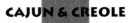

LOUISIANA CHICKEN STRIPS
(SERVES 4)

½ tsp	cayenne pepper	2 mL
½ tsp	paprika	2 mL
½ tsp	sage	2 mL
½ tsp	white pepper	2 mL
¼ tsp	ground ginger	1 mL
¼ tsp	black pepper	1 mL
¼ tsp	thyme	1 mL
1 tsp	oregano	5 mL
1½ tbsp	olive oil	25 mL
4	boneless, skinless chicken breasts, in strips	4
1½ cups	chicken stock, heated	375 mL
¼ cup	black bean sauce or soy sauce	50 mL
1 tsp	cornstarch	5 mL
2 tbsp	cold water	30 mL
	salt	

- Mix spices, herbs and oil together in small bowl and set aside.

- Heat cast iron pan over medium heat. When hot, add spice mixture to pan and cook 1 minute.

- Add chicken strips, salt lightly and brown 3 minutes over medium heat. Remove chicken from pan and set aside.

- Pour chicken stock and bean sauce into pan; mix well and cook 3 minutes.

- Dissolve cornstarch in cold water; stir into sauce and cook 1 more minute.

- Return chicken to pan, stir and simmer 3 minutes. Accompany with vegetable garnish.

Vegetable Garnish

1 tbsp	butter	15 mL
1	zucchini, halved lengthwise and sliced	1
12	radishes, sliced	12
12	cherry tomatoes, halved	12
12	snow peas, strings and ends removed	12
	salt and pepper	

- Heat butter in saucepan over medium heat. Add vegetables and season well. Cover and cook 3 minutes.

1 SERVING:	258 CALORIES	8 g CARBOHYDRATE	29 g PROTEIN
	12 g FAT	3.6 g FIBER	

TOMATO OYSTER SAUCE

(SERVES 4)

¼ tsp	cayenne pepper	1 mL
½ tsp	fennel seed	2 mL
¼ tsp	thyme	1 mL
½ tsp	basil	2 mL
½ tsp	celery seed	2 mL
½ tsp	black pepper	2 mL
¼ tsp	ground ginger	1 mL
36	shucked oysters with their juice	36
2 tbsp	butter	30 mL
1	onion, chopped	1
3	green onions, chopped	3
½	green pepper, chopped	½
2 tbsp	chopped jalapeño pepper	30 mL
28-oz	can tomatoes, drained and chopped	796-mL
	pinch saffron	
	salt	

■ Mix spices and herbs together and set aside.

■ Pour oysters with their juices into saucepan. Cover with cold water and poach 3 minutes over medium-low heat. Drain and set aside.

■ Heat butter in cast iron pan over medium heat. Add spice mixture, stir and cook 1 minute.

■ Add onions, and sweet and hot peppers. Season with salt, mix and cook 4 minutes over medium heat. Stir in tomatoes and continue cooking 4 minutes. Season to taste with salt.

■ Stir in drained oysters and simmer 3 to 4 minutes. Serve over fresh pasta.

---

1 SERVING: 193 CALORIES   17 g CARBOHYDRATE   13 g PROTEIN
8 g FAT   2.9 g FIBER

SHRIMP LAFAYETTE
(SERVES 4)

2 tbsp	butter	30 mL
1	onion, chopped	1
2	green peppers, chopped	2
1 tbsp	chopped jalapeño pepper	15 mL
4	tomatoes, peeled, seeded and chopped	4
2	garlic cloves, blanched, peeled and chopped	2
¼ tsp	cayenne pepper	1 mL
¼ tsp	black pepper	1 mL
¼ tsp	white pepper	1 mL
¼ tsp	brown sugar	1 mL
¼ cup	shrimp stock*	50 mL
1¼ lbs	fresh shrimp, peeled and deveined	625 g
	salt	

■ Heat half of butter in cast iron pan over medium heat. Add onion and both peppers. Cook 10 minutes over low heat, stirring occasionally.

■ Add tomatoes, garlic, spices and brown sugar. Mix well and cook 10 minutes over low heat.

■ Incorporate shrimp stock and continue cooking 10 minutes, stirring occasionally. Remove from heat and set aside.

■ Heat remaining butter in frying pan over medium heat. Add shrimp and cook 3 to 4 minutes. Mix once during cooking.

■ Add shrimp to tomato mixture, mix and let simmer 2 minutes over low heat. Serve over hot pasta.

Shrimp Stock

2 cups	water	500 mL
	shells from shrimp	
	salt and pepper	

■ Pour water into saucepan. Add shells from shrimp and season. Boil 15 minutes. Strain liquid.

1 SERVING:	272 CALORIES	11 g CARBOHYDRATE	40 g PROTEIN
	8 g FAT	2.5 g FIBER	

Boil shells from shrimp in water to make shrimp stock.

Cook onion, sweet and hot peppers in butter.

Add tomatoes, garlic, spices and brown sugar. Mix and cook over low heat.

Incorporate shrimp stock.

Sauté shrimp.

Add shrimp to tomato mixture and simmer.

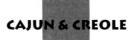

CREOLE CURRIED LAMB
(SERVES 4 TO 6)

4 lbs	boneless lamb shoulder	1.8 kg
1 tbsp	chopped fresh ginger	15 mL
1 tbsp	ground coriander	15 mL
1 tbsp	cumin	15 mL
1 tsp	curry powder	5 mL
1 tsp	basil	5 mL
¼ tsp	cayenne pepper	1 mL
2 tbsp	olive oil	30 mL
2	large onions, cubed	2
3	garlic cloves, blanched, peeled and puréed	3
4 tbsp	flour	60 mL
4 cups	chicken stock, heated	1 L
1	jalapeño pepper, chopped	1
1 tbsp	butter	15 mL
1	plantain banana, sliced	1
	salt and pepper	

■ Preheat oven to 350 °F (180 °C).

■ Trim fat from lamb and cut meat into 1-in (2.5-cm) cubes. Set aside.

■ Mix spices and herbs together in small bowl; set aside.

■ Heat oil in ovenproof sauté pan over high heat. Add half of cubed lamb and sear on all sides. Season with salt and pepper. Remove lamb from pan and set aside.

■ Repeat procedure for remaining lamb. Set all seared lamb aside.

■ Add onions and garlic to hot pan. Cook 6 minutes over medium-high heat. Mix once during cooking.

■ Stir in spice mixture and cook 4 minutes. Return lamb to pan and stir well. Sprinkle in flour, mix and cook 5 minutes.

■ Add chicken stock and jalapeño pepper; season with salt. Mix and bring to boil. Cover and cook in oven for 1½ hours.

■ Several minutes before stew is cooked, heat butter in frying pan over medium heat. Add sliced plantain and cook 1 minute on each side. Gently stir plantain into stew. Serve over egg noodles.

1 SERVING:	683 CALORIES	15 g CARBOHYDRATE	75 g PROTEIN
	36 g FAT	1.7 g FIBER	

Creole Curried Lamb

SPICY SAUCE FOR CHICKEN
(SERVES 6)

½ tsp	savory	2 mL
1 tsp	oregano	5 mL
¼ tsp	thyme	1 mL
¼ tsp	cayenne pepper	1 mL
½ tsp	black pepper	2 mL
¼ cup	dry white wine	50 mL
3 tbsp	butter	45 mL
3	dry shallots, peeled and chopped	3
4 tbsp	flour	60 mL
3 cups	chicken stock, heated	750 mL
1	small jalapeño pepper, finely chopped	1
	salt	

■ Place all spices and herbs in small bowl. Add wine, mix and let stand 1 hour.

■ Heat butter in saucepan over medium heat. Add shallots and cook 4 minutes over low heat.

■ Add flour and mix well. Cook 3 minutes, browning flour over low heat. Pour in chicken stock and mix well. Add spice mixture and jalapeño pepper.

■ Season with salt and cook 16 minutes over low heat. Do not cover.

■ Serve with chicken.

1 SERVING:	103 CALORIES	9 g CARBOHYDRATE	2 g PROTEIN
	6 g FAT	0 g FIBER	

POT LUCK STEW

(SERVES 4 TO 6)

3 tbsp	flour	45 mL
4-lb	bottom round roast, tied	1.8-kg
½ tsp	black pepper	2 mL
½ tsp	cayenne pepper	2 mL
½ tsp	sage	2 mL
½ tsp	thyme	2 mL
½ tsp	oregano	2 mL
3	garlic cloves, blanched, peeled and puréed	3
2 tbsp	olive oil	30 mL
1 cup	cranberry sauce	250 mL
2 cups	beef stock, heated	500 mL
4 tbsp	horseradish	60 mL
3	cloves	3
2	onions, cut in 6	2
8	whole dry shallots, peeled	8
2	large carrots, pared and cut in 3	2
	salt	

■ Preheat oven to 350 °F (180 °C).

■ Rub flour into meat. Set aside.

■ Mix herbs and spices (except cloves), garlic and oil together. Heat ovenproof casserole over medium heat. When hot, add spice mixture and cook 1 minute.

■ Add roast and sear on all sides. Season with salt. Add cranberry sauce and beef stock. Bring to boil. Cover and cook 2½ to 3 hours in oven.

■ One hour before end of cooking, add horseradish, cloves and vegetables.

■ If the stew sauce is not thick enough, dissolve 1 tbsp (15 mL) cornstarch in 3 tbsp (45 mL) cold water. Mix this into sauce and bring to boil. Cook 1 minute.

1 SERVING:	714 CALORIES	42 g CARBOHYDRATE	88 g PROTEIN
	22 g FAT	2.1 g FIBER	

FILET OF FLOUNDER WITH OYSTER SAUCE

(SERVES 4)

½ tsp	white pepper	2 mL
½ tsp	black pepper	2 mL
¼ tsp	dry mustard	1 mL
¼ tsp	cayenne pepper	1 mL
½ tsp	celery seed	2 mL
¼ tsp	ground ginger	1 mL
1 cup	flour	250 mL
4	flounder filets	4
1 cup	milk	250 mL
3 tbsp	butter	45 mL
1½ cups	Oyster Sauce, heated (see page 384)	375 mL

■ Place spices in mortar and grind together with pestle. Mix flour with spices.

■ Dip filets in milk, then dredge in spiced flour.

■ Heat butter in cast iron pan over medium heat. Add filets and cook 3 minutes on each side. Remove fish and serve with Oyster Sauce.

1 SERVING:	547 CALORIES	39 g CARBOHYDRATE	30 g PROTEIN
	30 g FAT	1.6 g FIBER	

Grind spices together in mortar.

Mix flour with spices.

Dip filets in milk.

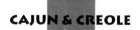

Dredge filets in spiced flour.

Add filets to hot butter in cast iron pan.

Turn filets over and continue cooking.

CREOLE BEEF CASSEROLE

(SERVES 4 TO 6)

1 tbsp	bacon fat	15 mL
4 lbs	round roast, cubed	1.8 kg
2	onions, cubed	2
2	garlic cloves, smashed and chopped	2
2	bay leaves, crushed	2
½ tsp	thyme	2 mL
3	parsley sprigs	3
2	cloves	2
5 tbsp	flour	75 mL
3 cups	beef stock, heated	750 mL
1 cup	sherry	250 mL
	pinch cayenne pepper	
	salt and pepper	

■ Preheat oven to 300 °F (150 °C).

■ Heat bacon fat in ovenproof casserole over high heat. Add half of meat and sear on all sides for 15 minutes. Season with salt and pepper; remove meat and set aside. Sear remaining meat using same procedure.

■ Return all meat to casserole. Add onions, garlic, herbs and spices. Mix and cook 4 to 5 minutes over medium heat. Season with salt and pepper.

■ Sprinkle in flour and mix well. Cook 6 minutes over low heat. Stir several times during cooking.

■ Pour in beef stock and sherry. Mix well and bring to boil. Cover and cook 2 hours in oven. Serve with fresh pasta.

1 SERVING: 589 CALORIES   10 g CARBOHYDRATE   86 g PROTEIN
19 g FAT   0 g FIBER

FETTUCCINE IN CREAM

(SERVES 4)

1 tbsp	butter	15 mL
½ tsp	white pepper	2 mL
⅓ tsp	cayenne pepper	1.5 mL
½ tsp	oregano	2 mL
½ tsp	celery seed	2 mL
2	garlic cloves, smashed and chopped	2
1	onion, finely chopped	1
2 cups	light cream	500 mL
½ cup	grated Parmesan cheese	125 mL
4	portions cooked spinach fettuccine, hot *	4
	pinch nutmeg	
	salt and pepper	

■ Heat butter in saucepan over medium heat. Add seasonings, garlic and onion. Mix and cook 4 minutes over low heat.

■ Incorporate cream and bring to boil over medium heat. Stir and continue cooking 8 minutes over low heat.

■ Stir in cheese and simmer 3 minutes.

■ Add hot cooked pasta, mix well and simmer several minutes. Serve.

* Use fresh pasta if available.

1 SERVING:	450 CALORIES	41 g CARBOHYDRATE	13 g PROTEIN
	26 g FAT	0 g FIBER	

OYSTER SAUCE
(SERVES 4 TO 6)

1 cup	shucked oysters with their juice	250 mL	
2½ cups	cold water	625 mL	
¼ tsp	black pepper	1 mL	
¼ tsp	white pepper	1 mL	
¼ tsp	ground basil	1 mL	
1	garlic clove, blanched, peeled and puréed	1	
3 tbsp	butter	45 mL	
1	onion, chopped	1	
3 tbsp	flour	45 mL	
¼ cup	heavy cream	50 mL	
	pinch nutmeg		
	pinch cayenne pepper		
	salt		

■ Pour oysters with their juice in bowl. Pour in cold water and refrigerate 8 hours.

■ Drain oysters and pour liquid into small saucepan, reserving oysters. Bring to gentle boil; cook 3 to 4 minutes over low heat.

■ Mix peppers and basil with garlic; set aside.

■ Heat butter in second saucepan or cast iron pan. Add onion and cook 4 minutes over low heat. Add flour, mix and cook 1 minute over low heat.

■ Gradually incorporate liquid from oysters; whisk constantly. Add spice mixture and heavy cream. Mix well and cook 12 minutes over low heat, stirring frequently. The sauce should become quite thick. If desired, place oysters in sauce and simmer 3 minutes. Serve with a variety of dishes.

1 SERVING:	149 CALORIES	7 g CARBOHYDRATE	5 g PROTEIN
	11 g FAT	0 g FIBER	

Place oysters with their juice in bowl. Add cold water and refrigerate 8 hours.

Drain oysters and pour liquid into saucepan.

Cook onion in hot butter.

Add flour, mix and cook 1 minute.

Incorporate liquid from oysters.

Add spice mixture and cream.

STUFFED LAMB CHOPS
(SERVES 4)

2 tbsp	butter	30 mL
2	green onions, chopped	2
½	yellow pepper, chopped	½
½	green pepper, chopped	½
3	slices ham, chopped	3
3	slices bread, crusts removed, bread soaked in chicken stock	3
½ tsp	cayenne pepper	2 mL
½ tsp	black pepper	2 mL
½ tsp	paprika	2 mL
½ tsp	celery salt	2 mL
1 tsp	oregano	5 mL
½ tsp	thyme	2 mL
1½ tbsp	olive oil	25 mL
8	lamb chops, 1 in (2.5cm) thick	8
	salt	

■ Heat butter in saucepan over medium heat. Add green onions, peppers, and ham. Cook 4 minutes.

■ Squeeze out excess liquid from soaked bread. Add bread to vegetables in pan; season with salt. Mix and cook 4 minutes over high heat.

■ Transfer mixture to food processor. Blend 5 seconds, then let cool.

■ Place all spices, herbs and oil in bowl; mix together.

■ Make a large incision in each lamb chop and stuff with vegetable/bread mixture.

■ Heat cast iron pan over medium heat. When hot, add spice mixture to pan and cook 1 minute.

■ Add stuffed lamb chops and cook 4 minutes on each side for "pink" lamb. Continue cooking a little longer if you prefer lamb well done.

■ Accompany with strong mustard or a spicy sauce.

1 SERVING:	627 CALORIES	12 g CARBOHYDRATE	63 g PROTEIN
	36 g FAT	1.1 g FIBER	

CAJUN SHRIMP ON SKEWERS

(SERVES 4)

2	garlic cloves, blanched, peeled and puréed	2
½ tsp	cayenne pepper	2 mL
½ tsp	black pepper	2 mL
½ tsp	white pepper	2 mL
½ tsp	thyme	2 mL
1 tsp	oregano	5 mL
3 tbsp	melted butter	45 mL
¼ cup	shrimp stock (see page 374)	50 mL
1¼ lbs	shrimp, shelled and deveined	625 g
1	lemon, thinly sliced	1

■ Mix garlic, spices, herbs and melted butter together in small bowl; set aside.

■ Pour shrimp stock into bowl. Add spice mixture and shrimp. Mix well and let stand 15 minutes.

■ Preheat grill at high.

■ Alternate shrimp and slices of lemon on metal skewers. Baste with shrimp stock marinade.

■ Oil grill and add shrimp skewers. Cook 3 minutes. Turn skewers over and cook 2 minutes. Baste with marinade during cooking.

1 SERVING:	247 CALORIES	2 g CARBOHYDRATE	37 g PROTEIN
	10 g FAT	0 g FIBER	

CRAB AND EGGPLANT COQUILLE

(SERVES 4 TO 6)

2	eggplants	2
2 tbsp	butter	30 mL
1	onion, finely chopped	1
1	yellow pepper, chopped	1
2 tbsp	chopped jalapeño pepper	30 mL
2	garlic cloves, smashed and chopped	2
¼ tsp	cayenne pepper	1 mL
¼ tsp	black pepper	1 mL
½ tsp	fennel seed	2 mL
7 oz	crab meat, thawed	200 g
½ cup	grated Parmesan cheese	125 mL
	salt and pepper	

■ Cut eggplants in half lengthwise and sprinkle flesh with salt. Let stand 30 minutes at room temperature. Rinse under cold water to remove salt and juices.

■ Preheat oven to 400 °F (200 °C).

■ Pat eggplants dry and arrange, flesh-side up, in roasting pan. Place in oven and cook 30 minutes. Remove from oven and hollow out shells. Set aside.

■ Heat butter in cast iron pan over medium heat. Add onion, yellow pepper, jalapeño pepper and garlic. Stir and cook 3 minutes.

■ Add spices, mix and cook 2 minutes. Mix in eggplant flesh. Season and cook 6 to 7 minutes.

■ Mix in crab meat; correct seasoning. Add 3 tbsp (45 mL) Parmesan, mix and cook 4 minutes over low heat.

■ Fill eggplant shells (or coquille dishes) with mixture. Top with remaining cheese and cook 8 minutes in oven at 350 °F (180 °C).

1 SERVING:	141 CALORIES	6 g CARBOHYDRATE	11 g PROTEIN
	8 g FAT	1.5 g FIBER	

Use spoon to remove cooked eggplant flesh from shells.

Cook onion, peppers and garlic in hot butter.

Add spices, mix and cook 2 minutes.

Mix in eggplant flesh. Season with salt and pepper; cook 6 to 7 minutes.

Add crab meat. Season to taste.

Add 3 tbsp (45 mL) of cheese.

CHUNK MEAT CHILI
(SERVES 4 TO 6)

Part I

2½ cups	dried kidney beans	625 mL
2½ lbs	boneless blade steak, cut in ½-in (1.2-cm) cubes	1.2 kg
1	celery stalk, cubed	1
1	onion, cubed	1
1	bay leaf	1
2	cloves	2
	salt and pepper	

■ Soak beans in cold water 8 hours. Drain and set aside.

■ Place meat and drained beans in large saucepan. Pour in enough cold water to cover ingredients by 1 in (2.5 cm). Bring to boil over high heat. Skim off foam.

■ Drain meat and beans; return to saucepan. Pour in enough cold water to cover ingredients by 1 in (2.5 cm). Add celery, onion, bay leaf and cloves. Season well. Partly cover and bring to boil. Cook 1½ hours over medium heat.

Part II

¼ tsp	ground cloves	1 mL
½ tsp	celery seeds	2 mL
1 tsp	basil	5 mL
½ tsp	cumin	2 mL
2½ tbsp	chili powder	40 mL
¼ tsp	cayenne pepper	1 mL
¼ tsp	thyme	1 mL
1 tbsp	oregano	15 mL
1 tsp	black pepper	5 mL
½	jalapeño pepper, chopped	½
1½ tbsp	olive oil	25 mL
1	large onion, chopped	1
3	garlic cloves, smashed and chopped	3
3	carrots, pared and sliced	3
1	yellow pepper, cubed medium	1
1	red pepper, cubed medium	1
2 tbsp	flour	30 mL
28-oz	can tomatoes, drained and chopped	796-mL
2 cups	beef stock, heated	500 mL
	salt	

■ Mix spices, herbs and jalapeño pepper together; set aside.

■ Heat oil in large saucepan over medium heat. Add onion and garlic; cook 3 minutes over low heat. Add carrots and peppers; mix well.

■ Stir in seasoning mixture. Mix very well (important). Cook 5 minutes over medium heat. Sprinkle flour over vegetables, stir well and cook 3 minutes over low heat.

■ Add tomatoes and beef stock; correct seasoning with salt. Mix and cook 40 minutes, partly covered, over low heat.

■ When meat is cooked, drain bean and meat mixture, reserving ½ cup (125 mL) of the cooking liquid.

■ Add meat and beans to vegetable mixture. Add reserved cooking liquid and mix well. Partly cover and cook 20 minutes over low heat. If desired, serve with sour cream and Cheddar cheese.

1 SERVING:	207 CALORIES	35 g CARBOHYDRATE	10 g PROTEIN
	3 g FAT	12.2 g FIBER	

Chunk Meat Chili

STUFFED ROAST CHICKEN
(SERVES 4)

3	whole dry shallots, peeled	3
¼ cup	wine vinegar	50 mL
¼ cup	water	50 mL
1	chicken liver, cleaned	1
3	dry shallots, chopped	3
¼ tsp	thyme	1 mL
1 tbsp	chopped fresh parsley	15 mL
½ tsp	sage	2 mL
1 tsp	basil	5 mL
¼ tsp	black pepper	1 mL
5	slices French bread, crusts removed and bread soaked in chicken stock	5
3½-4 lb	fresh chicken, cleaned	1.6-1.8 kg
4 tbsp	melted butter	60 mL
	lemon juice	
	salt and pepper	

■ Preheat oven to 400 °F (200 °C).

■ Place whole shallots in small bowl. Add wine vinegar and water; mix and let stand 12 minutes.

■ Chop chicken liver and place in second bowl. Add chopped shallots and seasonings; mix well. Squeeze out excess liquid from bread; add bread to bowl. Mix well and set stuffing aside.

■ Season cavity of chicken with salt and pepper. Stuff, truss and place chicken in roasting pan. Brush skin with melted butter and sprinkle with lemon juice. Season outside of bird and place in oven at 400 °F (200 °C). Cook 30 minutes.

■ Reduce oven heat to 375 °F (190 °C) and continue cooking chicken for 1 hour. Baste chicken 3 to 4 times with shallot/vinegar mixture during cooking.

■ Once chicken is cooked, remove from oven. Carve and serve with Spicy Sauce for Chicken (see page 378).

1 SERVING:	638 CALORIES	30 g CARBOHYDRATE	66 g PROTEIN	
	28 g FAT	1.4 g FIBER		

VERSATILE CAJUN SAUCE

(SERVES 6 TO 8)

3 tbsp	olive oil	45 mL
2	garlic cloves, smashed and chopped	2
1	onion, chopped	1
¼	stalk celery, diced	¼
2	dry shallots, peeled and chopped	2
2	green peppers, chopped	2
4 tbsp	flour	60 mL
3 cups	beef stock, heated	750 mL
¼ tsp	pepper	1 mL
¼ tsp	cayenne pepper	1 mL
¼ tsp	thyme	1 mL
1 tsp	tomato paste	5 mL
	salt	

■ Heat oil in saucepan over medium heat. Add garlic and vegetables; cook 7 minutes over low heat, stirring occasionally.

■ Mix in flour and cook 7 minutes over low heat to brown flour.

■ Pour in beef stock and whisk to incorporate. Add all seasonings and tomato paste. Cook 18 minutes over low heat, stirring occasionally.

■ Strain sauce through fine sieve.

■ Serve sauce with chicken, beef or sausages.

1 SERVING:	93 CALORIES	9 g CARBOHYDRATE	1 g PROTEIN
	6 g FAT	1.0 g FIBER	

CAJUN BUTTER

(SERVES 8 TO 10)

¼ tsp	black pepper	1 mL
¼ tsp	white pepper	1 mL
¼ tsp	sage	1 mL
1 tsp	chopped jalapeño pepper	5 mL
2	garlic cloves, blanched, peeled and puréed	2
½ lb	unsalted butter, soft	250 g
	pinch cayenne pepper	
	juice of ½ lemon	
	salt	

■ Mix spices, jalapeño pepper and garlic together in bowl. Add butter and mix until well incorporated. Season with salt and lemon juice. Mix again.

■ Place butter on double sheet of aluminum foil. Roll in a cylindrical shape and twist ends shut. Freeze and use as needed.

1 SERVING:	206 CALORIES	0 g CARBOHYDRATE	0 g PROTEIN
	23 g FAT	0 g FIBER	

TASTY PEPPER SHRIMP
(SERVES 4)

2	garlic cloves, puréed	2
½ tsp	cayenne pepper	2 mL
½ tsp	black pepper	2 mL
½ tsp	white pepper	2 mL
½ tsp	thyme	2 mL
1 tsp	oregano	5 mL
2 tbsp	butter	30 mL
¾ lb	fresh mushrooms, cleaned and cut in 3	375 g
2	green onions, chopped	2
1½ lbs	fresh shrimp, shelled and deveined	750 g
⅓ cup	shrimp stock (see page 374)	75 mL
2 tbsp	beurre manié (see page 155)	30 mL
	salt	

■ Grind garlic, peppers, thyme and oregano together in mortar.

■ Heat butter in cast iron pan over medium heat. Add spice mixture and cook 1 minute.

■ Add mushrooms and green onions. Season with salt, stir and cook 4 minutes.

■ Add shrimp and cook 3 minutes. Stir once during cooking. Remove shrimp from pan and set aside.

■ Increase heat to high and pour in shrimp stock. Bring to boil and cook 2 minutes. Whisk in beurre manié.

■ Return shrimp to pan and cook 1 minute over low heat. Serve over rice.

1 SERVING:	340 CALORIES	7 g CARBOHYDRATE	47 g PROTEIN
	14 g FAT	2.6 g FIBER	

Grind garlic, spices and herbs together in mortar.

Cook spice mixture in hot butter.

Add mushrooms and green onions. Cook 4 minutes.

Add shrimp and cook 3 minutes.

Remove shrimp from pan. Pour in shrimp stock and bring to boil.

Incorporate beurre manié using whisk.

BREADED VEAL CUTLETS

(SERVES 4)

4	medium veal cutlets	4
½ tsp	white pepper	2 mL
¼ tsp	paprika	1 mL
1 tsp	finely chopped fresh parsley	5 mL
2	garlic cloves, blanched, peeled and puréed	2
½ cup	flour	125 mL
2	eggs, beaten	2
¼ cup	light cream	50 mL
2 tbsp	butter	30 mL
1 tbsp	olive oil	15 mL
	breadcrumbs	
	salt	

■ Place each veal cutlet between two sheets of waxed paper. Pound with smooth side of mallet to flatten.

■ Mix spices, parsley and garlic together. Spread half of mixture over one side of each veal cutlet.

■ Incorporate remaining spices into flour. Dredge veal in flour.

■ Mix beaten eggs with cream. Dip veal in eggs, then coat well in breadcrumbs. Season with salt.

■ Heat butter and oil in frying pan over medium heat. Add veal and cook 2 minutes on each side. Serve.

1 SERVING: 417 CALORIES   17 g CARBOHYDRATE   26 g PROTEIN
27 g FAT   0 g FIBER

PORK CUTLETS STUFFED WITH CHEESE

(SERVES 4)

¼ tsp	dry mustard	1 mL
¼ tsp	black pepper	1 mL
½ tsp	ground oregano	2 mL
¼ tsp	ground thyme	1 mL
¼ tsp	ground ginger	1 mL
¼ tsp	cayenne pepper	1 mL
8	large pork cutlets, ¼ in (0.65 cm) thick	8
4	slices prosciutto	4
4	slices Havarti cheese	4
1	egg, beaten	1
1½ cups	breadcrumbs	375 mL
2 tbsp	olive oil	30 mL
	salt	

■ Preheat oven to 350 °F (180 °C).

■ Mix spices and herbs together; set aside.

■ Place each cutlet between two sheets of waxed paper. Flatten with smooth side of mallet.

■ Season meat with spice mixture. Lay 4 cutlets flat on counter. Cover each with slice of prosciutto and slice of cheese. Trim stuffing so that it does not overhang pork.

■ Position remaining 4 cutlets on top. Pound edges of cutlets together using mallet. Season with salt.

■ Dip stuffed cutlets in beaten egg, then coat in breadcrumbs.

■ Heat oil in ovenproof frying pan over medium heat. Add stuffed cutlets and cook 3 minutes on each side. Transfer pan to oven and continue cooking 8 to 10 minutes.

■ Serve with fresh vegetables.

1 SERVING:	540 CALORIES	25 g CARBOHYDRATE	38 g PROTEIN
	32 g FAT	1.0 g FIBER	

CAJUN HAMBURGERS

(SERVES 4)

1½ lbs	lean ground beef	750 g
1	egg	1
1	large onion, chopped and cooked	1
2	garlic cloves, smashed and chopped	2
1 tsp	Dijon mustard	5 mL
1 tsp	Worcestershire sauce	5 mL
½ tsp	black pepper	2 mL
½ tsp	cayenne pepper	2 mL
½ tsp	white pepper	2 mL
½ tsp	paprika	2 mL
1 tsp	oregano	5 mL
2 tbsp	olive oil	30 mL
1½ cups	beef stock, heated	375 mL
1 tbsp	cornstarch	15 mL
3 tbsp	cold water	45 mL
	salt	

■ Place beef in mixer. Add egg, cooked onion, garlic, mustard and Worcestershire sauce. Season with salt and mix several minutes to incorporate well.

■ Shape mixture into 4 large patties. Set aside.

■ Mix spices and herbs together; set aside.

■ Heat cast iron pan over medium heat. When hot, pour in oil. Add spice mixture and cook 1 minute.

■ Add hamburgers and cook 8 minutes. Turn patties over 3 to 4 times during cooking.

■ Remove hamburgers from pan and keep hot.

■ Pour beef stock into same pan. Boil 3 to 4 minutes.

■ Dissolve cornstarch in cold water; stir into sauce and cook 1 minute. Pour sauce over hamburgers and serve with potatoes.

1 SERVING:	400 CALORIES	5 g CARBOHYDRATE	41 g PROTEIN
	24 g FAT	0 g FIBER	

Place beef in mixer. Add egg, onion, garlic, mustard and Worcestershire sauce. Season with salt and blend together.

Shape mixture into large patties.

Cook spices in hot oil.

Add hamburgers and cook
8 minutes. Turn patties over
3 to 4 times during cooking.

Pour beef stock into hot pan.

Incorporate dissolved cornstarch
into sauce.

BLACKENED SCALLOPS

(SERVES 4)

1 tsp	paprika	5 mL
1 tsp	black pepper	5 mL
1 tsp	white pepper	5 mL
½ tsp	cayenne pepper	2 mL
1 tsp	oregano	5 mL
1 tsp	rosemary	5 mL
1 tbsp	olive oil	15 mL
1	green pepper, diced	1
1	yellow pepper, diced	1
1	dry shallot, peeled and chopped	1
1 lb	scallops	500 g
4	small portions cooked pasta, hot	4
	pinch thyme	
	salt	

■ Mix spices and herbs, except salt, with oil in small bowl; set aside.

■ Heat cast iron pan over high heat. When hot, add spice mixture to pan and cook 1 minute. Stir constantly!

■ Add peppers and shallot; mix and cook 2 minutes over high heat.

■ Add scallops. Mix well and cook 3 minutes over high heat. Stir once during cooking and season with salt.

■ Serve over hot pasta. If desired, sprinkle with lemon juice.

1 SERVING:	336 CALORIES	42 g CARBOHYDRATE	31 g PROTEIN
	5 g FAT	0 g FIBER	

BAKED EGGS WITH MUSHROOMS

(SERVES 4)

3 tbsp	melted butter	45 mL
½ lb	fresh mushrooms, cleaned and diced small	250 g
1 tbsp	chopped fresh parsley	15 mL
1	dry shallot, peeled and finely chopped	1
2 tbsp	dry white wine	30 mL
4	large eggs	4
	salt and pepper	

■ Preheat oven to 325 °F (160 °C). Have ready 4 ramequins.

■ Heat 2 tbsp (30 mL) butter in nonstick frying pan. When melted, add mushrooms, parsley and shallot; season well. Cook 3 minutes over high heat.

■ Pour in wine and continue cooking 2 minutes. Set aside.

■ Divide remaining butter between ramequins. Take half of mushroom mixture and spoon equal amounts into dishes.

■ Place 1 egg in each dish and top with remaining mushroom mixture. Bake 10 to 15 minutes in oven.

---

1 SERVING:	189 CALORIES	6 g CARBOHYDRATE	8 g PROTEIN
	14 g FAT	1.7 g FIBER	

EGGS SURPRISE

(SERVES 4)

2 tbsp	butter	30 mL
1 tbsp	flour	15 mL
1 cup	hot milk	250 mL
8	large eggs	8
½ cup	grated Gruyère cheese	125 mL
	salt and pepper	
	pinch nutmeg	

■ Preheat oven to 375 °F (190 °C). Grease a large baking dish with half of butter; set aside.

■ Heat remaining butter in saucepan over medium heat. Sprinkle in flour and mix well; cook 1 minute over low heat.

■ Pour in milk and mix well; season with salt, pepper and nutmeg. Cook 8 to 10 minutes over low heat, stirring occasionally. Set aside.

■ Separate eggs, with whites all in one bowl and each yolk in a separate dish.

■ Beat egg whites until stiff, then fold into white sauce. Pour this into baking dish.

■ Using back of soup spoon, shape 8 spaced indentations in the white sauce/egg whites mixture. Carefully slide an egg yolk into each little hole.

■ Sprinkle cheese over and bake 10 to 15 minutes in oven.

1 SERVING:	295 CALORIES	7 g CARBOHYDRATE	18 g PROTEIN
	22 g FAT	0 g FIBER	

SUNNY-SIDE-UP EGGS ON TOMATOES
(SERVES 4)

2 tbsp	olive oil	30 mL
2	tomatoes, peeled and diced	2
1	small garlic clove, smashed and chopped	1
1 tsp	chopped fresh parsley	5 mL
4	large eggs	4
	pinch oregano	
	salt and pepper	

■ Heat half of oil in nonstick frying pan over high heat. Add tomatoes, garlic, parsley and oregano; season well. Cook 7 to 8 minutes over medium heat. Transfer mixture to heated platter and set aside, keeping hot.

■ Add remaining oil to frying pan over medium-high heat. Break in eggs and season. Cover and cook 3 to 4 minutes until whites are set.

■ Slide eggs out onto hot tomato mixture and serve.

1 SERVING:	155 CALORIES	3 g CARBOHYDRATE	7 g PROTEIN
	13 g FAT	1.0 g FIBER	

STUFFED EGGS SAFFRON

(SERVES 4)

8	hard-boiled eggs	8
1 cup	thick white sauce, heated	250 mL
¼ tsp	saffron	1 mL
1 tbsp	chopped fresh parsley	15 mL
4 tbsp	breadcrumbs	60 mL
2 tbsp	melted butter	30 mL
	salt and pepper	

■ Preheat oven to 375 °F (190 °C).

■ Slice eggs in half lengthwise and carefully remove yolks. Arrange whites in baking dish.

■ Place yolks in fine sieve and force through into bowl. Add white sauce and mix well. Add saffron, parsley and seasonings; mix again.

■ Using spoon, fill egg whites with yolk mixture. Sprinkle tops with breadcrumbs and moisten each with few drops melted butter.

■ Cook 5 minutes in oven. Serve with various breads, if desired.

1 SERVING:	358 CALORIES	12 g CARBOHYDRATE	15 g PROTEIN
	28 g FAT	0 g FIBER	

MUSHROOM SOUFFLÉ OMELET
(SERVES 2)

4 tbsp	butter	60 mL
¼ lb	fresh mushrooms, cleaned and sliced	125 g
1 tbsp	chopped fresh parsley	15 mL
1 tsp	lemon juice	5 mL
4	large eggs, separated	4
⅓ cup	light cream	75 mL
	salt and pepper	

■ Heat half of butter in frying pan over medium heat. Add mushrooms, season and cook 5 minutes over high heat. Sprinkle in parsley and lemon juice; mix well and set pan aside.

■ Place egg yolks in large bowl and add cream; mix well and set aside. Beat egg whites in separate bowl until they form soft peaks, then using spatula fold whites into egg yolks.

■ Heat remaining butter in large nonstick pan over high heat. When bubbling, pour in eggs and cook 1 minute. Shake pan back and forth, stirring eggs to help layers cook.

■ When eggs have taken shape but are still soft, cover omelet with sautéed mushrooms. Continue cooking 1 minute.

■ Using spatula, begin rolling omelet away from you while tilting pan in the direction of the roll. With pan held at a 45° angle, hold edge of plate up against bottom lip of pan. Turn omelet out onto plate by turning pan upside-down. Serve.

1 SERVING:	444 CALORIES	6 g CARBOHYDRATE	15 g PROTEIN
	40 g FAT	1.7 g FIBER	

SCRAMBLED EGGS MAGDA

(SERVES 4)

8	large eggs, beaten	8	
1 tbsp	chopped fresh parsley	15 mL	
1 tsp	chopped fresh chives	5 mL	
½ cup	grated Gruyère cheese	125 mL	
1 tbsp	Dijon mustard	15 mL	
2 tbsp	butter	30 mL	
	salt and pepper		

■ Place eggs, herbs, cheese and mustard in mixing bowl; mix well.

■ Heat butter in large nonstick frying pan over medium-high heat.

■ Pour eggs into pan and cook 1 minute; season. Stir quickly; cook 1 minute. Stir quickly; continue cooking until eggs are soft on top.

■ Serve with croutons and garnish with orange slices, if desired.

1 SERVING: 245 CALORIES 1 g CARBOHYDRATE 15 g PROTEIN
20 g FAT 0 g FIBER

TASTY SHRIMP CANAPÉ SPREAD
(SERVES 10)

1½ lbs	cooked shrimp, peeled and deveined	750 g
8	garlic cloves, blanched and peeled	8
2	dry shallots, peeled and chopped	2
2 tbsp	chopped fresh parsley	30 mL
¼ tsp	paprika	1 mL
1 tsp	Worcestershire sauce	5 mL
¼ lb	soft butter	125 g
	juice of 1 lemon	
	pinch cayenne pepper	
	salt and pepper	

- Place all ingredients in food processor. Blend 1 minute and correct seasoning.

- Transfer mixture to bowl, cover and refrigerate 1 hour.

- Serve shrimp spread on toasted bread as an accompaniment to drinks.

1 SERVING:	185 CALORIES	3 g CARBOHYDRATE	19 g PROTEIN
	11 g FAT	0 g FIBER	

Choose fresh shrimp.

To cook shrimp, place in saucepan. Add cold water to cover and drop in slices of lemon.

Bring to boil. Remove saucepan from heat and let shrimp stand in hot liquid for 3 minutes.

Remove shells.

To devein shrimp, slit backs with paring knife.

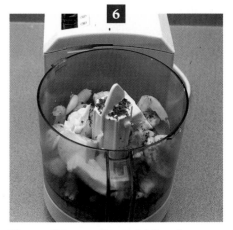

Place all ingredients in food processor and blend 1 minute.

Old-Fashioned Meatballs in Tomato Sauce

OLD-FASHIONED MEATBALLS IN TOMATO SAUCE

(SERVES 6)

1 tbsp	olive oil	15 mL ·
1	onion, chopped	1
1	celery stalk, diced	1
½	small hot pepper, chopped	½
2	garlic cloves, smashed and chopped	2
28-oz	can tomatoes, drained and chopped	796-mL
½ tsp	oregano	2 mL
½ tsp	basil	2 mL
1 tbsp	chopped fresh parsley	15 mL
5½-oz	can tomato paste	156-mL
½ cup	light beef stock, heated	125 mL
½ lb	lean ground beef	250 g
½ lb	lean ground veal	250 g
¼ tsp	chili powder	1 mL
1	beaten egg white	1
1	onion, finely chopped and blanched	1
1 tbsp	sunflower oil	15 mL
	pinch brown sugar	
	salt and pepper	

■ Heat olive oil in nonstick saucepan over medium heat. Add chopped onion, celery, hot pepper and garlic; cook 4 to 5 minutes over medium-low heat, covered.

■ Stir in tomatoes, dash of salt and pepper, brown sugar, oregano, basil, parsley, tomato paste and beef stock. Bring to boil and continue cooking 25 minutes over medium heat, uncovered.

■ Meanwhile, place beef and veal in food processor. Add chili powder and season with pepper. Process 15 seconds.

■ Add egg white and blanched onion; process until meat forms a ball. Shape mixture into small meatballs about 1 in (2.5 cm) in diameter.

■ Heat sunflower oil in nonstick frying pan over medium-high heat. Add meatballs and cook 7 to 9 minutes, depending on size. Turn to brown all sides and season once during cooking.

■ Discard excess fat from meatballs, then add to tomato sauce. Simmer 5 minutes before serving over hot pasta.

---

1 SERVING: 291 CALORIES   14 g CARBOHYDRATE   17 g PROTEIN
11 g FAT   1.6 g FIBER

CHICKEN WITH ARTICHOKES
(SERVES 4)

1 tbsp	butter	15 mL
4	boneless chicken breasts	4
1 tbsp	olive oil	15 mL
4	artichoke hearts, cut in three	4
½ lb	fresh mushrooms, cleaned and cut in three	250 g
1	dry shallot, peeled and chopped	1
3 tbsp	cognac	45 mL
1½ cups	chicken stock, heated	375 mL
1 tbsp	cornstarch	15 mL
3 tbsp	cold water	45 mL
2 tbsp	heavy cream	30 mL
1 tsp	chopped fresh parsley	5 mL
	salt and pepper	

■ Heat butter in sauté pan over medium heat. Add chicken and season well. Cover and cook 5 minutes on each side over very low heat.

■ Meanwhile, heat oil in frying pan. Add artichoke hearts, mushrooms and shallot. Season, cover and cook 5 minutes over medium heat.

■ Add cognac and cook 2 minutes over high heat. Do not cover.

■ Pour in chicken stock and correct seasoning. Continue cooking 5 minutes over low heat.

■ Dissolve cornstarch in cold water. Incorporate into sauce in frying pan. Stir in cream and simmer 1 minute.

■ Place cooked chicken in sauce and simmer 3 minutes. Sprinkle with parsley and serve.

1 SERVING:	297 CALORIES	12 g CARBOHYDRATE	30 g PROTEIN
	12 g FAT	1.6 g FIBER	

Cook chicken in hot butter.

Heat oil in frying pan. Add artichoke hearts, mushrooms and shallot. Season, cover and cook 5 minutes.

Add cognac and cook 2 minutes over high heat.

Pour in chicken stock and correct seasoning. Cook over low heat.

Thicken sauce with dissolved cornstarch. Stir in cream and simmer.

Place cooked chicken in sauce to simmer before serving.

BONELESS CHICKEN WITH CARAMELIZED ONIONS

(SERVES 4)

1½ tbsp	olive oil	25 mL
2	onions, peeled and sliced	2
4	boneless chicken breasts	4
1 tsp	teriyaki sauce	5 mL
½ cup	Gruyère cheese	125 mL
	juice of 1 lemon	
	salt and pepper	

■ Heat half of oil in frying pan over medium heat. Add onions and cook 15 minutes, stirring occasionally. Season during cooking. Onions should become golden brown. Remove onions from pan and set aside.

■ Heat remaining oil in same pan. Add chicken and season with salt and pepper. Cook 5 minutes on each side over medium heat.

■ Add teriyaki sauce and lemon juice. Cook 1 minute.

■ Transfer chicken breasts to ovenproof baking dish and top with onions. Sprinkle with cheese.

■ Broil 3 minutes in oven.

1 SERVING: 245 CALORIES 4 g CARBOHYDRATE 30 g PROTEIN 12 g FAT 0 g FIBER

SAFFRON CHICKEN WINGS

(SERVES 4)

2 tbsp	olive oil	30 mL
2 lbs	chicken wings	900 g
1	large onion, chopped	1
2	garlic cloves, smashed and chopped	2
1	red pepper, sliced	1
1½ cups	chopped tomatoes	375 mL
2 tbsp	tomato paste	30 mL
½ tsp	saffron	2 mL
½ tsp	basil	2 mL
1 cup	chicken stock, heated	250 mL
	pinch crushed chilies	
	salt and pepper	

■ Preheat oven to 350 °F (180 °C).

■ Heat oil in ovenproof sauté pan over medium heat. Add chicken wings and season; cook 6 minutes on each side. Remove wings from pan and set aside.

■ Add onion and garlic to hot pan; cook 4 minutes over medium heat. Add red pepper, tomatoes and tomato paste. Season, mix well and add seasonings, except crushed chilies. Mix again and cook 5 to 6 minutes over medium heat.

■ Pour in chicken stock, return chicken wings to pan and sprinkle in crushed chilies. Mix, cover and cook 18 to 20 minutes in oven.

1 SERVING:	593 CALORIES	12 g CARBOHYDRATE	47 g PROTEIN
	40 g FAT	2.2 g FIBER	

PORK CHOPS PROVENÇALE

(SERVES 4)

1 tbsp	vegetable oil	15 mL
4	boneless pork chops, ¾ in (2 cm) thick, trimmed of fat	4
2	green onions, chopped	2
2	garlic cloves, smashed and chopped	2
2	dry shallots, peeled and chopped	2
28-oz	can tomatoes, drained and chopped	796-mL
½ tsp	oregano	2 mL
1 cup	chicken stock, heated	250 mL
1 tbsp	tomato paste	15 mL
	salt and pepper	

■ Heat oil in large frying pan over medium heat. When hot, add chops and cook 4 to 5 minutes. Turn chops over, season well and continue cooking 4 to 5 minutes; adjust time depending on thickness. Remove pork and keep hot.

■ Add green onions, garlic and shallots to pan; cook 2 minutes over high heat. Mix in tomatoes and oregano; season well. Cook 5 to 6 minutes over medium heat.

■ Pour in chicken stock and cook 3 to 4 minutes. Mix in tomato paste and cook another 3 to 4 minutes. Serve sauce over pork chops.

1 SERVING:	347 CALORIES	15 g CARBOHYDRATE	30 g PROTEIN
	19 g FAT	2.4 g FIBER	

PORK CHOPS WITH PICKLES

(SERVES 4)

1 tbsp	vegetable oil	15 mL
4	boneless pork chops, ¾ in (2 cm) thick, trimmed of fat	4
2	onions, sliced	2
1	celery stalk, sliced ½ in (1.2 cm) thick	1
3 tbsp	wine vinegar	45 mL
1½ cups	beef stock or consommé, heated	375 mL
1 tbsp	tomato paste	15 mL
2	large pickles, in julienne	2
1 tbsp	cornstarch	15 mL
3 tbsp	cold water	45 mL
1 tbsp	chopped fresh parsley	15 mL
	salt and pepper	

■ Heat oil in large frying pan over medium heat. When hot, add chops and cook 4 to 5 minutes. Turn chops over, season and continue cooking 4 to 5 minutes; adjust time depending on thickness. When cooked, remove and keep warm.

■ Add onions and celery to frying pan and cook 7 minutes over high heat. Pour in wine vinegar and cook 3 minutes.

■ Add beef stock, tomato paste and pickles; mix well. Cook 3 to 4 minutes, still over high heat.

■ Dissolve cornstarch in cold water; stir into sauce until well incorporated. Cook 2 minutes over high heat, then pour over pork chops, sprinkle with parsley and serve.

1 SERVING: 313 CALORIES   7 g CARBOHYDRATE   29 g PROTEIN
            19 g FAT   1.2 g FIBER

BAKED CHICKEN WINGS

(SERVES 4)

2 tbsp	olive oil	30 mL
2 lbs	chicken wings	900 g
4	dry shallots, peeled and chopped	4
2	garlic cloves, smashed and chopped	2
½ lb	fresh mushrooms, cleaned and sliced	250 g
1 cup	dry white wine	250 mL
1 tbsp	tarragon	15 mL
½ tsp	oregano	2 mL
1½ cups	chopped tomatoes	375 mL
1 cup	chicken stock, heated	250 mL
1 tbsp	cornstarch	15 mL
3 tbsp	cold water	45 mL
	salt and pepper	

■ Heat oil in ovenproof sauté pan over medium heat. Add chicken wings and season; cook 6 minutes on each side. Remove wings from pan and set aside.

■ Place shallots and garlic in hot pan. Cook 2 minutes over medium heat. Add mushrooms, season and cook 5 minutes over high heat.

■ Pour in wine and add seasonings; cook another 3 minutes.

■ Add tomatoes and chicken stock; stir and cook 3 minutes over medium heat.

■ Meanwhile, preheat oven to 350 °F (180 °C).

■ Return chicken to pan and stir. Cover and finish cooking 18 to 20 minutes in oven.

■ Remove pan from oven and place on stove. Dissolve cornstarch in cold water and incorporate into sauce. Bring to boil for 2 minutes and serve.

1 SERVING: 667 CALORIES 17 g CARBOHYDRATE 50 g PROTEIN 40 g FAT 4.1 g FIBER

Sear chicken wings in hot oil.

Remove browned wings and set aside.

Cook shallots and garlic 2 minutes. Add mushrooms, season and cook 5 minutes over high heat.

Pour in wine and add seasonings; cook another 3 minutes.

Add tomatoes and chicken stock; stir and cook 3 minutes over medium heat.

Return chicken to pan.

VEAL CHOPS SAVOYARDE
(SERVES 4)

2 tbsp	butter	30 mL
4	veal chops, ¾ in (2 cm) thick, trimmed of fat	4
¼ cup	dry vermouth	50 mL
4	slices Black Forest ham	4
1½ cups	white sauce, heated	375 mL
1 cup	grated Gruyère cheese	250 mL
	salt and pepper	
	dash paprika	

- Heat butter in large frying pan over medium heat. Add chops and cook 4 to 5 minutes. Turn chops over, season and continue cooking 4 to 5 minutes; adjust time depending on size.

- Transfer cooked veal to baking dish. Pour vermouth into frying pan and cook 1 minute over high heat; pour over chops. Cover each with slice of ham, layer of white sauce and layer of cheese. Season and sprinkle with paprika.

- Broil 3 minutes to melt cheese, and serve.

1 SERVING: 627 CALORIES 8 g CARBOHYDRATE 57 g PROTEIN
39 g FAT 0 g FIBER

MUSTARD GRILLED PORK CHOPS

(SERVES 4)

1 tbsp	oil	15 mL	
4	boneless pork chops, ¾ in (2 cm) thick, trimmed of fat	4	
1½ tbsp	Dijon mustard	25 mL	
2 tbsp	breadcrumbs salt and pepper	30 mL	

■ Heat oil in large frying pan over medium heat. Add chops and cook 4 to 5 minutes. Turn chops over, season well and continue cooking 4 to 5 minutes; adjust time depending on thickness.

■ Preheat broiler.

■ Spread mustard over one side of chops and top with breadcrumbs. Place in oven and broil 3 to 4 minutes. Serve.

1 SERVING: 293 CALORIES   2 g CARBOHYDRATE   28 g PROTEIN
19 g FAT   0 g FIBER

TOMATO MUSHROOM CHICKEN

(SERVES 4)

½ cup	flour	125 mL
3½ lbs	chicken, cleaned and cut into 8 pieces	1.6 kg
2 tbsp	butter	30 mL
1 lb	fresh mushrooms, cleaned and halved	500 g
1 tbsp	oil	15 mL
1	large onion, diced large	1
28-oz	can tomatoes, drained and coarsely chopped	796-mL
1 tbsp	curry powder	15 mL
½ tsp	oregano	2 mL
	salt and pepper	
	paprika	
	few drops Tabasco sauce	

■ Mix flour with salt, pepper and paprika; dredge chicken pieces in flour mixture.

■ Heat butter in large skillet over medium heat. Add chicken and cook 15 minutes, turning pieces over twice.

■ Add mushrooms, season and continue cooking 10 to 12 minutes.

■ Meanwhile, heat oil in frying pan over high heat. Add onion and cook 4 minutes. Add tomatoes and all seasonings including Tabasco; cook 8 to 10 minutes over medium heat.

■ Spoon mixture over chicken and serve.

1 SERVING:	610 CALORIES	29 g CARBOHYDRATE	67 g PROTEIN
	25 g FAT	5.7 g FIBER	

TANGY PORK SPARERIBS

(SERVES 4)

4½ lbs	pork spareribs	2 kg
¼ cup	olive oil	50 mL
¼ cup	lemon juice	50 mL
2 tbsp	wine vinegar	30 mL
2 tbsp	teriyaki sauce	30 mL
3	blanched garlic cloves, chopped	3
½ cup	chili sauce	125 mL
½ cup	ketchup	125 mL
¼ cup	beef stock, heated	50 mL
	salt and pepper	
	few drops Tabasco sauce	

■ Place ribs in large roasting pan. Mix oil, lemon juice, vinegar, teriyaki sauce, garlic and Tabasco together; pour over pork. Cover with plastic wrap and marinate 6 hours in refrigerator; turn ribs over once.

■ Preheat oven to 350 °F (180 °C).

■ Remove ribs from pan and set aside. Pour marinade into saucepan; add chili sauce, ketchup and beef stock. Season, mix well and cook 8 minutes over medium heat.

■ Place ribs in clean roasting pan and brush generously with marinade. Cook 1½ hours, basting every 15 minutes. Serve with any remaining sauce.

1 SERVING:	1500 CALORIES	20 g CARBOHYDRATE	91 g PROTEIN
	118 g FAT	0 g FIBER	

HUNTER VEAL
(SERVES 4)

1 tbsp	butter	15 mL
2 tbsp	olive oil	30 mL
4	medium veal scallops, cut in strips 1 in (2.5 cm) wide	4
½ lb	fresh mushrooms, cleaned and halved	250 g
1	dry shallot, peeled and finely chopped	1
3 tbsp	flour	45 mL
2 cups	chicken stock, heated	500 mL
¼ cup	sour cream	50 mL
1 tsp	chopped fresh parsley	5 mL
	salt and pepper	

■ Heat half of butter and half of oil in frying pan over medium heat. Add half of veal and cook 1 minute. Turn strips over, season and cook 1 more minute. Remove veal and set aside.

■ Add remaining veal to pan and repeat procedure. Set all veal aside.

■ Heat remaining butter and oil in same pan. Add mushrooms and shallot. Season and cook 4 minutes.

■ Sprinkle flour over mushrooms, stir and cook 1 minute.

■ Mix in chicken stock and cook 6 minutes over low heat.

■ Add veal to pan. Stir in sour cream and simmer 2 minutes. Sprinkle with parsley and serve.

1 SERVING:	245 CALORIES	10 g CARBOHYDRATE	13 g PROTEIN
	17 g FAT	1.8 g FIBER	

Cook veal strips 1 minute on each side.

Add mushrooms and shallot to hot pan. Cook 4 minutes.

Sprinkle in flour, stir and cook 1 minute.

Mix in chicken stock and cook over low heat.

Add veal to pan.

Stir in sour cream.

GROUND LAMB PATTIES WITH VEGETABLE MEDLEY
(SERVES 4)

1 lb	lean ground lamb	500 g
1 tbsp	chopped fresh parsley	15 mL
½ tsp	cayenne pepper	2 mL
1 tsp	tarragon	5 mL
1	garlic clove, smashed and chopped	1
2 tbsp	olive oil	30 mL
½	zucchini, in sticks	½
12	snow peas, strings removed	12
½	green pepper, in sticks	½
12	yellow beans, pared	12
½	red pepper, in sticks	½
1	boiled onion, quartered	1
8	cooked Brussels sprouts	8
	salt and pepper	

■ Place lamb, parsley, cayenne pepper, tarragon, garlic, salt and pepper in bowl; mix together until well combined. Shape into 4 patties.

■ Heat half of oil in large frying pan over medium heat. Add lamb patties and cook 10 to 12 minutes, turning over 4 times. Season to taste and set patties aside, keeping hot.

■ Add remaining oil to pan, still over medium heat. Add all vegetables and season generously. Cover and cook 4 minutes.

■ Serve vegetables with lamb. If desired, top with garlic butter or maître d'hôtel butter (see page 158).

1 SERVING:	292 CALORIES	12 g CARBOHYDRATE	30 g PROTEIN
	14 g FAT	6.2 g FIBER	

HAMBURGER STEAK WITH ONIONS

(SERVES 4)

1¼ lbs	lean ground beef	625 g
½ cup	cooked chopped onions	50 mL
1	egg	1
1 tbsp	chopped fresh parsley	15 mL
2 tbsp	olive oil	30 mL
2	medium onions, sliced	2
2	green peppers, sliced	2
1½ cups	beef stock, heated	375 mL
1 tsp	cornstarch	5 mL
2 tbsp	cold water	30 mL
	few drops Worcestershire sauce	
	salt and pepper	

■ Place ground beef, cooked chopped onions, egg, parsley and Worcestershire sauce in food processor; blend 2 to 3 minutes. When meat forms ball, remove and shape into 4 patties.

■ Heat oil in large frying pan over medium heat. Add patties and cook 8 to 10 minutes, depending on thickness, turning over 2 to 3 times to avoid charring.

■ When cooked, remove from pan and set aside, keeping hot.

■ Add sliced onions to same frying pan and cook 6 minutes over medium heat. Add peppers and cook another 4 minutes.

■ Pour in beef stock, mix well and correct seasoning. Dissolve cornstarch in cold water; stir into sauce until well incorporated.

■ Bring to boil, then spoon onion sauce over hamburger steaks and serve.

1 SERVING:	363 CALORIES	7 g CARBOHYDRATE	35 g PROTEIN
	22 g FAT	1.1 g FIBER	

HAMBURGER STEAK ITALIAN-STYLE

(SERVES 4)

1¼ lbs	lean ground beef	625 g
1	medium onion, chopped and cooked	1
2	blanched garlic cloves, chopped	2
1	egg	1
1 tbsp	curry powder	15 mL
1 tbsp	chopped fresh parsley	15 mL
2 tbsp	olive oil	30 mL
1	carrot, pared and diced small	1
1	garlic clove, smashed and chopped	1
1	celery stalk, diced small	1
28-oz	can tomatoes, drained and chopped	796-mL
2 tbsp	tomato paste	30 mL
1 tsp	oregano	5 mL
	salt and pepper	
	few drops Worcestershire sauce	

■ Place beef, onion, blanched garlic, egg, curry powder, parsley, salt and pepper in food processor; blend 3 minutes. When mixture forms ball, remove and shape meat into 4 patties.

■ Heat oil in large frying pan over medium heat. Add patties and cook 8 to 10 minutes, depending on thickness. Turn patties over 2 to 3 times to avoid charring.

■ When cooked, remove patties and set aside, keeping hot.

■ Add carrot, remaining garlic and celery to frying pan; cook 4 minutes over medium heat.

■ Mix in tomatoes, tomato paste, oregano and Worcestershire sauce. Cook 7 minutes over medium heat.

■ Correct seasoning and serve tomato sauce with hamburger steaks.

1 SERVING:	396 CALORIES	14 g CARBOHYDRATE	36 g PROTEIN
	22 g FAT	2.6 g FIBER	

CHICKEN WITH SHALLOT SAUCE
(SERVES 4)

3 tbsp	butter	45 mL
4	boneless chicken breasts	4
2	dry shallots, peeled and chopped	2
3 tbsp	chopped fresh basil	45 mL
1 tbsp	chopped fresh parsley	15 mL
¼ cup	dry white wine	50 mL
1 cup	chicken stock, heated	250 mL
1 tsp	brown sugar	5 mL
1 tbsp	cornstarch	15 mL
3 tbsp	cold water	45 mL
	juice of 1 lime	
	salt and freshly ground pepper	

■ Heat half of butter in frying pan over medium heat. Add chicken, season and cook 4 minutes. Turn chicken over and continue cooking 5 minutes. Set aside.

■ Heat remaining butter in sauté pan over medium heat. Add shallots, basil, parsley and wine. Season, cover and cook 3 minutes.

■ Stir in chicken stock, brown sugar and lime juice. Cook 6 minutes over low heat.

■ Dissolve cornstarch in cold water. Stir into sauce and quickly bring to boil. Cook 1 minute.

■ Place chicken in sauce and simmer 2 minutes over low heat. Serve.

1 SERVING:	253 CALORIES	7 g CARBOHYDRATE	28 g PROTEIN
	12 g FAT	0 g FIBER	

EGGPLANT-STUFFED VEAL

(SERVES 4)

1	medium eggplant	1
2 tbsp	olive oil	30 mL
4	large veal scallops	4
3	green onions, chopped	3
¼ cup	dry white wine	50 mL
1 cup	chicken stock, heated	250 mL
1 tbsp	cornstarch	15 mL
3 tbsp	cold water	45 mL
	salt and pepper	

■ Preheat oven to 375 °F (190 °F).

■ Peel eggplant and slice ½ in (1.2 cm) thick. Place slices on cookie sheet and brush lightly with olive oil. Season and cook 12 minutes in oven. Remove and set aside.

■ Place each veal scallop between two sheets of waxed paper. Using smooth side of wooden mallet, pound until thin. Remove paper.

■ Place two slices of eggplant on each piece of veal. Wrap meat over eggplant and secure bundles with string.

■ Heat remaining oil in sauté pan over medium heat. Add veal bundles and cook 4 minutes, browning both sides.

■ Add green onions and cook 2 minutes. Pour in wine, season and cook 3 minutes.

■ Remove veal from pan and set aside.

■ Add chicken stock to pan and cook 2 minutes over medium heat. Dissolve cornstarch in cold water; mix into sauce and cook 1 minute.

■ Return veal to pan and simmer 3 minutes over very low heat. Serve.

1 SERVING:	177 CALORIES	5 g CARBOHYDRATE	11 g PROTEIN
	12 g FAT	1.2 g FIBER	

Slice eggplant into ½-in (1.2-cm) thick rounds.

Place slices on cookie sheet and brush lightly with olive oil. Season and cook in oven.

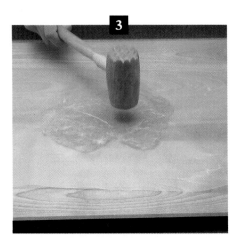

Flatten veal between two sheets of waxed paper.

Place two slices of eggplant on each piece of veal.

Wrap sides of meat over eggplant.

Finish wrapping ends, then secure bundles with string.

MARINATED CALF LIVER

(SERVES 4)

4	slices calf liver	4	
½ cup	dry white wine	125 mL	
2 tbsp	tarragon vinegar	30 mL	
1	bay leaf	1	
2	garlic cloves, smashed and chopped	2	
2 tbsp	melted butter	30 mL	
1 tsp	olive oil	5 mL	
1 tbsp	chopped fresh parsley	15 mL	
	salt and pepper		
	few drops lemon juice		

■ Place calf liver in baking dish. Add wine, tarragon vinegar, bay leaf and garlic; season well. Marinate 1 hour in refrigerator.

■ Heat butter and oil in large frying pan over medium heat. Drain liver, reserving marinade. Add liver and cook 2 minutes on each side; adjust time depending on thickness.

■ Remove liver and keep warm. Add marinade to pan and cook 3 minutes over high heat. Add parsley and few drops lemon juice; correct seasoning. Mix well, pour over liver and serve.

1 SERVING:	301 CALORIES	5 g CARBOHYDRATE	25 g PROTEIN
	18 g FAT	0 g FIBER	

BREADED LAMB CHOPS
(SERVES 4)

8	loin lamb chops	8
½ cup	seasoned flour	125 mL
2	eggs, beaten	2
1 cup	breadcrumbs	250 mL
2 tbsp	olive oil	30 mL
2 tbsp	red currant jelly	30 mL
1½ cups	beef stock, heated	375 mL
¼ cup	port wine	50 mL
1 tbsp	cornstarch	15 mL
3 tbsp	cold water	45 mL
1 tbsp	chopped fresh parsley	15 mL
	salt and pepper	

■ Preheat oven to 375 °F (190 °C).

■ Trim fat from lamb chops and scrape about 1 in (2.5 cm) of bone clean. Place between 2 sheets of waxed paper; flatten with mallet. Dredge chops in flour, then dip in beaten eggs and coat with breadcrumbs.

■ Heat oil in large ovenproof frying pan over medium heat. When hot, add chops and cook 3 minutes. Turn chops over, season and continue cooking 2 minutes. Transfer to oven and continue cooking 6 to 8 minutes; adjust time depending on size and preference.

■ Meanwhile, place currant jelly in saucepan over medium heat. Pour in beef stock and port wine; season, mix well, bring to boil and continue cooking 5 minutes.

■ Dissolve cornstarch in cold water; stir into sauce until well incorporated. Add parsley and simmer 3 minutes over low heat.

■ Spoon sauce over cooked lamb chops and serve.

1 SERVING:	758 CALORIES	53 g CARBOHYDRATE	65 g PROTEIN
	30 g FAT	1.0 g FIBER	

LAMB CHOPS WITH WHOLE SHALLOTS
(SERVES 4)

1½ cups	water	375 mL
¾ lb	dry shallots, peeled and left whole	375 g
1 tbsp	butter	15 mL
1 tsp	chopped fresh tarragon	5 mL
½ cup	dry white wine	125 mL
1¼ cups	chicken stock, heated	300 mL
1 tbsp	cornstarch	15 mL
3 tbsp	cold water	45 mL
1 tsp	olive oil	5 mL
8	lamb chops, most of fat removed	8
1 tsp	chopped fresh parsley	5 mL
	rind of ¼ orange, in julienne	
	salt and pepper	

■ Pour 1½ cups (375 mL) water in saucepan set over medium heat. Add salt and bring to boil. Add shallots and cook 8 minutes. Remove from heat and drain well.

■ Return shallots to saucepan. Add butter, tarragon and orange rind. Cook 2 minutes over high heat. Pour in wine and cook 2 more minutes.

■ Add chicken stock and bring to boil. Reduce heat to low and cook 3 minutes. Dissolve cornstarch in cold water; incorporate into sauce. Season and simmer sauce over low heat during preparation of lamb.

■ Heat oil in frying pan over medium heat. Add lamb chops and cook 3 minutes. Turn chops over, season, and continue cooking 3 minutes. If chops are very thick, cook 2 minutes longer.

■ Serve lamb with shallot sauce. Sprinkle with parsley.

1 SERVING:	543 CALORIES	18 g CARBOHYDRATE	57 g PROTEIN	
	25 g FAT	0 g FIBER		

Cook whole shallots in boiling water.

Drain shallots and return to saucepan. Add butter, tarragon and orange rind. Cook 2 minutes over high heat.

Pour in wine and cook 2 more minutes.

Add chicken stock and bring to boil.

Remove most of fat from lamb chops.

Cook lamb chops in hot oil.

Spicy Lamb Meatballs with Vegetable Sauce

SPICY LAMB MEATBALLS WITH VEGETABLE SAUCE
(SERVES 4)

1 lb	lean ground lamb	500 g
1 tbsp	chopped fresh parsley	15 mL
1 tsp	curry powder	5 mL
½ tsp	ground anise	2 mL
½ tsp	cayenne pepper	2 mL
1	dry shallot, peeled and chopped	1
1	large egg	1
1 tbsp	olive oil	15 mL
1	celery stalk, sliced	1
1	medium onion, sliced	1
1	red pepper, diced	1
¼ lb	fresh mushrooms, cleaned and halved	125 g
1½ cups	beef stock, heated	375 mL
1 tbsp	tomato paste	15 mL
1 tbsp	cornstarch	15 mL
3 tbsp	cold water	45 mL
	salt and pepper	

■ Place lamb in bowl with parsley, curry powder, anise and cayenne pepper; mix well. Lightly season with salt and pepper, add shallot and egg; mix again until completely incorporated. Shape meat into medium-size meatballs.

■ Preheat oven to 350 °F (180 °C).

■ Heat oil in large ovenproof frying pan over medium heat. Add meatballs (do not overcrowd pan) and cook 6 to 7 minutes, browning on all sides. Remove from pan and set aside.

■ Add celery and onion to hot frying pan. Cook 3 to 4 minutes over medium heat.

■ Add red pepper and mushrooms; season and cook 2 minutes. Pour in beef stock and stir in tomato paste; cook 1 minute.

■ Dissolve cornstarch in cold water; stir into sauce and cook 2 minutes over low heat.

■ Return meatballs to sauce and cover pan. Transfer to oven and finish cooking 15 minutes. Serve with hot pasta.

1 SERVING:	254 CALORIES	11 g CARBOHYDRATE	30 g PROTEIN
	10 g FAT	2.2 g FIBER	

CHICKEN SOUBISE

(SERVES 4)

2	whole chicken breasts, skinned and split in 2	2
2 tbsp	butter	30 mL
2	medium onions, thinly sliced and blanched 3 minutes	2
1 tbsp	chopped fresh parsley	15 mL
1	green pepper, thinly sliced	1
1	red pepper, thinly sliced	1
2 cups	chicken stock, heated	500 mL
1 tbsp	cornstarch	15 mL
3 tbsp	cold water	45 mL
	salt and pepper	
	Worcestershire sauce	

■ Season chicken breasts and set aside.

■ Heat butter in large skillet over medium heat. Add blanched onions (be sure they are well drained) and cook 5 to 6 minutes over medium-high heat.

■ Add chicken, season well and continue cooking 6 to 7 minutes.

■ Add parsley and both peppers. Season well and cook another 6 minutes over medium heat.

■ Remove cooked chicken and keep hot on serving platter.

■ Pour chicken stock into skillet and bring to boil. Dissolve cornstarch in cold water and stir into sauce until well incorporated. Cook 1 minute over low heat.

■ Correct seasoning and add Worcestershire sauce to taste. Pour over chicken and serve.

1 SERVING: 222 CALORIES 8 g CARBOHYDRATE 28 g PROTEIN
9 g FAT 1.0 g FIBER

CHICKEN WITH SAUSAGE AND PEPPERS

(SERVES 4)

1 tbsp	olive oil	15 mL
4	boneless chicken breasts	4
2	Italian sausages	2
1	red onion, sliced in rings	1
1	red pepper, in wide strips	1
1	green pepper, in wide strips	1
2	garlic cloves, peeled and cut in three	2
1½ cups	chicken stock, heated	375 mL
1 tbsp	cornstarch	15 mL
3 tbsp	cold water	45 mL
	salt and pepper	

■ Heat oil in large frying pan over medium heat. Add chicken and sausages. Season and cook 3 to 4 minutes on each side. Remove chicken from pan and set aside.

■ Cover pan and continue cooking sausages about 8 minutes, depending on thickness. Remove from pan and set aside.

■ Add onion to hot pan and cook 4 minutes over medium heat.

■ Add peppers and garlic; cook 5 minutes. Season well. Pour in chicken stock and cook 1 minute.

■ Dissolve cornstarch in cold water. Incorporate into sauce in pan and cook 1 minute.

■ Return chicken to pan and simmer 3 minutes in sauce. Slice sausages and add to pan. Simmer 1 minute and serve.

1 SERVING:	358 CALORIES	7 g CARBOHYDRATE	38 g PROTEIN
	20 g FAT	1.0 g FIBER	

CHINESE ROLLS STUFFED WITH EGGPLANT

(SERVES 4)

Stuffing

1 tbsp	olive oil	15 mL
2	green onions, chopped	2
2	dry shallots, chopped	2
2	garlic cloves, smashed and chopped	2
1 tbsp	chopped fresh parsley	15 mL
1 tbsp	basil	15 mL
½ lb	fresh mushrooms, chopped	250 g
½ cup	chopped roasted red pepper	125 mL
½	eggplant, peeled and diced	½
½ cup	ricotta cheese	125 mL
	salt and pepper	

Rolls

1 tbsp	flour	15 mL
3 tbsp	cold water	45 mL
8	egg roll wrappers	8
	oil	

■ To make stuffing, heat oil in frying pan over medium heat. Add green onions, shallots and garlic. Cook 3 minutes.

■ Add herbs and mushrooms. Season, mix and cook 2 minutes.

■ Add roasted red pepper and eggplant; mix well. Partly cover and cook 15 minutes over medium heat. Stir once during cooking process.

■ Stir in cheese and cook 2 minutes. Set stuffing aside.

■ To prepare rolls, preheat oil in deep fryer to 375 °F (190 °C).

■ Dissolve flour in cold water to make a paste.

■ Spread each egg roll wrapper flat on counter. Spoon some eggplant stuffing in center of each wrapper. Roll up as illustrated in technique, using flour paste to seal edges.

■ Deep fry in hot oil 3 to 4 minutes, or adjust time depending on size. Serve hot with the sauce.

(continued)

Sauté green onions, shallots and garlic in hot oil.

Add herbs and mushrooms. Season, mix and cook 2 minutes.

Add roasted red pepper and eggplant; mix well. Partly cover and cook 15 minutes over medium heat.

Sauce

1 tsp	olive oil	5 mL
2	green onions, chopped	2
28-oz	can tomatoes, drained and chopped	796-mL
3 tbsp	Chinese black bean sauce	45 mL
2 tbsp	chopped fresh basil	30 mL

■ Heat oil in small saucepan over medium heat. Add green onions and cook 2 minutes.

■ Add tomatoes, season and cook 10 minutes.

■ Add remaining ingredients, mix and cook 2 minutes. Mix again and serve with egg rolls.

1 SERVING: 438 CALORIES 76 g CARBOHYDRATE 11 g PROTEIN
10 g FAT 4.8 g FIBER

Stir in cheese and cook 2 minutes.

Stuff egg roll wrappers and roll up.

Brush edges of wrappers with flour paste and seal edges shut.

HAM STEAKS GLAZED WITH MAPLE SYRUP
(SERVES 4)

1 tbsp	maple syrup	15 mL
1 tbsp	melted butter	15 mL
4	cooked ham steaks, ¾ in (2 cm) thick	4
	juice ½ lemon	
	freshly ground pepper	

■ Preheat oven to 375 °F (190 °C).

■ Mix maple syrup with butter and lemon juice. Place ham steaks on ovenproof platter and brush mixture on both sides. Season with pepper.

■ Change oven setting to broil. Set platter on top oven rack and broil 4 minutes on each side.

■ Serve.

1 SERVING:	189 CALORIES	4 g CARBOHYDRATE	25 g PROTEIN
	8 g FAT	0 g FIBER	

VEAL CHOPS AND FRESH BLACKBERRIES

(SERVES 4)

1 tbsp	olive oil	15 mL
8	veal chops, trimmed of fat	8
1	dry shallot, peeled and chopped	1
½ cup	dry white wine	125 mL
1½ cups	veal or beef stock, heated	375 mL
1 tbsp	cornstarch	15 mL
2 tbsp	cold water	30 mL
1 cup	blackberries, washed	250 mL
1 tbsp	chopped fresh parsley	15 mL
	salt and pepper	

■ Preheat oven to 350 °F (180 °C).

■ Heat oil in ovenproof frying pan over medium heat. Add chops and cook about 4 minutes on each side, depending on thickness. Remove meat from pan and set aside.

■ Add shallot and wine to hot pan. Cook 3 minutes over high heat. Stir in veal stock and season; cook 5 minutes.

■ Dissolve cornstarch in cold water and incorporate into sauce. Add berries and veal chops. Place in oven and cook 5 minutes.

■ Sprinkle with parsley and serve.

1 SERVING:	545 CALORIES	9 g CARBOHYDRATE	48 g PROTEIN
	33 g FAT	2.9 g FIBER	

PORK STRIPS WITH BAMBOO SHOOTS

(SERVES 4)

3 tbsp	vegetable oil	45 mL
2 tbsp	chopped fresh ginger root	30 mL
3	green onions, chopped	3
2	celery stalks, sliced	2
½ lb	fresh mushrooms, cleaned and cut in 3	250 g
2 lbs	pork loin, trimmed of fat and cut in strips	900 g
2 tbsp	soy sauce	30 mL
½ cup	dry white wine	125 mL
½ cup	canned bamboo shoots, drained	125 mL
1	garlic clove, smashed and chopped	1
1½ cups	chicken stock, heated	375 mL
1 tsp	cornstarch	5 mL
2 tbsp	cold water	30 mL
	salt and pepper	

■ Heat oil in skillet over medium heat. Add ginger, green onions and celery; cook 1 minute over high heat. Add mushrooms, season, and continue cooking 3 minutes; remove vegetables and set aside.

■ Add pork and stir-fry 4 minutes, seasoning during cooking. Remove meat and set aside.

■ Stir in soy sauce and wine; cook 3 more minutes. Mix in bamboo shoots, garlic and chicken stock; bring to boil.

■ Dissolve cornstarch in cold water; stir into sauce until well incorporated. Return vegetables and meat to pan and season well; cook 6 minutes over low heat.

---

1 SERVING: 591 CALORIES 9 g CARBOHYDRATE 60 g PROTEIN
33 g FAT 4.0 g FIBER

PORK SAUTÉED WITH ZUCCHINI
(SERVES 4)

2 tbsp	olive oil	30 mL
1	zucchini, halved lengthwise and sliced	1
2	celery stalks, sliced	2
2	apples, cored, peeled and sliced in wedges	2
2	garlic cloves, smashed and chopped	2
8	pork cutlets, trimmed of fat and cut in strips	8
1 tbsp	chopped fresh parsley	15 mL
	salt, pepper, paprika	

■ Heat half of oil in frying pan over high heat. Add vegetables, apples and garlic; season well. Cook 3 minutes.

■ Turn vegetables over and continue cooking 3 minutes over medium heat. Remove vegetables and apples from pan and set aside.

■ Heat remaining oil in pan over medium heat. Add meat and cook 2 minutes on each side. Season with salt and pepper.

■ Return vegetables and apples to pan with pork. Add parsley, season and sprinkle lightly with paprika. Cook 2 minutes to reheat, then serve.

■ Accompany with boiled new potatoes.

1 SERVING:	611 CALORIES	13 g CARBOHYDRATE	56 g PROTEIN
	37 g FAT	2.5 g FIBER	

SMOKED SALMON ON POTATO PANCAKES
(SERVES 4)

4	large potatoes	4
1	onion, grated	1
3 tbsp	flour	45 mL
1	large egg, separated	1
2 tbsp	olive oil	30 mL
16	thin slices smoked salmon	16
	sour cream	
	salt and pepper	

■ Peel and grate potatoes. Place grated potatoes in large bowl and cover with cold water. Let stand 15 minutes, then drain well. Squeeze out excess liquid from potatoes.

■ Place potatoes in bowl of electric mixer. Add onion and flour and season. Mix well. Add egg yolk and mix again.

■ Very lightly beat egg white and incorporate into mixture.

■ Shape mixture into small pancakes. Refrigerate 1 hour.

■ Heat half of oil in frying pan over medium heat. Add half of potato pancakes and cook 5 minutes on each side. Season well. Remove pancakes from pan and keep hot in oven. Add remaining oil and repeat procedure for remaining pancakes.

■ Roll slices of salmon and serve on potato pancakes. Accompany with sour cream.

1 SERVING:	296 CALORIES	35 g CARBOHYDRATE	10 g PROTEIN
	13 g FAT	3.0 g FIBER	

Squeeze out excess liquid from grated potatoes.

Place potatoes in bowl of mixer. Add grated onion.

Add flour, season and mix well.

Add egg yolk and mix again.

Add very lightly beaten egg white and incorporate into mixture.

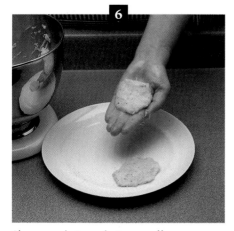

Shape mixture into small pancakes.

WINE-BRAISED PORK TENDERLOIN WITH MUSHROOMS

(SERVES 4)

1 tbsp	olive oil	15 mL
2 tbsp	butter	30 mL
2	pork tenderloins, trimmed of fat	2
1	onion, chopped	1
1	garlic clove, smashed and chopped	1
1 lb	fresh mushrooms, cleaned and halved	500 g
½ cup	dry white wine	125 mL
2 cups	chicken stock, heated	500 mL
2 tbsp	tomato paste	30 mL
½ tsp	oregano	2 mL
1 tbsp	cornstarch	15 mL
3 tbsp	cold water	45 mL
	salt and pepper	

■ Preheat oven to 350 °F (180 °C).

■ Heat oil and butter in large ovenproof sauté pan over medium heat. When hot, add pork and sear 10 to 12 minutes on all sides, seasoning during cooking. Remove pork and set aside.

■ Add onion and garlic to pan; cook 3 minutes. Add mushrooms and season well; increase heat to high and cook 5 minutes.

■ Pour in wine and cook 3 minutes. Add chicken stock, tomato paste and oregano; mix well. Return pork to pan, cover and cook 25 minutes in oven.

■ Remove pork from pan, slice about ½ in (1.2 cm) thick and set aside.

■ Dissolve cornstarch in cold water; stir into sauce until well incorporated. Season and cook 1 minute. Return meat to sauce and simmer 2 minutes over low heat. Serve.

1 SERVING:	365 CALORIES	11 g CARBOHYDRATE	39 g PROTEIN
	16 g FAT	3.4 g FIBER	

Wine-Braised Pork Tenderloin with Mushrooms

BANDE DE POMMES

(SERVES 4 TO 6)

1 lb	flaky dough (see page 482)	500 g
3 to 4	cooking apples jam of choice beaten egg granulated sugar	3 to 4

■ Preheat oven to 375 °F (190 °C).

■ Roll out flaky dough ¼ in (0.65 cm) thick on lightly floured surface. Use ruler to measure rectangle of about 5 x 15 in (13 x 38 cm). Using pastry wheel, cut out rectangle and transfer to cookie sheet. Prick dough with fork.

■ Cut out 4 strips of dough about ¾ in (2 cm) wide; 2 long enough for the sides and 2 for the ends. Position strips of dough on rectangle using a little beaten egg to affix overlapping corners.

■ Spread a thin layer of jam on bottom of dough.

■ Core, peel and cut apples in wedges ½ in (1.2 cm) thick. Arrange apples over jam on dough. Apples should not rest on borders.

■ Brush borders of dough with beaten egg. Sprinkle with sugar and bake 30 minutes in oven.

Note: If desired, refer to the illustrated technique of Strawberry Bande de Fruits on page 488.

1 SERVING:	565 CALORIES	60 g CARBOHYDRATE	7 g PROTEIN
	33 g FAT	2.2 g FIBER	

FAR BRETON

(SERVES 6)

4	large eggs	4
½ cup	granulated sugar	125 mL
1 cup	all-purpose flour	250 mL
3 tbsp	rum	45 mL
¼ cup	marmalade	50 mL
½ cup	sultana raisins	125 mL
2 cups	milk	500 mL
	pinch salt	
	icing sugar	

■ Preheat oven to 350 °F (180 °C). Butter a 1¾-in (4.5-cm) deep baking dish, 11¾ x 7½ in (30 x 19 cm) in size.

■ Place eggs and sugar in bowl; beat together. Add flour and salt; beat to incorporate.

■ Add rum, marmalade and raisins; beat well. Pour in milk and beat to incorporate.

■ Pour batter into baking dish and bake 50 to 55 minutes or until golden brown. Let cool in baking dish and serve cold.

■ Cut into squares and sprinkle with icing sugar. Serve with maple syrup, if desired.

1 SERVING: 350 CALORIES 60 g CARBOHYDRATE 10 g PROTEIN
6 g FAT 1.0 g FIBER

FRESH FIG LOAF

(SERVES 6 TO 8)

4	large eggs, beaten	4
4 tbsp	brown sugar	60 mL
½ cup	peanut oil	125 mL
1½ cups	cake flour, sifted	375 mL
1 tsp	baking powder	5 mL
½ tsp	baking soda	2 mL
1 lb	fresh figs, peeled and chopped	500 g
2 tbsp	rum	30 mL
½ cup	pecan halves	125 mL

■ Preheat oven to 350 °F (180 °C). Use 2½-in (6.5-cm) deep loaf pan that is about 9¼ x 5¼ in (23.5 x 13 cm) in size. Line bottom of pan with waxed paper of exact size. Butter waxed paper and sides of pan.

■ Mix beaten eggs with sugar. Add oil and whisk to incorporate.

■ Sift flour with baking powder and soda. Add ⅓ to egg batter and beat well. Repeat for remaining flour.

■ Stir in figs, rum and pecans. Pour batter into mold and bake in middle of oven for 55 to 60 minutes.

■ When cake is done, remove and let cool slightly before unmolding. Finish cooling on wire rack.

1 SERVING:	475 CALORIES	52 g CARBOHYDRATE	8 g PROTEIN
	25 g FAT	3.2 g FIBER	

CHOCOLATE LAYER CAKE
(SERVES 8 TO 10)

10	large eggs, separated	10
1	whole large egg	1
⅔ cup	granulated sugar	150 mL
⅓ cup	unsweetened cocoa	75 mL
1 cup	pastry flour, sifted	250 mL
3 oz	semi-sweet chocolate	90 g
2 cups	heavy cream	500 mL
½ cup	apricot jam	125 mL

■ Preheat oven to 350 °F (180 °C). Grease 10-in (25-cm) springform cake pan with oil. Line with sheet of oiled waxed paper; set aside.

■ Place egg yolks and whole egg in mixing bowl. Add 3 tbsp (45 mL) granulated sugar and beat with electric hand mixer 3 to 4 minutes until thick. Incorporate cocoa using spatula.

■ In separate bowl, beat egg whites until stiff. Add remaining granulated sugar and continue beating to incorporate. Fold into cocoa mixture.

■ Sift flour over cocoa mixture and fold in using spatula. Pour batter into prepared mold and bake 35 minutes or until cake tests done.

■ Remove cake from oven and let cool slightly in pan. Turn upside-down onto wire rack and carefully remove mold. Slowly peel off waxed paper. Cool completely.

■ Using long knife, slice cake evenly to make 2 layers. Set aside.

■ Melt chocolate in double boiler and cool. Beat cream until quite stiff, then fold in chocolate.

■ To assemble cake, place bottom layer on platter and spread with half of jam. Cover with layer of chocolate whipped cream. Set top cake layer in place and spread with remaining jam and chocolate cream. Use pastry bag for decorative effect. Chill and serve.

1 SERVING:	525 CALORIES	47 g CARBOHYDRATE	12 g PROTEIN
	32 g FAT	0 g FIBER	

Chocolate Layer Cake

GÉNOISE – BASIC SPONGE CAKE

(2 GÉNOISE CAKES)

6	large eggs, at room temperature	6
½ tsp	vanilla	2 mL
½ cup	granulated sugar	125 mL
1 cup	all-purpose flour	250 mL
3 tbsp	melted unsalted butter, tepid	45 mL
	pinch salt	

■ Preheat oven to 350 °F (180 °C). Use 2 cake pans, each 8½ in (21.5 cm) in diameter and 1¾ in (4.5 cm) deep. Prepare cake pans as illustrated in the technique.

■ Place saucepan half-filled with water on stove over low heat. Bring water to simmer.

■ Place eggs, vanilla and sugar in stainless steel bowl. Set bowl on saucepan. Beat egg mixture with electric hand mixer for 3 minutes. During this time check that water is not too hot or eggs will begin cooking.

■ Remove bowl from pan and place on counter. Continue beating until batter becomes very thick and forms ribbons. Avoid overbeating batter; 5 minutes at the most.

■ Add salt to flour and sift ⅓ over batter. Fold in with spatula. Repeat for remaining flour. Fold in tepid, melted butter and divide batter between cake pans.

■ Bake in middle of oven for 25 minutes.

■ When cakes are cooked, remove from oven and let stand 4 minutes in pans. Turn upside-down on wire rack and let cool slightly before peeling off waxed paper.

■ Cool cakes completely before assembling.

1 CAKE:	847 CALORIES	107 g CARBOHYDRATE	26 g PROTEIN
	35 g FAT	2.3 g FIBER	

Cut out 2 circles of waxed paper to fit bottom of each cake pan. Dot a little butter on bottom of pan and position waxed paper on top. Butter sides of pan and top of waxed paper, then dust with flour.

Place eggs, vanilla and sugar in stainless steel bowl.

Set bowl on saucepan containing simmering water.

Beat with electric hand mixer for 3 minutes. Do not allow water to become too hot or eggs will begin cooking.

Use flour sifter to incorporate flour gradually. Fold in with spatula.

Fold in tepid, melted butter.

PASTRY CREAM FOR FRUIT TARTS

6	large egg yolks	6
⅔ cup	granulated sugar	150 mL
½ cup	all-purpose flour	125 mL
¼ tsp	salt	1 mL
2 cups	hot milk	500 mL
1 tsp	vanilla	5 mL
1 tbsp	orange liqueur (Cointreau)	15 mL
1 tbsp	unsalted butter	15 mL

■ Place egg yolks and sugar in bowl; beat together 2 to 3 minutes using electric hand mixer. Eggs should turn pale yellow and thicken.

■ Whisk in flour and salt. Pour in half of hot milk; whisking constantly. Whisk in vanilla.

■ Pour mixture into heavy-bottomed saucepan. Whisk in remaining milk and bring to boil over medium-low heat; whisk constantly. As cream cooks, it will thicken. Use wooden spoon to scrape out corners of pan.

■ When cream starts to boil, reduce heat to low. Continue cooking 5 to 6 minutes. Cream should be thick.

■ Transfer cream to bowl and whisk in liqueur and butter. Cover with sheet of waxed paper touching surface. Lift up one corner of paper to create air space and let cool completely.

■ Press waxed paper snug against cream and refrigerate.

1 RECIPE:	1593 CALORIES	214 g CARBOHYDRATE	45 g PROTEIN
	58 g FAT	2.3 g FIBER	

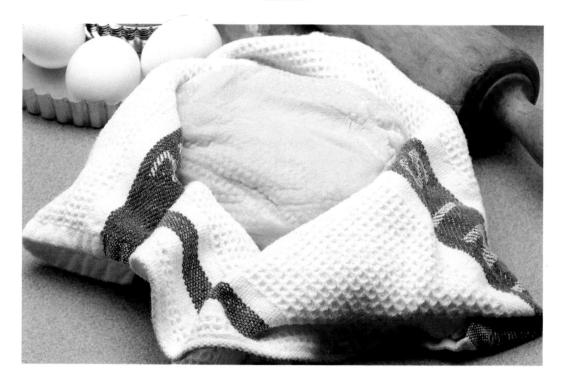

SWEET DOUGH

This dough is used for open-faced fruit tarts,
tartelettes, Gâteau St-Honoré and Bande de Fruits.

1 lb	all-purpose flour	500 g
¼ cup	granulated sugar	50 mL
¼ tsp	salt	1 mL
½ lb	unsalted butter, softened and cut in pieces	250 g
2	extra-large eggs	2
1	egg yolk	1
3-4 tbsp	cold water	45-60 mL

■ Place flour on work surface and make a well in center. Add all remaining ingredients to the well.

■ Use a pastry scraper or your fingers to gather up ingredients into a ball. Add a bit of water if dough is too dry. Use the heel of your hand and knead small amounts of the dough against the work surface. This technique helps combine the ingredients. The dough should become smooth and uniform.

■ At this point the dough is ready to use. To store dough for later use, dust with flour and place in clean cloth. Refrigerate. Let dough stand at room temperature for 2 hours before using.

---

1 RECIPE: 4000 CALORIES   424 g CARBOHYDRATE   70 g PROTEIN
225 g FAT   4.0 g FIBER

CHART HOUSE MUD PIE

(SERVES 8 TO 10)

7-oz	package chocolate wafers, crushed	200-g
½ cup	soft butter	125 mL
3 cups	chocolate ice cream	750 mL
3 cups	vanilla ice cream	750 mL
1 cup	chocolate fudge sauce	250 mL

■ Mix crushed wafers with butter. Spread into bottom of 10-in (25-cm) springform cake pan.

■ Set ice cream containers on counter until ice cream is pliable, but not melting. Place ice creams in bowl of electric mixer or mix by hand, whichever works best. Mix ice creams just enough for marbled effect.

■ Fill cake pan, using spatula to help shape ice cream.

■ Drizzle top with chocolate fudge sauce. Place in freezer just until chocolate hardens, then cover top with sheet of waxed paper. Finish freezing 12 hours before slicing.

■ If desired, serve with whipped cream.

1 SERVING: 560 CALORIES   64 g CARBOHYDRATE   4 g PROTEIN
            32 g FAT   0 g FIBER

BAKED APPLES WITH RAISINS

(SERVES 6)

6	baking apples, cored	6
2 tbsp	butter	30 mL
2 tbsp	brown sugar	30 mL
1 tbsp	cinnamon	15 mL
3 tbsp	rum	45 mL
¼ cup	honey	50 mL
½ cup	sultana raisins	125 mL
½ cup	water	125 mL
1 tbsp	cornstarch	15 mL
3 tbsp	cold water	45 mL
	juice of 1 orange	

■ Preheat oven to 350 °F (180 °C).

■ Score skin of apples around perimeter as illustrated in picture. Place apples in baking dish.

■ Cream butter with brown sugar. Spoon into cavities of apples and stuff with cinnamon, rum, orange juice, honey and raisins. Pour ½ cup (125 mL) water into bottom of baking dish.

■ Bake 40 minutes or until apples are soft. The cooking time may vary depending on the type of apple used.

■ When cooked, remove apples from pan and set aside. Place pan on stove over medium heat. Cook 3 minutes. Dissolve cornstarch in 3 tbsp (45 mL) cold water; stir into cooking liquid. Cook 1 minute, then serve with apples.

■ Serve apples warm with ice cream if desired.

1 SERVING:	252 CALORIES	50 g CARBOHYDRATE	0 g PROTEIN
	4 g FAT	1.9 g FIBER	

CHOCOLATE PASTRY CREAM

4 oz	semi-sweet chocolate	125 g
2¼ cups	milk	550 mL
½ tsp	vanilla	2 mL
5	large egg yolks, at room temperature	5
½ cup	superfine sugar	125 mL
½ cup	all-purpose flour	125 mL
2 tbsp	unsalted butter, softened	30 mL
	pinch salt	

■ Place chocolate in stainless steel bowl. Set bowl over saucepan half-filled with simmering water. Check that bottom of bowl does not touch water. Adjust heat to low and let chocolate melt without stirring. When melted, remove bowl from pan and let stand on counter.

■ Meanwhile, pour milk, vanilla and salt in heavy-bottomed saucepan. Bring to boiling point, then remove from heat.

■ Place egg yolks and sugar in bowl. Beat with electric hand mixer until well incorporated and color changes to pale yellow. Add flour and incorporate with wooden spoon.

■ Pour in half of hot milk and mix quickly to incorporate. Return saucepan containing remaining milk to stove over low heat. Pour egg mixture from bowl into saucepan, whisking to incorporate.

■ Cook cream over low heat until it becomes very thick; about 5 to 6 minutes. Whisk constantly. Use wooden spoon to scrape out corners of pan.

■ Turn off heat. Whisk in melted chocolate, then butter. Transfer cream to bowl . Cover with sheet of waxed paper touching surface. Lift up one corner of the paper to create an air space.

■ Let cream cool completely at room temperature before refrigerating.

1 RECIPE:	2232 CALORIES	223 g CARBOHYDRATE	56 g PROTEIN
	124 g FAT	2.3 g FIBER	

Melt chocolate in double boiler over low heat. Bottom of bowl should not touch water below. Do not stir during melting process.

Use electric hand mixer to mix egg yolks with sugar.

Notice color change to pale yellow. Incorporate flour with wooden spoon.

Incorporate half of hot milk to egg yolk mixture.

Pour dissolved egg yolk mixture into saucepan containing remaining milk. Cook cream over low heat, whisking constantly. At the end of cooking, cream should be thick and smooth.

Turn off heat. Whisk in melted chocolate, then butter.

CARROT CAKE

(SERVES 8)

1½ cups	granulated sugar	375 mL
½ cup	brown sugar	125 mL
1½ cups	vegetable oil	375 mL
2 cups	all-purpose flour, sifted	500 mL
1½ tsp	baking powder	7 mL
2 tsp	cinnamon	10 mL
1 tsp	baking soda	5 mL
1 tsp	salt	5 mL
5	large eggs	5
2½ cups	grated carrots	625 mL
1 cup	golden raisins	250 mL
1 tbsp	flour	15 mL
1 tbsp	grated lemon rind	15 mL

■ Preheat oven to 350 °F (180 °C). Butter sides and bottom of 9½-in (24-cm) springform cake pan with depth of 2½ in (6.5 cm). Set aside.

■ Place both sugars and oil in bowl. Whisk together.

■ In second bowl, sift in flour, baking powder, cinnamon, baking soda and salt. Incorporate dry ingredients into sugar mixture using electric hand mixer.

■ Add eggs, one at a time, mixing well between each addition. Use electric hand mixer.

■ Incorporate carrots. Dust raisins with 1 tbsp (15 mL) flour and stir into batter. Mix in lemon rind.

■ Pour batter into cake pan and bake 60 to 70 minutes.

■ When cake is done, remove from oven and let stand in mold 5 minutes. Unmold and finish cooling on wire rack.

■ Serve plain or with icing.

1 SERVING:	897 CALORIES	106 g CARBOHYDRATE	7 g PROTEIN
	50 g FAT	2.2 g FIBER	

BUTTER CREAM FROSTING

1 cup	superfine sugar	250 mL
½ cup	water	125 mL
5	large egg yolks	5
1 tsp	vanilla	5 mL
½ lb	butter, softened	250 g

■ Place sugar and water in small saucepan. Do not stir. Cook over low heat until temperature reaches 220 °F (104 °C).

■ Meanwhile, place egg yolks and vanilla in mixing bowl. Use electric beater and beat at medium speed for 2 minutes.

■ Remove sugar syrup from heat and whisk vigorously. Slowly pour the syrup into the beaten egg yolks while beating at medium speed. Continue beating 12 minutes until mixture turns white in color and becomes very thick.

■ Place butter in separate bowl. Use electric beater and beat 30 seconds at medium speed.

■ Pour half of egg yolk mixture into bowl containing butter. Beat 10 seconds at medium speed.

■ Pour in remaining yolk mixture and continue beating 10 seconds or less until smooth. If you overbeat the mixture, the butter cream will become grainy.

■ Transfer the butter cream to a clean bowl. Cover with sheet of plastic wrap touching surface and refrigerate until desired spreading consistency is reached.

■ Use as a filling for layer cakes and for decoration.

1 RECIPE:	2981 CALORIES	210 g CARBOHYDRATE	16 g PROTEIN
	231 g FAT	0 g FIBER	

CARAMEL-COATED CREAM PUFFS
(SERVES 6 TO 8)

8	cream puffs (see page 472)	8
1½ cups	Chocolate Pastry Cream (see page 462)	375 mL
½ cup	granulated sugar	125 mL
3 tbsp	cold water	45 mL
⅓ cup	cold water	75 mL
	few drops lemon juice	

■ Make a hole in bottom of each cream puff as illustrated in the technique. Use pastry bag to fill cream puffs with Chocolate Pastry Cream. Set aside.

■ Place sugar, 3 tbsp (45 mL) water and lemon juice in saucepan. Cook over medium heat until liquid becomes a deep golden color. Do not stir!

■ Remove from heat and briefly plunge bottom of pan in bowl of cold water. Return pan to stove over medium heat. Pour in remaining water and, without stirring, cook another 30 seconds.

■ Remove pan from heat and place on counter. Carefully dip tops of cream puffs in hot caramel. Set aside to cool, then refrigerate to serve cold.

1 SERVING: 401 CALORIES 48 g CARBOHYDRATE 10 g PROTEIN
19 g FAT 0 g FIBER

Use a flat, plain tip to make a hole in bottom of each cream puff.

Use a pastry bag to fill cream puffs with Chocolate Pastry Cream.

Cook sugar, water and lemon juice in saucepan over medium heat. Do not stir!

As soon as sugar syrup reaches the caramel stage, briefly plunge bottom of pan into bowl of cold water.

Return pan to stove over medium heat and pour in second measure of water. Cook 30 seconds.

Dip tops of cream puffs in caramel while it is still hot.

BANANAS FOSTER À LA SIENNA

(SERVES 4)

2 tbsp	butter	30 mL
3 tbsp	brown sugar	45 mL
2	large bananas, sliced	2
3 tbsp	banana liqueur	45 mL
3 tbsp	rum	45 mL
	juice of 1 orange	
	juice of ½ lemon	
	vanilla ice cream	

■ Heat butter in frying pan over medium heat. When melted, add sugar and mix well. Cook until golden brown.

■ Add sliced bananas and mix well; cook 1 minute.

■ Add fruit juices, mix and continue cooking 1 minute.

■ Add liqueur and rum; flambée. Mix well and serve over vanilla ice cream.

1 SERVING:	409 CALORIES	57 g CARBOHYDRATE	3 g PROTEIN
	13 g FAT	1.9 g FIBER	

ALMOND TARTELETTES

(SERVES 4 TO 6)

½ lb	Flaky Dough (see page 482)	250 g
½ cup	ground almonds	125 mL
⅓ cup	superfine sugar	75 mL
1 tsp	all-purpose flour	5 mL
1	large egg white beaten egg	1

■ Preheat oven to 400 °F (200 °C).

■ Use tartelette molds with a diameter of about 4 in (10 cm).

■ Roll out flaky dough on floured surface ⅛ in (0.3 cm) thick. Line molds with dough. Prick bottoms with fork and brush sides with beaten egg. Set aside.

■ Place ground almonds, sugar and flour in bowl. Mix and add egg white. Incorporate thoroughly.

■ Place 2 tbsp (30 mL) of almond mixture in each mold. Bake 16 minutes.

■ Cool before serving.

1 SERVING: 424 CALORIES   39 g CARBOHYDRATE   7 g PROTEIN
27 g FAT   0 g FIBER

UPSIDE-DOWN PEACH CAKE

(SERVES 6 TO 8)

⅓ cup	butter	75 mL
⅓ cup	granulated sugar	75 mL
1	large egg	1
1 tsp	vanilla	5 mL
1 cup	pastry flour	250 mL
1 tbsp	baking powder	15 mL
½ cup	light cream	125 mL
2	large egg whites, beaten stiff	2
¼ cup	brown sugar	50 mL
2 cups	sliced peeled peaches*	500 mL
	extra granulated sugar	

■ Preheat oven to 350 °F (180 °C). Generously butter 23-cm (9-in) cake pan; set aside.

■ Place butter, granulated sugar, whole egg and vanilla in large bowl. Using electric hand mixer, beat 2 minutes or until mixture becomes thick.

■ Sift flour and baking powder together. Using wooden spoon, incorporate half of flour into egg mixture in bowl.

■ Pour in cream and mix well. Add remaining flour and continue mixing until well incorporated.

■ Fold in beaten egg whites until no trace of white can be seen; set batter aside.

■ Sprinkle brown sugar over bottom of prepared cake pan, then cover with sliced peaches in circle pattern.

■ Pour in batter and bake 1 hour in middle of oven, or until cake tests done.

■ When done, remove cake from oven and let cool in pan. Turn out onto ovenproof serving platter and sprinkle with a little granulated sugar. Place in oven, 6 in (15 cm) from broiler element, and broil 3 to 4 minutes. Slice and serve.

*Use fresh peaches if in season. Canned peaches should be well drained.

1 SERVING:	290 CALORIES	41 g CARBOHYDRATE	5 g PROTEIN
	12 g FAT	1.3 g FIBER	

Upside-Down Peach Cake

CREAM PUFF DOUGH

This dough is used to make Cream Puffs, Éclairs,
Paris-Brest and Gâteau St-Honoré

1 cup	water	250 mL	
¼ tsp	salt	1 mL	
4 tbsp	unsalted butter	60 mL	
1 tbsp	granulated sugar	15 mL	
1 cup	all-purpose flour	250 mL	
4	large eggs	4	
	beaten egg		

■ Preheat oven to 375 °F (190 °C). Butter and
lightly flour cookie sheet.

■ Place water, salt, butter and sugar in heavy-
bottomed saucepan. Cook over medium heat.
Continue cooking for 2 minutes after liquid
starts to boil.

■ Reduce heat to low. Add all of flour and mix
rapidly with wooden spoon. Cook dough until it
no longer sticks to spoon or fingers when pinched.
Be sure to mix constantly.

■ Remove pan from heat and transfer mixture
to bowl. Let cool 3 minutes.

■ Incorporate eggs one at time, mixing well
between additions. Mixture must regain its
smooth texture before next egg is added. The
finished dough should be shiny and smooth.

■ Fit pastry bag with plain, round tip. Fill pastry
bag with dough and squeeze out shapes of your
choice: the size of an egg for cream puffs or 4-in
(10-cm) long strips for éclairs. Leave space
between each.

■ Brush tops of shapes with beaten egg,
smoothing tails left by pastry bag. Let stand
at room temperature for 20 minutes.

■ Bake 35 minutes in oven. Turn off heat and
position door ajar. Let stand 45 minutes.

■ When cold, fill with your choice of pastry cream
or whipped cream. Glaze tops with caramel or
chocolate.

1 RECIPE:	1271 CALORIES	119 g CARBOHYDRATE	39 g PROTEIN
	71 g FAT	2.0 g FIBER	

Place water, salt and butter in
heavy-bottomed saucepan.

Add sugar and melt over medium
heat. Continue cooking 2 minutes
after liquid starts to boil.

Reduce heat to low and add all
of flour. Mix rapidly with wooden
spoon.

Cook dough over low heat until it no longer sticks to spoon or fingers when pinched. Be sure to mix constantly.

Transfer dough to bowl and let cool 3 minutes.

Incorporate eggs one at a time, mixing well between additions. Mixture must regain its smooth texture before next egg is added.

GÂTEAU ST-HONORÉ
(SERVES 8)

½ lb	Flaky Dough *or* Sweet Dough (see pages 482 and 459)	250 g
1	recipe Cream Puff Dough (see page 472)	1
8	cream puffs	8
2½ cups	Pastry Cream #2 (see page 498)	625 mL
½ cup	Almond Sugar (see page 478)	125 mL
½ cup	granulated sugar	125 mL
3 tbsp	cold water	45 mL
1½ cups	whipped cream	375 mL
	beaten egg	
	few drops lemon juice	

■ Preheat oven to 375 °F (190 °C). Butter and flour cookie sheet.

■ Roll out flaky dough ⅛ in (0.3 cm) thick on lightly floured surface. Place dough on cookie sheet. Position 10-in (25-cm) flan ring on dough; use pastry wheel to trim away excess dough, leaving circle. Remove flan ring and prick dough with fork.

■ Fit pastry bag with medium plain, round tip. Tracing edge of flaky dough circle, squeeze out even ring of cream puff dough. Squeeze out two more rings; one on the inside, adjacent to the first ring and the other on top of both rings.

■ Brush rings with beaten egg and set cookie sheet aside for 15 minutes.

■ Place cookie sheet in oven and bake 35 minutes. Turn off heat and position door ajar; let stand 45 minutes.

■ To assemble cake, begin by stuffing cream puffs with some of pastry cream. Mix almond sugar with remaining pastry cream and set aside.

■ Place sugar, water and lemon juice in saucepan. Cook over medium heat until liquid becomes a deep golden color. Do not stir.

■ When caramelized, briefly plunge bottom of pan in bowl of cold water. Place saucepan on counter and let stand several minutes.

■ Carefully dip tops of cream puffs in caramel. To anchor cream puffs on ring border of cake, let excess caramel drip onto the spot where you plan to place cream puff. Position cream puff, glazed side up, on ring. Repeat technique for remaining cream puffs.

■ Fill center of cake with remaining pastry cream. Decorate with whipped cream.

■ Set aside in cool place until serving.

---

1 SERVING: 813 CALORIES   88 g CARBOHYDRATE   16 g PROTEIN
43 g FAT   1.0 g FIBER

Gâteau St-Honoré

APPLES WITH SABAYON

(SERVES 4)

5	medium-size apples	5
½ cup	granulated sugar	125 mL
1 tbsp	cinnamon	15 mL
½ cup	golden raisins	125 mL
2 tbsp	finely chopped lemon rind	30 mL
4 tbsp	rum	60 mL
4	egg yolks	4
1	whole egg	1
4 tbsp	granulated sugar	60 mL
¼ cup	dry white wine	50 mL
4 tbsp	coffee liqueur (Tia Maria)	60 mL

■ Core, peel and slice apples. Place in a saucepan with ½ cup (125 mL) sugar, cinnamon, raisins, lemon rind and rum. Cover and cook 10 minutes over medium heat. Stir 2 to 3 times during cooking.

■ Remove saucepan from stove and let cool. Divide apples between 4 glass coupes and set aside.

■ Place all eggs in stainless steel bowl. Add remaining sugar, wine and liqueur. Place bowl over saucepan half-filled with hot water set over low heat. Beat with electric beater at low speed until mixture triples in volume.

■ Pour sabayon over apples and serve.

1 SERVING: 515 CALORIES   89 g CARBOHYDRATE   5 g PROTEIN
7 g FAT   2.3 g FIBER

TIA MARIA CREAM FOR BERRIES

(SERVES 4)

4	large egg yolks	4
3 tbsp	superfine sugar	45 mL
¾ cup	milk, scalded	175 mL
4 tbsp	Tia Maria liqueur	60 mL

■ Place egg yolks and sugar in stainless steel bowl. Beat 2 minutes with electric beater.

■ Pour in hot milk and continue beating until frothy – about 30 seconds.

■ Place bowl over saucepan half-filled with boiling water over medium heat. Whisk cream constantly until it becomes thick enough to coat the back of a spoon – about 5 to 6 minutes. During cooking, cream will stick to sides of bowl. When this happens, remove bowl from heat and whisk vigorously to incorporate fully. Return bowl over saucepan and resume cooking.

■ When cream is cooked, remove bowl from heat and add liqueur. Continue whisking until cool. Cover with plastic wrap touching surface and refrigerate until cold. Serve with fresh berries in season.

1 SERVING:	183 CALORIES	17 g CARBOHYDRATE	5 g PROTEIN
	7 g FAT	0 g FIBER	

PARIS-BREST

(SERVES 8 TO 10)

Almond Sugar

1 cup	icing sugar	250 mL
⅓ cup	slivered almonds	75 mL

Cake Assembly

1	recipe Cream Puff Dough (see page 472)	1
1½ cups	heavy cream	375 mL
1 tsp	vanilla	5 mL
2 tbsp	icing sugar	30 mL
1	recipe Pastry Cream #2 (see page 498)	1
	beaten egg	
	sliced almonds	

■ Place ingredients for almond sugar in small saucepan over low heat. Cook until mixture becomes caramel; stir constantly!

■ Pour into oiled cookie sheet and set aside until cold. Break into pieces and blend in food processor until powdered. Store in airtight container until ready to mix with pastry cream.

■ Preheat oven to 375 °F (190 °C). Butter and lightly flour cookie sheet.

■ Use rim of 9-in (23-cm) cake pan to trace circle on cookie sheet. Fit pastry bag with large plain, round tip and fill with cream puff dough. Tracing marked circle, squeeze out even ring of dough about 1 in (2.5 cm) wide.

■ Squeeze out two more rings; one on the inside, adjacent to the first ring and the other on top of both rings. Brush rings with beaten egg and sprinkle with sliced almonds. Let stand at room temperature for 30 minutes.

■ Place cake in oven and bake 45 minutes. Turn off heat and position door ajar; let cake stand another 45 minutes.

■ Meanwhile, prepare whipped cream. Place heavy cream and vanilla in bowl of mixer and beat until firm. Add icing sugar and beat 30 seconds longer. Refrigerate.

(continued)

Butter and flour cookie sheet. Use rim of 9-in (23-cm) cake pan to trace circle on cookie sheet.

Tracing marked circle, squeeze out even ring of dough about 1 in (2.5 cm) wide. Squeeze out another ring, tracing the inside edge of the first ring.

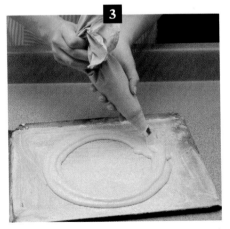

Squeeze out a third ring on top of both rings.

■ To assemble cake, have all ingredients ready on counter. Using a long knife with serrated blade, slice lid off cake. Mix 2 cups (500 mL) of pastry cream with ½ cup (125 mL) of almond sugar and fill bottom of cake.

■ Using pastry bag, add whipped cream over pastry cream and position lid. Decorate top of cake with rosettes of whipped cream and sprinkle with icing sugar, if desired.

1 SERVING:	600 CALORIES	64 g CARBOHYDRATE	12 g PROTEIN
	32 g FAT	0 g FIBER	

Brush rings with beaten egg.

Sprinkle with sliced almonds and let stand at room temperature.

Slice lid off cooked cake.

WHITE CAKE
(SERVES 6 TO 8)

6	large eggs	6
¾ cup	granulated sugar	175 mL
¼ tsp	vanilla	1 mL
1 cup	sifted pastry flour with pinch salt	250 mL

■ Preheat oven to 400 °F (200 °C). Line 9-in (23-cm) springform cake pan with buttered and floured waxed paper. Set aside.

■ Place eggs, sugar and vanilla in stainless steel bowl. Place bowl over saucepan half-filled with hot water over medium heat. Beat ingredients with electric beater 3 minutes or until mixture becomes very thick.

■ Remove bowl from saucepan. Divide flour into thirds and incorporate ⅓ at a time by sifting over batter. Fold well between each addition.

■ Pour batter into prepared mold and bake 35 to 40 minutes. Let cake cool slightly before unmolding.

■ Serve cake plain or divide into 2 layers and decorate.

1 SERVING:	218 CALORIES	36 g CARBOHYDRATE	7 g PROTEIN
	5 g FAT	0 g FIBER	

FRESH RASPBERRY COUPE
(SERVES 4)

1½ cups	fresh raspberries, cleaned	375 mL
2 tbsp	orange liqueur (Cointreau)	30 mL
1 cup	Pastry Cream for Fruit Tarts (see page 458)	250 mL
1½ cups	whipped cream	375 mL

■ Divide half of raspberries between 4 dessert glasses. Sprinkle each with half of liqueur.

■ Add thin layer of pastry cream and thin layer of whipped cream.

■ Continue layering ingredients in same order until used. Refrigerate 1 hour before serving.

1 SERVING: 597 CALORIES   63 g CARBOHYDRATE   12 g PROTEIN
31 g FAT   4.3 g FIBER

WHITE ICING

3½ cups	icing sugar	875 mL
3	large egg whites	3
¼ tsp	vanilla	1 mL

■ Sift 2 cups (500 mL) of icing sugar in bowl of electric mixer. Add egg whites and mix 1 minute at low speed.

■ Increase to medium speed and continue mixing 1 minute.

■ Increase to full speed and continue mixing 6 minutes.

■ Add vanilla and mix just to incorporate. Sift in 1 cup (250 mL) of icing sugar and mix 3 minutes.

■ Sift in remaining icing sugar and mix 2 minutes.

■ Use to frost a variety of cakes.

1 RECIPE: 2572 CALORIES 633 g CARBOHYDRATE 10 g PROTEIN
0 g FAT   0 g FIBER

FLAKY DOUGH

This dough is used for Bande de Fruits, Tartelettes, Gâteau St-Honoré and other pastries.

1 lb	unsalted butter	500 g
1¼ lb	all-purpose flour	625 g
1 cup	water	250 mL
1 tsp	salt	5 mL

■ Place butter on lightly floured surface and flatten slightly with rolling pin. Set aside at room temperature.

■ Place flour on counter and make a well in center Add some of water and salt to well. Gather mixture towards middle using fingers or pastry scraper. Add more water as needed. Shape into ball when incorporated.

■ Cut a crisscross on top of dough as illustrated in technique.

■ Roll out dough, making a four-leaf clover shape. Do not roll too thin.

■ Place block of butter in middle of dough. Wrap ends of dough over butter to cover completely. Ideally, butter and dough should be of the same consistency. If butter is too hard or too soft, it will not incorporate well during rolling.

■ Roll out dough into thick rectangle. Always roll from the center towards the edges. Do not press too hard or butter will come through dough. Fold dough into 3 as illustrated. Wrap in clean cloth and refrigerate 30 minutes.

■ Position dough on lightly floured counter with narrow, open edge facing you. Roll out into rectangular shape about ½ in (1.2 cm) thick. Fold in 3 and mark dough with two fingertips. This indicates the second turn, or completion of the rolling and folding technique. Wrap in cloth and refrigerate 30 minutes.

■ Make 4 more turns following the same technique. Always roll out the dough with the narrow, open edge facing you. Do not overwork dough and dust away any leftover flour on dough at the end of each turn. Remember to mark dough with the correct number of fingers to keep count of the turns.

■ Store dough in refrigerator in plastic wrap. When needed, cut off a piece widthwise and bring to room temperature before rolling.

| 1 RECIPE: | 5892 CALORIES | 476 g CARBOHYDRATE | 70 g PROTEIN |
| | 412 g FAT | 4.0 g FIBER | |

Shape dough into ball when mixed.

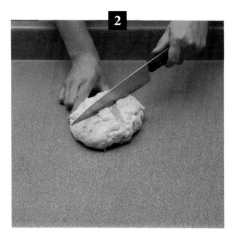

Cut a deep crisscross on top of dough and flatten to form four-leaf clover shape.

Roll out dough, following the four-leaf clover shape. Do not roll too thin. Place block of butter in middle of dough.

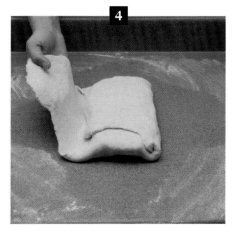

Wrap ends of dough over butter to cover completely.

After dough has been rolled into thick rectangle, fold dough equally into three. This represents the completion of the first turn.

To keep track of the turns, mark dough with the correct number of fingertips.

RASPBERRY FRUIT PIE

(SERVES 6 TO 8)

Dough

1½ cups	sifted flour	375 mL
⅓ cup	unsalted butter	75 mL
3 tbsp	shortening	45 mL
1	beaten egg	1
2 tbsp	granulated sugar	30 mL
3-4 tbsp	cold water	45-60 mL
	pinch salt	
	beaten egg	

Filling

½ cup	granulated sugar	125 mL
½ cup	cold water	125 mL
2½ cups	fresh raspberries, washed	625 mL
2 tbsp	fruit jelly	30 mL

■ To make dough, sift flour and salt into large bowl. Make well in middle; add butter, shortening, 1 beaten egg and sugar. Incorporate well with pastry cutter.

■ Add water and incorporate with fingertips; knead dough to form ball. Lightly flour dough and wrap in clean cloth; chill 1 hour. Remove dough from refrigerator and let warm to room temperature.

■ Preheat oven to 425 °F (220 °C).

■ Roll out dough ⅛ in (0.3 cm) thick. Line 10-in (25-cm) fluted tart pan with removable bottom. Press dough snug against inside corners of pan to prevent shrinkage.

■ Use rolling pin to trim off excess dough overlapping sides of pan. Crimp edges with fingers. Prick bottom with fork and line with waxed paper. Fill with baking weights and brush edges of dough with beaten egg.

■ Cook in bottom half of oven 15 minutes. Transfer to counter, remove paper and weights and let cool.

■ To make filling, place sugar and water in small saucepan. Bring to boil and cook until it reaches temperature of 230 °F (110 °C) on candy thermometer.

■ Place raspberries in bowl and pour in syrup; mix well and let marinate until pie crust is ready to use.

■ To assemble tart, scoop out berries from bowl using slotted spoon and transfer to pie crust.

■ Place syrup from berries in saucepan and mix in fruit jelly. Cook 2 minutes over medium heat, then let cool.

■ Glaze berries with fruit jelly syrup, slice and serve.

1 SERVING:	352 CALORIES	50 g CARBOHYDRATE	5 g PROTEIN
	15 g FAT	4.4 g FIBER	

Raspberry Fruit Pie

GÉNOISE CAKE WITH RASPBERRIES

(SERVES 6 TO 8)

1	Génoise Cake (see page 456)	1
3 tbsp	orange liqueur	45 mL
3 cups	whipped cream	750 mL
3 cups	fresh raspberries *or* berries in season, cleaned	750 mL

■ Use long knife with serrated blade to cut génoise cake into two equal layers.

■ Position bottom layer, crust-side down, on flat cake platter. Sprinkle half of liqueur over cake. Fit pastry bag with star tip and pipe a layer of whipped cream over cake. Cover cream with a layer of raspberries.

■ Position top layer and sprinkle with remaining liqueur. Spread entire cake with thin covering of whipped cream. Pipe remaining cream decoratively around base and on top of cake. Decorate with berries.

1 SERVING:	352 CALORIES	25 g CARBOHYDRATE	5 g PROTEIN
	24 g FAT	4.4 g FIBER	

FRESH CHERRY TART

(SERVES 6 TO 8)

	Sweet Dough	
	(see page 459)	
	beaten egg	
¼ cup	superfine sugar	50 mL
1 lb	large fresh cherries, pitted	500 g

■ Preheat oven to 400 °F (200 °C).

■ Roll out dough on lightly floured surface ⅛ in (0.3 cm) thick. Line 8-in (20-cm) fluted tart pan with removable bottom. Press dough snug against inside corners of pan to prevent shrinkage.

■ Use rolling pin to trim off excess dough overlapping sides of pan. Crimp edges of dough with fingers. Prick bottom of dough with fork and line with waxed paper. Fill with baking weights or dried beans. Bake 18 minutes.

■ Remove tart pan from oven and decrease oven heat to 375 °F (190 °C). Remove weights and waxed paper. Brush dough with beaten egg and sprinkle some sugar over crust.

■ Toss cherries with remaining sugar, then arrange in tart shell. Bake 25 minutes in oven.

■ If desired, brush cherries with fruit syrup.

■ Cool and serve plain or with whipped cream.

1 SERVING:	643 CALORIES	75 g CARBOHYDRATE	12 g PROTEIN
	33 g FAT	3.6 g FIBER	

STRAWBERRY BANDE DE FRUITS

(SERVES 6 TO 8)

Strawberry Glaze

1½ cups	fresh strawberries, cleaned and hulled	375 mL
¼ cup	granulated sugar	50 mL
2 tbsp	orange liqueur	30 mL

Assembly

1 lb	fresh strawberries, cleaned and hulled	500 g
2 tbsp	liqueur of your choice	30 mL
2 tbsp	granulated sugar	30 mL
1 lb	Flaky Dough (see page 482)	500 g
1¼ cups	Pastry Cream #2 (see page 498)	300 mL
	beaten egg	

■ Place glaze ingredients in small saucepan. Cook 8 minutes over medium heat. Pass through sieve into bowl and set aside.

■ Preheat oven to 400 °F (200 °C).

■ Place whole strawberries in bowl with liqueur and sugar. Marinate 45 minutes.

■ Meanwhile, roll out flaky dough ¼ in (0.65 cm) thick on lightly floured surface. Use ruler to measure rectangle of about 5 x 15 in (13 x 38 cm). Using pastry wheel, cut out rectangle and transfer to cookie sheet. Prick with fork and brush with beaten egg.

■ Cut out 4 strips of dough about ¾ in (2 cm) wide; 2 long enough for the sides and 2 for the ends. Position strips of dough on rectangle using a little beaten egg to affix overlapping corners. Brush tops of strips with beaten egg.

■ Bake 18 minutes in oven. Remove from oven and let stand at room temperature until cold.

■ Spread layer of pastry cream over bottom of dough. Drain strawberries and arrange on cream. Brush fruit with strawberry glaze.

1 SERVING:	648 CALORIES	68 g CARBOHYDRATE	10 g PROTEIN
	35 g FAT	2.6 g FIBER	

Roll out flaky dough ¼ in (0.65 cm) thick on lightly floured surface.

Use ruler to measure rectangle of about 5 x 15 in (13 x 38 cm). Use pastry wheel to cut out dough.

Transfer rectangle of dough to cookie sheet. Prick with fork and brush with beaten egg.

Cut out 4 strips of dough about ¾ in (2 cm) thick for sides and ends.

Position strips of dough on rectangle using a little beaten egg or water under each, overlapping corner. This technique will secure border during cooking.

Brush tops of strips with beaten egg.

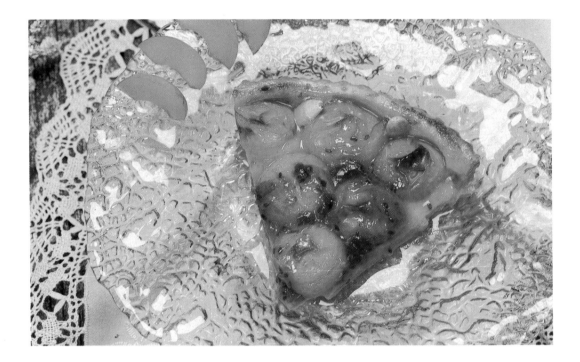

PLUM TART

(SERVES 6 TO 8)

	Sweet Dough (see page 459)	
¼ cup	apricot jelly	50 mL
25	fresh ripe plums, halved and pitted	25
2 tbsp	superfine sugar	30 mL
	beaten egg	

■ Preheat oven to 400 °F (200 °C).

■ Roll out dough on lightly floured surface ⅛ in (0.3 cm) thick. Line 9½-in (23-cm) fluted tart pan with removable bottom. Press dough snug against inside corners of pan to prevent shrinkage.

■ Use rolling pin to trim off excess dough overlapping sides of pan. Crimp edges of dough with fingers. Prick bottom of dough with fork.

■ Melt apricot jelly in small saucepan. When cooled, brush some over bottom of tart shell. Arrange plums in a circle starting from outside of tart. Brush remaining jelly over plums and sprinkle with sugar.

■ Brush edges of dough with beaten egg and bake 35 to 40 minutes. Cool and serve.

1 SERVING: 745 CALORIES   100 g CARBOHYDRATE   12 g PROTEIN
33 g FAT   7.4 g FIBER

CREAMY BAKED CHEESECAKE

(SERVES 8 TO 10)

Crumb Crust

1 cup	graham cracker crumbs	250 mL
¼ cup	granulated sugar	50 mL
¼ cup	melted butter	50 mL

Cake

3	½-lb (250-g) packages cream cheese, at room temperature	3
1½ cups	granulated sugar	375 mL
1 cup	light cream	250 mL
1 tbsp	vanilla	15 mL
5 tbsp	all-purpose flour	75 mL
2	large eggs	2

■ Preheat oven to 350 °F (180 °C). Combine graham cracker crumbs, ¼ cup (50 mL) sugar and melted butter. Press into bottom of buttered 9½-in (24-cm) springform cake pan, with a depth of 2½ in (6.5 cm).

■ Bake crumb crust 10 minutes. Remove and set aside.

■ Place cream cheese in bowl of electric mixer and beat until creamy. Add sugar and beat to incorporate.

■ Add light cream, vanilla and flour. Beat until incorporated. Scrape down sides of bowl as needed.

■ Add eggs and beat once more. Pour batter into prepared cake pan. Bake 55 minutes.

■ When cheesecake is cooked, remove from oven and let stand on counter to cool. Refrigerate at least 8 hours before slicing. Serve plain or with sliced fruit.

---

1 SERVING: 600 CALORIES   55 g CARBOHYDRATE   9 g PROTEIN
            38 g FAT   0 g FIBER

BORDELAISE TARTELETTES

(SERVES 6 TO 8)

½ lb	Flaky Dough (see page 482)	500 g
¾ cup	granulated sugar	175 mL
5	large egg yolks	5
1	large egg	1
½ cup	all-purpose flour	125 mL
2 cups	hot milk	500 mL
2 tbsp	rum	30 mL
	beaten egg	
	icing sugar	

■ Use 4-in (10-cm) diameter tartelette molds with a depth of ¾ in (2 cm).

■ Roll out dough on lightly floured surface ⅛ in (0.3 cm). Line molds and prick bottoms with fork; set aside. Cut remaining dough into thin strips to arrange on top of filling; set aside.

■ Place sugar and egg yolks in stainless steel bowl. Beat together with electric hand mixer. Beat in whole egg and sift flour over batter; mix well.

■ Add hot milk and rum; mix well. Set bowl on saucepan half-filled with hot water over low heat. Cook mixture until it becomes very thick, stirring constantly.

■ Remove bowl from stove and cover with waxed paper. Let cool at room temperature.

■ Preheat oven to 400 °F (200 °C). When cream filling is cold, mix well and spoon into molds. Position thin strips of dough over filling in grid pattern. Trim off excess dough and crimp edges. Brush with beaten egg.

■ Bake 15 to 18 minutes.

■ Remove tartelettes from oven and sprinkle with icing sugar. Let cool before serving.

1 SERVING:	645 CALORIES	68 g CARBOHYDRATE	12 g PROTEIN
	36 g FAT	0 g FIBER	

RASPBERRY TARTELETTES

(SERVES 6 TO 8)

½ lb	Flaky Dough (see page 482)	250 g
½ cup	ground almonds	125 mL
⅓ cup	superfine sugar	75 mL
1	large egg white	1
	pinch of flour	
	few drops lemon juice	
	beaten egg	
	fresh raspberries, cleaned	
	extra sugar	

■ Use 4-in (10-cm) diameter tartelette molds with a depth of ¾ in (2 cm).

■ Preheat oven to 400 °F (200 °C).

■ Roll out dough on lightly floured surface ⅛ in (0.3 cm) thick. Line molds and prick bottoms with fork; set aside.

■ Mix almonds, superfine sugar, egg white, flour and lemon juice together in bowl. Divide mixture between molds and brush edge of dough with beaten egg. Bake 15 minutes.

■ Remove molds from oven and arrange raspberries on top. Sprinkle with sugar and bake 3 minutes.

■ Remove tartelettes from oven and let cool before serving.

1 SERVING:	309 CALORIES	31 g CARBOHYDRATE	4 g PROTEIN
	19 g FAT	2.1 g FIBER	

CHOCOLATE ÉCLAIRS
(SERVES 6 TO 10)

2 cups	heavy cream, cold	500 mL
1 tsp	vanilla	5 mL
2 tbsp	icing sugar	30 mL
4 oz	good quality semi-sweet chocolate	125 g
1 tbsp	cold water	15 mL
12	éclairs (see page 472)	12

■ Pour cream and vanilla in bowl of electric mixer. Beat until firm. Add icing sugar and beat another 30 seconds, but no longer. Set aside in refrigerator.

■ Place chocolate in stainless steel bowl. Set over saucepan half-filled with hot water. Check that bowl does not touch water. Melt over very low heat.

■ When melted, thin chocolate with 1 tbsp (15 mL) cold water. Dip tops of éclairs in warm chocolate. If preferred, spread chocolate with spatula.

■ When chocolate on tops of éclairs has set, carefully slice shells open using knife with serrated blade. Fill with whipped cream and serve.

1 SERVING:	470 CALORIES	24 g CARBOHYDRATE	8 g PROTEIN
	38 g FAT	0 g FIBER	

Choose good quality semi-sweet chocolate for the best taste and shine. Melt in double boiler over very low heat.

When chocolate is melted, add small amount of cold water and incorporate with whisk.

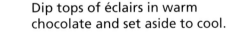

Dip tops of éclairs in warm chocolate and set aside to cool.

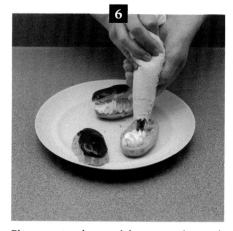

When chocolate is set, cut shells open using knife with serrated blade. Try to make opening in middle of éclairs and cut all the way through.

You can use whipped cream to fill éclairs or a variety of pastry creams. If you choose whipped cream, be sure to beat firm.

Fit a pastry bag with a star tip and fill bottom of each éclair. Replace tops.

PASTRY CREAM #1

2 cups	milk	500 mL
1 tsp	vanilla	5 mL
5	extra-large egg yolks	5
¼ cup	granulated sugar	50 mL
½ cup	all-purpose flour	125 mL
2 tbsp	orange liqueur (Cointreau)	30 mL
1 tbsp	butter	15 mL
	pinch salt	

■ Pour milk and vanilla into heavy-bottomed saucepan and bring to boiling point. Set aside.

■ Separate eggs and egg yolks in large bowl with sugar. Beat 3 minutes using electric hand mixer.

■ Fold in flour and salt; mix well. Gradually add milk while stirring with wooden spoon.

■ Pour mixture back into saucepan and cook over medium heat until thick. Stir constantly and do not let mixture boil. Reduce heat to low and continue cooking 5 to 6 minutes. Stir constantly.

■ When thick, remove saucepan from heat and stir in liqueur and butter. Pour into clean bowl and cover with sheet of waxed paper. Lift up one corner of paper to create air space and let cool completely. Press waxed paper snug against cream and refrigerate. Use this pastry cream in a variety of recipes.

1 RECIPE:	1250 CALORIES	135 g CARBOHYDRATE	42 g PROTEIN
	52 g FAT	2.3 g FIBER	

ITALIAN MERINGUE

1 cup	powdered fruit sugar	250 mL
4	large egg whites	4
½ tsp	vanilla	2 mL

■ Sift sugar into stainless steel bowl. Place over saucepan half-filled with hot water set over low heat.

■ Add egg whites and vanilla to bowl and begin beating with electric hand mixer at low speed. Water should be simmering. When egg whites start to take shape increase speed to medium and continue beating steadily.

■ Just before meringue starts to peak, increase speed to high for final 30 seconds of beating. You can test meringue by turning bowl upside-down. Egg whites should remain firmly in place.

■ Remove bowl from saucepan and continue beating at high speed until meringue becomes cold.

■ Use as a fancy topping for broiled fruits or to make meringue cookies.

1 RECIPE:	900 CALORIES	212 g CARBOHYDRATE	13 g PROTEIN
	0 g FAT	0 g FIBER	

ELEGANT RICE PUDDING

(SERVES 6 TO 8)

½ cup	sultana raisins	125 mL
3 tbsp	rum	45 mL
½ cup	long grain rice, rinsed	125 mL
3½ cups	2% milk, scalded	875 mL
1 tsp	grated lemon rind	5 mL
1 tsp	grated orange rind	5 mL
¼ cup	granulated sugar	50 mL
¼ cup	brown sugar	50 mL
1 tsp	vanilla	5 mL
3	egg yolks	3
1 cup	light cream	250 mL
	cinnamon to taste	

■ Marinate raisins in rum for 15 minutes.

■ Preheat oven to 375 °F (190 °C). Have ready 6-cup (1.5-L) soufflé mold.

■ Meanwhile, cook rice 10 minutes in boiling water. Drain well but do not rinse.

■ Place hot rice in bowl. Add milk, fruit rinds, both sugars, vanilla and marinated raisins. Mix well.

■ Pour mixture into soufflé dish and set in roasting pan. Add enough hot water to roasting pan to measure 2 in (5 cm) deep and bake 15 minutes.

■ Beat egg yolks with light cream. Stir into rice mixture. Reduce oven heat to 325 °F (160 °C) and continue cooking for 45 minutes.

■ When pudding is cooked, remove from oven and mix in cinnamon to taste. Let cool, then refrigerate until cold. Serve in tall glasses for a fancy presentation.

1 SERVING: 313 CALORIES   42 g CARBOHYDRATE   8 g PROTEIN
11 g FAT   0 g FIBER

PASTRY CREAM #2

Use this pastry cream for Paris-Brest, Gâteau St-Honoré, etc.

2 cups	milk	500 mL
1 tbsp	vanilla	15 mL
7	extra-large egg yolks	7
¾ cup	granulated sugar	175 mL
½ cup	all-purpose flour	125 mL
2 tbsp	rum	30 mL
1 tbsp	butter	15 mL
	pinch salt	

■ Heat milk and vanilla in heavy-bottomed saucepan just to boiling point.

■ Place egg yolks and sugar in stainless steel bowl. Using whisk, mix yolks until well incorporated.

■ Beat egg yolk mixture with electric hand mixer until color turns pale yellow, about 2 to 3 minutes.

■ Add flour and salt; whisk just to incorporate. Add 1 cup (250 mL) of hot milk and whisk well.

■ Place saucepan containing remaining milk on stove over medium-low heat. Pour contents of bowl into saucepan, whisking constantly.

■ Cook cream over low heat until very thick, about 5 to 6 minutes. You must whisk constantly and occasionally use wooden spoon to scrape out corners of pan. Lift pan off heat while scraping out corners.

■ Remove pan from heat and stir in rum and butter. Transfer cream to bowl and cover with sheet of waxed paper. Lift up one corner of the paper to create air space.

■ Let cream cool completely at room temperature before refrigerating.

1 RECIPE:	1798 CALORIES	240 g CARBOHYDRATE	48 g PROTEIN
	64 g FAT	2.3 g FIBER	

Place egg yolks and sugar in stainless steel bowl.

Using whisk, mix yolks until well incorporated.

Beat egg yolk mixture with electric hand mixer until color turns pale yellow, about 2 to 3 minutes. Incorporate flour and salt.

Add 1 cup (250 mL) of hot milk and mix well.

Pour contents of bowl into saucepan containing remaining milk. Cook cream over low heat until very thick, whisking constantly.

Use wooden spoon to scrape out corners of pan. This technique prevents the build-up of cooked egg which would otherwise result in a lumpy pastry cream.

GOLDEN MOLASSES APPLE CAKE

(SERVES 6 TO 8)

2	large eggs	2
2	large egg yolks	2
1 cup	brown sugar	250 mL
½ cup	molasses	125 mL
3	apples, cored, peeled and diced small	3
1 tbsp	grated orange rind	15 mL
1½ cups	pastry flour	375 mL
2 tsp	baking soda	10 mL
2 tsp	baking powder	10 mL
2 tbsp	cinnamon	30 mL
	pinch salt	

■ Preheat oven to 300 °F (150 °C). Line bottom of 9-in (23-cm) springform cake pan with circle of waxed paper. Butter paper and sides of pan.

■ Place all eggs in bowl. Add brown sugar and molasses. Beat 3 minutes with electric hand mixer.

■ Stir in apples and orange rind.

■ Sift flour, baking soda, baking powder, cinnamon and salt together. Place in sifter and re-sift over cake batter while incorporating with wooden spoon.

■ Pour batter into cake pan and cook 60-65 minutes or until cake is done.

■ Cool in pan slightly before unmolding. Finish cooling on wire rack. Serve with whipped cream.

1 SERVING:	465 CALORIES	102 g CARBOHYDRATE	6 g PROTEIN
	4 g FAT	1.8 g FIBER	

FRUIT IN ZABAGLIONE

(SERVES 4)

4	egg yolks	4
¼ cup	granulated sugar	50 mL
⅓ cup	medium-dry white wine	75 mL
½ cup	heavy cream, whipped	125 mL
	fresh fruit in season	1

■ Place egg yolks in stainless steel bowl. Add sugar and beat with electric hand mixer until thick.

■ Place saucepan half-filled with hot water on stove over low heat. Set bowl containing egg yolks over saucepan. Pour in wine and beat for 8 minutes or until thick.

■ Remove bowl from saucepan and continue beating with electric hand mixer until cold.

■ Gently whisk whipped cream into mixture. Serve in large dessert glasses and garnish with chocolate shavings or fresh fruits in season. Strawberries and raspberries are ideal.

1 SERVING:	195 CALORIES	17 g CARBOHYDRATE	4 g PROTEIN
	11 g FAT	1.7 g FIBER	

STRAWBERRY GALETTE
(SERVES 4 TO 6)

3	large eggs	3
⅓ cup	granulated sugar	75 mL
1 tbsp	coffee liqueur (Tia Maria)	15 mL
⅓ cup	all-purpose flour, sifted	75 mL
⅓ cup	granulated sugar	75 mL
⅓ cup	water	75 mL
2 cups	fresh strawberries, washed and hulled	500 mL
2 tbsp	orange liqueur (Cointreau)	30 mL
1 cup	heavy cream, whipped	250 mL

■ Preheat oven to 350 °F (180 °C). Butter 8-in (20-cm) springform cake pan. Completely line with buttered waxed paper; set aside.

■ Place eggs in large bowl and add ⅓ cup (75 mL) sugar. Pour in coffee liqueur and beat with electric hand mixer 4 to 5 minutes until thick.

■ Resift flour over mixture and incorporate by folding with spatula. No trace of flour should be visible.

■ Pour batter into prepared mold. Bake in middle of oven 30 minutes or until cake tests done.

■ Remove cake from oven and turn upside-down onto wire rack to unmold. Wait until cake is quite cool before peeling off waxed paper, then flip right-side-up onto cake plate.

■ Place ⅓ cup (75 mL) sugar in small saucepan and add water. Cook over high heat until mixture reaches temperature of 230 °F (110 °C) on a candy thermometer. Remove from heat and pour syrup over strawberries. Add orange liqueur and marinate 30 minutes.

■ When ready to serve, spread whipped cream over cake and top with glazed strawberries.

1 SERVING:	308 CALORIES	40 g CARBOHYDRATE	5 g PROTEIN
	12 g FAT	1.6 g FIBER	

APPLE JELLY COMPOTE

(SERVES 4 TO 6)

⅓ cup	granulated sugar	75 mL
⅓ cup	apple jelly	75 mL
1 tbsp	grated lemon rind	15 mL
1 tbsp	grated orange rind	15 mL
3 tbsp	light rum	45 mL
5	McIntosh apples, cored, peeled and sliced	5
1 tbsp	cinnamon	15 mL
½ cup	golden raisins	125 mL

■ Place sugar, apple jelly, grated fruit rinds and rum in small saucepan. Cook 4 minutes over medium heat.

■ Place sliced apples in large saucepan. Add fruit syrup and mix very well. Add cinnamon and raisins; cook, partly covered, 18 minutes over medium heat.

■ Transfer mixture to blender and purée.

■ Cool and serve plain, with yogurt or with ice cream.

1 SERVING:	262 CALORIES	60 g CARBOHYDRATE	1 g PROTEIN
	0 g FAT	1.9 g FIBER